MR BRENNAN

WOODFIELD

MR BRENNAN

WOODFIELD

PRACTICAL
GRAPHIC DESIGN
TECHNIQUES

PRACTICAL
GRAPHIC DESIGN
TECHNIQUES

EDITED BY LYDIA DARBYSHIRE

TIGER BOOKS INTERNATIONAL
LONDON

A QUINTET BOOK

This edition first published in 1991 by
Tiger Books International PLC
London

ISBN 1-85501-178-6

This book was designed and produced by
Quintet Publishing Limited
6 Blundell Street
London N7 9BH

Designer: Tony Jones
Photographers: John Heseltine, John Wyand,
Michael Freeman, Clive Boden, Malcolm Hoare and
Larry Bray
Project Editor: Laura Sandelson
Editor: Lydia Darbyshire

Typeset in Great Britain by
En to En Typesetters, Tunbridge Wells
Manufactured in Singapore by
Chroma Graphics (Overseas) PTE. LTD.
Printed in Spain by
Gráficas Estella, S.A.

The material in this publication previously
appeared in *Graphic Designer's Handbook,
Introduction to Graphic Design* and *Studio Secrets
for the Graphic Artist.*

Picture Credits
Page 7: Robert Opie Collection. Page 22-23 Rob Shone. Page 29 (top
and left): Photo Images. Page 93 (top): Marshall Editions. Page 99 (left):
The Moving Picture Company/Electronic Paintbox. Page 99 (centre and
right): Computer Animator/Bruce Carter. Page 100-101: Chrysalis Visual
Programming. Page 102: Robert Opie Collection. Page 103 (top): Pavilion
Books/Guy Rycart. Page 116: Crabtree & Evelyn/Tessa Traegar.

CONTENTS

INTRODUCTION

The task of a graphic designer is to communicate a message to his or her audience successfully through the organization of words and images. The graphic designer Paul Rand defined the designer as being 'like a juggler, demonstrating his skills by manipulating various ingredients in a given space'. This is an apt description although it does not give adequate credit to the aesthetic judgements involved.

The principle, however, remains basically the same whether it is applied to the design of a letterhead or to the creation of computer-generated television images. A well-designed poster or book may appear to be the result of almost casual effort on the part of the designer, but this is rarely the case. More often it is the result of a lengthy process, including experimenting with many options until a satisfactory one is found.

Good design has to take into consideration the practical constraints imposed by a client's brief — the budget, schedule and audience. The designer acts as a go-between, carrying a message from client to customer. To do this well, a designer must be familiar with all forms of graphic reproduction and be able to work with printers, photographers, illustrators and other technicians.

Laser scanners, digital cathode ray tubes, microprocessors — current design technology is sometimes as daunting for contemporary designers as a printing press might have been to a medieval scribe. Of course, the design task is now far more complex than it was for the scribe, working away in his cell. All that concerned him were his pens or brushes, paints or inks and the parchments on which his designs were directly created. Today's designers have a far more complex and daunting task. Although their aim remains the same, the technology involved in achieving it has multiplied to the point where it seems almost bewildering in its complexity. At no time in design history have designers been required to know and understand as much as they are today. To work effectively, it is often essential to break down or transcend the barriers that have been created, paradoxically enough, by technological progress. This can be achieved only by a thorough grounding in these self-same technologies insofar as their workings apply to the business of design. These facts have given rise to the profession of 'graphic designer'; the traditional role of the craftsman has now been swamped by technological advances.

Take typesetting, for instance. In today's typesetting industry old-style craftsmen are being replaced by, or transformed into, a new generation of technicians, whose prime allegiance is more to the micro-chip than to design traditions and aesthetics. This places an even greater responsibility on the designer. Not only must he or she respond to such innovations positively but, at the same time, police them, so that aesthetic standards are preserved. Much the same has happened in reproduction and printing and much the same knowledge and interest is required. As opposed to the medieval scribe, no modern designer can now design in isolation, but some designers, when faced with digital CRT machines, may have the same feelings as the scribe confronted with the first movable type.

To fulfil their responsibilities to the job, therefore, today's designers must accumulate a wealth of knowledge from a variety of previously unrelated sources. It is virtually impossible to gather this knowledge from any one source, so one of the aims of this book is to fill this gap. It aims to provide a guide to the technology of design by giving the designer access to information previously available only in lengthy and highly-specialized technical tomes. The only area not covered in detail is that of computer graphics, for the simple reason that the hardware capable of producing an image of acceptable resolution for general design purposes is still prohibitively expensive.

Like any profession, graphic design has its own vocabulary of jargon words and its own shorthand methods of notation, all impenetrable to an outsider. There are many short cuts in technique and procedure and an ever-increasing range of design-oriented new materials and equipment that can make any job easier and more successful. For students entering the profession or for practising graphic artists learning new tricks, there is a lot to keep up with. You may need to know in principle what a laser scanner can do, but in a day-to-day context, you will find that a simple can of lighter fluid is an indispensable graphic aid. This book is designed to demystify the jargon, explaining basic skills and the use of specific materials, equipment and technical processes. Selected projects show every stage of the graphic artist's work, from taking a brief to presenting finished artwork.

Graphic art is an exciting area — the presentation of a product can be largely responsible for its success or failure. The sudden success of a new magazine or advertising campaign shows how influential the graphic image can be, but many jobs are deliberately limited in range and intention — so it is no good entertaining fantasies of hi-tech styling when the job in hand is a simple black-and-white newspaper ad.

The first idea a graphic artist must absorb is that however confident and innovative the individual approach may be, design is basically a service: your responsibilities are to the client, the product and the market — to conveying information effectively in a way that suits all three. At the most basic level, remember that it's the client who pays the bill. This doesn't mean, however, that the customer is always right; good design, in a sense, comes from an efficient and sympathetic committee process. The client knows the product, whom it is for, how it has been presented in the past and where a possible new market lies. The artist is being asked to assemble a given number of elements and contribute the overall style and visual details that will make the product attractive, accessible and functional within its intended market. This means offering a creative individual approach; it does not mean imposing ideas on an unwilling audience.

EQUIPMENT AND MATERIALS

All graphic designers need a wide range of the best possible quality of equipment to enable them to work to the deadlines and to the high standards demanded today. This equipment ranges from tools that have changed little since their invention to those that have been recently developed for specific purposes using the latest technology. For example, while wood-cased pencils are very similar to those used in the 18th century, precision engineering has improved the reliability of clutch and propelling pencils. Erasers have also been developed to erase not only pencil, but also many inks.

Basic equipment for the graphic designer includes a good drawing board, good light, suitable measuring equipment — an inch and millimetre scale, a type scale and a steel straight-edge are essential tools — triangles (the adjustable kind are the most versatile), drawing equipment including a stylo-tipped fountain pen with a variety of different width nibs, and a basic variety of brushes. With deadlines to meet, the designer must be able to work quickly and accurately, so any device that can speed up work is invaluable.

The initial cost of equipping a studio is considerable, but this expenditure is normally spread over a period of time. Deciding what to buy will always depend on financial considerations, and before you invest in a major purchase, look carefully at methods of payment and whether you can afford it. If necessary take professional advice, but always be sure that you need the item and that it will pay for itself. Try to anticipate your future requirements and think of any labour-saving equipment as an investment. Will you need a larger plan chest (flat file) or PMT camera in a year's time? Are you choosing wisely and can you buy the item secondhand? Should you rent or lease?

If you are working freelance, there will always be items of equipment you would like but may not be able to afford. Once you buy or lease a photocopier that enlarges and reduces, you will wonder how you ever managed without one.

Get into the habit of checking your stock of materials, such as masking tape and adhesive, and have one main order every week to replenish it. To allow yourself to run out of basic materials is both inefficient and unnecessary.

It is wise to keep a good range of coloured papers to hand and to order specific colours as and when you need them. Coloured papers and boards are more economical to buy in packs, rather than individually. You should also keep well stocked with tracing and layout pads.

Graphic materials are expensive, so try to be as careful and as economical as possible. When using coloured papers, films and boards, don't throw the off-cuts away — there are bound to be occasions when a little scrap of a certain colour will save you the expense and delay of buying a new sheet. Look after the small items of equipment that you use daily, such as ruling pens (technical drawing pens) and set-squares (triangles). Keep your technical pens clean and use them regularly, otherwise they become blocked. A generally meticulous approach is one of the most important skills you must acquire. If you work in chaos, it will be reflected in the quality of your work and you will waste time.

▶ *A sharp pair of scissors and a scalpel (X-Acto knife) with a variety of blades are essential. Craft knives for cutting heavyweight materials such as cardboard, plastic, hardboard and wood are also useful; the handles are shaped for a sure grip and carry spare blades.*

▶ *Metal rules are often used for cutting but can be dangerous. A proper metal cutting edge ruler is much heavier and rubber-backed so that it will neither move nor slip.*

▼ *Cutting mats can be either transparent or coloured. The transparent kind can be used on a lightbox, while the coloured ones are for use on the desk. The surface does not break up with use and does not blunt blades. The grid printed on the surface can be used as a guide for squaring up illustrations or text.*

▼ *Knives with retractable, disposable blades, which can be snapped off when blunt, are convenient for those unused to changing blades, but they are something of a luxury.*

DESK EQUIPMENT

Pens and pencils

Drawing pencils   As many as 19 grades of pencil are available, ranging from the softest — EE, EB, 6B to B, HB — through F, which is of medium hardness, and from H to 9H — the hardest.

Carbon pencils   A recommended carbon pencil is Wolff's, which is available in degrees ranging from HH to BB. There are three degrees of black Conté pencils — No 1 medium (HB), No 2 soft (B) and No 3 extra soft (BB).

Coloured pencils   Three main types of coloured pencil are widely available. First, those with thick, comparatively soft leads are both waterproof and lightproof and can be bought in a wide variety of colours — Derwent produces 72 shades and Eagle 62. They do not smudge or erase easily, nor do they need to be fixed.

Second, the Veri-thin variety has, as the name implies, a thin, non-crumbling lead, which is useful for fine detailed work. They

are also waterproof, but only 36 to 40 shades are generally available. They do not smudge, but only a few colours are manufactured that are completely erasable.

The third group are those that are water-soluble. Used with water to produce washes of colour, these are something of a cross between pencils and watercolours and are made by various

Magic Marker is a specific trade name, but it is often applied generally to spirit-based coloured pens (felt-tipped marker pens), which are increasingly used in design work. They are available in an enormous range of colours with fine or broad tips, which can be reshaped using a scalpel (X-Acto knife). You can begin by keeping black and a good selection of greys before building up a wider range of colours. Letraset makes a range called Pantone Markers, and these can be matched directly in colour to a range of inks and papers. As markers are spirit-based, the colour bleeds outwards when they are used. It also bleeds through the paper, so be careful when working that your paper is not resting on anything important.

Their main virtue is that you can cover a large area of layout paper with an even colour, but it does take practice. Make your strokes quickly, otherwise a darker line appears where a fresh stroke of the pen overlaps one that has already dried. To cover a large area quickly, remove from inside the pen the piece of wadding, which is soaked in the colour, and use it horizontally with wide, sweeping strokes.

If you use a marker with a ruler, remember to clean the edge of the ruler first, otherwise the spirit in the pen will carry the dirt from the ruler onto your layout.

Get into good habits when using these pens, or you will get virtually no use out of them. If you leave markers in the sun or near a radiator they will dry out. Buy a black one and a good selection of greys and then build up the range as the need arises.

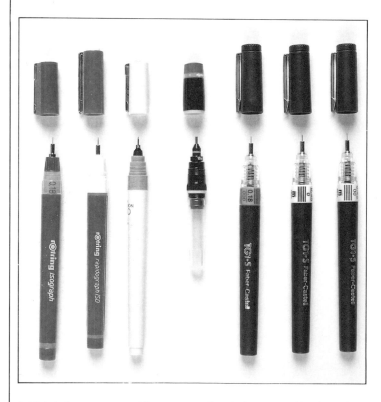

▲ *Technical pens are essential for accurate artwork and detail. Instead of a conventional nib they have a metal tube. The ink is fed through the tube, producing a consistent thickness of line.*

They also have removable nibs, so that a variety of point sizes can be bought. The pen must be held upright to assist the flow of ink, and some makes have been adapted to take non-clogging ink.

▲ *Mechanical pencils and lead-holders hold different thicknesses of leads and have a special sharpener attached. The leads can also vary in hardness — from B to H.*

with broad italic nibs to ones with fine, flexible copperplate nibs.

Reservoir pens are popular among draughtsmen and illustrators alike, in that their chief attraction is that they can be used with waterproof drawing inks of any type, for which there is a wide range of colours. Of this type, Pelikan Graphos pens have a range of 19 nibs, which are quickly interchangeable and so just as useful as stylo-tipped pens.

Fibre and felt-tipped pens   These are now produced in a vast range of types, mostly with a large selection of colours. Their main virtue is that they produce a dependable, flowing and consistent line, while their width sensitivity makes working with them similar to drawing with the tip of a brush. Many are made for specific uses, such as drawing on film for overhead projection purposes. They are also available in water-soluble and spirit-based permanent varieties, as well as in an almost daunting range of tip thicknesses.

Inks   Artists' drawing inks are waterproof and dry to a glossy film. They are available in an impressive variety of colours: for

manufacturers with either thick or thin leads and in ranges of up to about 36 colours.

Clutch pencils   A development of the propelling pencil, clutch pencils consist of a holder made of plastic or metal, or both, inside which is a sleeve that holds and protects the lead. The lead is secured in position by a clutch lock, which is released to project the lead forward by pressing a button at the end of the holder. Leads are available in a wide variety of softnesses and widths, the smallest of which is 0.2mm.

Pens   Apart from the traditional quills, reed-pens and dip-pens, fountain pens — particularly the stylo tipped variety — are the most useful for the designer. Stylo-tipped fountain pens are useful not only because of the wide range of 15 widths but also because they draw a line of consistent and unvarying width. Osmiroid drawing pens — now adapted to take black, non-clogging, water-proof drawing ink — are extremely useful. They range from those

▲ *Magic Marker pens, Pantone pens and Mecanorma pens are available in an enormous selection of colours. They are useful for covering large areas with flat colour in mock-ups and finished visuals. Pantone pens match the Pantone Matching System. Be careful, since most of these pens are spirit-based and so will bleed through normal paper onto the surface below.*

It is a good idea to put masking tape on the back of your set-square (triangle) or ruler. This raises the edge slightly and prevents ink from your technical pen from bleeding underneath. It also gives a cleaner line and stops your set-square or ruler slipping.

example, Grumbacher offers 17, Pelikan makes 18 and Winsor and Newton has 22. The range of black drawing inks, sometimes called Indian, is similarly impressive. Pelikan makes a variety of special coloured inks in filler bottles for use in Graphos and stylo-tipped pens, as well as special drawing inks for use on polyester drawing films.

Bottles of ink should always be shaken before use, since the pigment tends to settle at the bottom of the bottle if it is left unused for some time. Ink may evaporate slightly in summer while uncorked during a day's work, with the result that the colour becomes deeper and the ink thicker; the addition of just a small amount of distilled water (not a heavy dilution) will thin it again and cause an easier flow.

Rulers, protractors and triangles

A proper straight-edge metal ruler is very heavy and therefore good for use on cutting mats or thick cardboard. It should be rubber-backed so that it will not move or slip easily. A clear plastic ruler is useful for lining up type and is also easy to keep clean. Do not use your plastic ruler for cutting. A centring rule has zero in the middle and is most useful for centring type during paste-up. A parallel ruler will allow you to produce lines at a variety of distances that are always parallel.

A depth scale (pica measure) is used to calculate the number of typeset lines to a page in any given typesize. Metal type rulers are also available, and those made of brushed matt metal are easy to read. Buy a model that has point sizes and imperial and metric conversions. If you have to handle a lot of typeset matter, you might also find it useful to buy a printer's rule, which is a metal depth scale.

Use a protractor for dividing sections of a circle and for working out angles for pie-charts or other diagrams that show percentages of a circle. Right-angled triangles or set-squares are essential for squaring up work and for marking up consistent angles. They are available in 45 and 60 degree versions, and some have bevelled edges for easier use with ruling pens or stainless steel cutting edges. An adjustable set-square is particularly useful for diagrams and graphs as it can be used to set intermediate angles.

Compasses and dividers

An adjustable compass with an extension arm is useful if you want to produce a large circle since it enables you to keep your pen or the pencil point at a consistent angle of 45 degrees to the paper. Smaller compasses, however, have better locking devices if you have to repeat the same circumference. There are various attachments on the market so that you can fit technical pens to your compasses. If you have to draw extremely large circles, you may need a beam compass, which can be extended almost indefinitely, while pump compasses can draw circles of less than $\frac{1}{16}$in (1.5mm) in diameter. Always keep your compass lead sharpened for best results; an emery board is the easiest way.

Dividers enable you to make repeated and accurate measurements, and proportional dividers allow you to take a measurement and calculate whatever proportions you require.

▲ *Although these French curves look as though they may provide only a small number of shapes, the curve itself can be manipulated to produce almost any shape — the problem is remembering the movements when you wish to repeat it!*

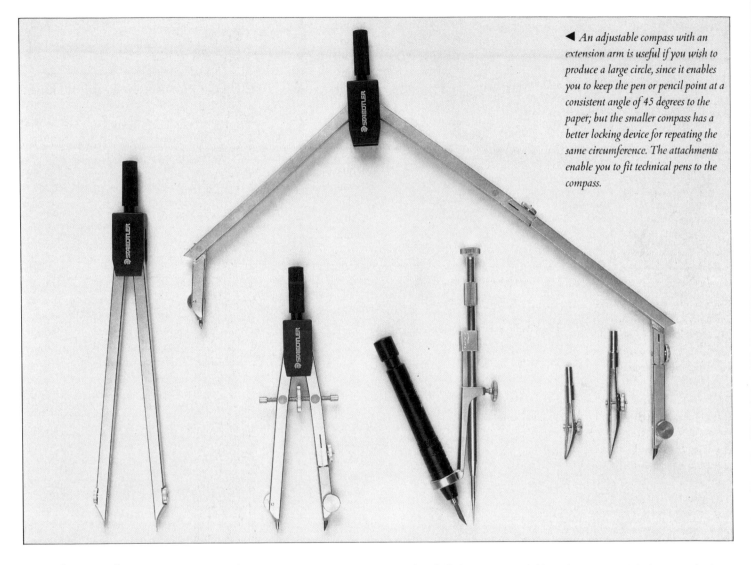

◄ *An adjustable compass with an extension arm is useful if you wish to produce a large circle, since it enables you to keep the pen or pencil point at a consistent angle of 45 degrees to the paper; but the smaller compass has a better locking device for repeating the same circumference. The attachments enable you to fit technical pens to the compass.*

Templates and curves

Templates come in all shapes and sizes and offer a practical way of drawing curves and circles accurately and quickly. They can be placed directly onto artwork and traced around. Some kinds also have a bevelled edge, which reduces the risk of smudging when used with a technical pen. Flexible snakes will bend to the curve you need, but they are not very precise and are difficult to use well. They come into their own when finished artwork has to be roughed out. Flexible curves are made with a lip so that you can draw a clean line with no risk of bleeding.

Paper

If you are to work effectively as a designer you must be prepared and able to meet deadlines. Make sure that you have adequate stocks of all the papers and films that you are likely to need. If you run out of any paper that you use fairly regularly, you are not running your studio efficiently. Be economical with your materials and save those small off-cuts — there are going to be occasions when a scrap of a colour will save you time and money.

There are many types of paper and card available, and you should be careful when buying to make sure that you get the kind you need for different types of work. Watercolour papers vary considerably in both weight and texture. All good watercolour papers have a right side that is carefully prepared and coated with size, but they often need to be stretched before they are suitable for taking the watercolour paint without buckling. 'Not' watercolour paper is the most commonly used paper for watercolours. The slightly rough surface receives wash and line artwork well.

Bristol board is a thin, smooth card that is suitable for technical illustration and three-dimensional work. Hot-pressed papers are hard and smooth and are ideal for pencil, pen and ink drawing as well as for line and wash. Cartridge paper is used for pencil work and early roughs, while line board takes all types of pen line work without the line feathering. Mistakes can be scratched out with a sharp scalpel (X-Acto knife). Cover papers, which are available in a wide range of colours, are mainly used for presentations and for display work.

Among the other papers that are available are marker paper, which is coated so that the colour from the marker does not bleed through, and high white layout paper, which has good resistance to marker bleed. You will also need pads of tracing paper, which should be smooth and transparent enough to be seen through and also smooth enough for fine ink and pencil work, and of layout paper, which is used for initial roughs and which is thin enough to allow type to show through but opaque enough to be drawn on.

You should also equip yourself with rolls or pads of acetate, which is used with presentations as a clear overlay to keep your work clean and also for separating artwork. Acetate is available in several weights, but, although it is ideal for presentations, it cracks when creased. Drafting film does not stretch or contract. It takes ink and paint, and mistakes can be scraped off with a scalpel (X-Acto knife). Blue tint drafting film is ideal for colour-separated line work. Clear coated film will accept all studio media, while photo-opaque film, which is sticky-backed, photographs as black and is used for masking areas on artwork. It takes pen and ink and is transparent on a lightbox.

Pantone Matching System

The Pantone Colour Specifier holds small samples of all the Pantone range on both coated and uncoated papers. The use of a Pantone swatch enables a printer to match colour exactly as a job is

---

When handling knives, always do so with extreme care. It is particularly easy to inflict serious injuries when changing a blade or using a plastic ruler to cut against. Use the correct implements — a proper metal cutting edge is not very expensive and will last for years. Wrap masking tape around old blades before you discard them, so no one else will cut themselves later.

When cutting paper or card, use the correct tool. A lightweight blade used to cut a thick piece of card will result in either a broken blade or damage to the edge you are cutting. This is all commonsense, but it is surprising how many accidents occur.

---

run. The complete range of more than 500 papers is available in matt finish and will accept most art media. The colours are also linked into a range of gloss papers and of sticky-back film, which is used mainly in presentation work.

Knives, blades and cutting tools

A sharp pair of scissors and a craft knife for cutting heavy cardboard are essential. You will also need a scalpel (X-Acto knife) with a variety of blades, which are specially made for different purposes — make sure you use the right blade for the right job. Blades can also be used for cutting or scraping marks off paper and board, so keep a selection in stock. Scapel (X-Acto knife) blades are dangerous: wrap masking tape around old blades before you dispose of them.

Knives that hold a range of interchangeable differently shaped blades are ideal for general studio use, while swivel knives are especially designed for cutting curves and complicated shapes in lightweight material such as film or paper. The blade rotates through 360 degrees, giving you fine control of the direction of cutting. Retractable knives have a single blade, which can be snapped off and disposed of as it is blunted, while disposable knives are convenient for those unused to changing blades.

Cutting mats are either transparent or green. The transparent ones are for use on a lightbox and the green ones for the desk. The surface does not break down with use and will not blunt your scalpel (X-Acto knife) blades. The grid printed on the surface can be used as a guide for squaring up photographs.

STUDIO EQUIPMENT

Airbrush

There are two types of airbrush mechanisms — single-action lever and double-action lever. Single action is the simplest form of airbrush, in which the only way of altering the pattern of spray is to increase or decrease the distance between the brush and the surface being sprayed. Though simple to maintain, this type of airbrush is suitable for general background work only.

The double-action brush is essential for the precision and detail required in much technical illustration. Its main advantage is that it allows the user to control the proportions of paint to air; as the lever is depressed air, not paint, is released through the brush, and only when it is pulled backwards does paint meet the airstream — the further back, the greater the amount of paint released. There are a wide range of airbrushes on the market today, and choice of a suitable instrument will depend on what it is to be used for.

The Aerograph Super 63 A-504 is a double-action lever model,

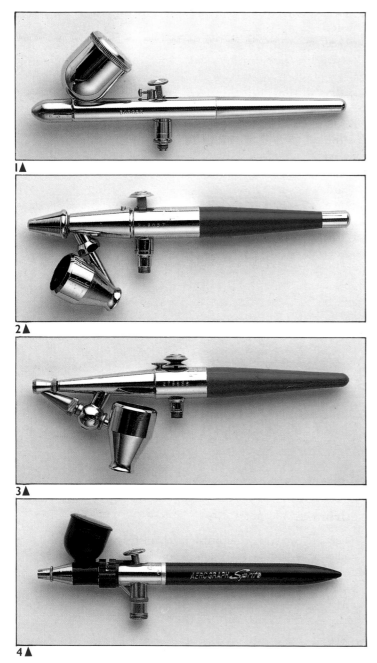

1▲

2▲

3▲

4▲

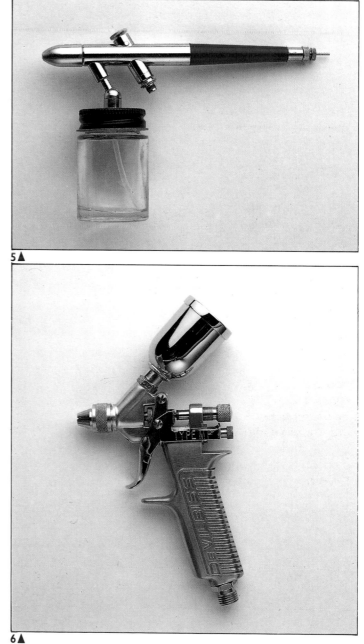

5▲

6▲

▲ The Badger 100 LG (top) is a simple two-way gravity-feed airbrush. It is quite cheap, but there is not a great deal of control. The Paasche H3 (second from top) is also at the cheaper end of the market. It is for rough work rather than precision, and is often used by model-makers. The Paasche VLS (third from top) is a better, precision, double-action airbrush. The De Vilbiss Sprite (bottom) is a medium-quality airbrush. It is a good working model, not too expensive and is suitable for students and hobbyists.

▲ ▲ The Badger 200 is a model-maker's airbrush and so, although it is very useful for large areas of flat colour, it is not suitable for detailed work. It has a fixed jet, just on and off – which is why it produces a constant flow.

▲ The De Vilbiss MP Spray Gun is a lightweight industrial airbrush. It is suitable for medium detail work or for spraying large amounts of colour. It is also useful for three-dimensional applications.

▲ *This double parallel motion assembly unit can be used for viewing negatives, positives or transparencies and doubles as a 'spotting' bench.*

giving precision control suitable for most types of work. The Super 63 E-504 is similar to the A-504, but has a coarser nozzle and a larger reservoir, so allowing a greater area to be covered in a shorter time. The Sprite is a simpler double-action type and, consequently, is less precise on line work. The Conograph is a single-action lever brush with detachable cups.

The Wold A1 is a double-action lever brush with two air caps — one coned and one flared. It can be used for work ranging from fine

When removing the air cap from an airbrush, always remove the needle first. If this simple precaution is ignored, there is the risk that both needle and air cap will be damaged. Unscrew the handle and loosen the nut locking the needle in position. Take the needle out about 1in (25mm), unscrew the air cap and remove the nozzle.

line rendering to broad wash tones. The Wold A2 is similar to the A1, but with an improved air cap assembly, while the M type has double the capacity of the A series, as it is fitted with a 1oz or 2oz (28 or 56g) jar, with interchangeable cups for any colour changes. The K-M is single-action with a wheel control that predetermines the volume of spray, handling large quantities of colour in a short time.

The Thayer and Chandler models AA and A are both double lever brushes that produce fine lines and broad coverage of tones. The C type's 2oz (56g) capacity makes it ideal for large areas, while the E and G1 models are ideal for display artists.

The Paasche AB is capable of producing the finest hairline thickness or dots and so it is ideally suited to freehand drawing and photographic retouching. The Paasche H1, H2 and H3 types are single-action control lever brushes with separate controls which can be pre-adjusted for colour and air. The air caps and colour nozzles are interchangeable to provide a range from fine line to broad spray. The Paasche V1 and V2 are both double-action, the former being suitable for fine work and the latter for medium rendering, and both being good for vignetting. Each has a micrometer line adjuster giving rapid setting from very fine to broad. The Paasche air eraser holds an abrasive instead of paint, which can erase ink and paint without streaking or smudging. It can also be used for blending highlights and shadows.

An airbrush is an extremely expensive item of equipment and should be treated with the utmost care. It should be thoroughly cleaned after use because, for example, dried paint may distort the shape of the air cap or even damage the nozzle, thus affecting the quality of spray. Dried paint can even render an airbrush ineffective if it gets into the workings.

The air supply to an airbrush should be maintained at an average pressure of 30lb per square in (2kg per square cm) and is available in a variety of sources — in an aerosol can, a refillable canister like that used by underwater divers, by a foot pump (hard work) or by an electric compressor. The last is the most efficient method because the air is supplied at much more constant pressure.

Drawing board

The type of drawing board you buy will depend partly on the space available in your studio and, of course, on how much you wish to pay. The most basic plain wooden board will probably need to be covered with a backing sheet of some kind, although plastic-covered table-top boards are available. These have the advantage that they can be stored away when not in use if space is short.

You will probably need a parallel-motion board, and these are available in a wide variety of styles and degrees of sophistication. Some have built-in light boxes for viewing transparencies, and others have boards that can be moved through 360 degrees.

▲ *To pre-release a character, rub gently with a burnisher, holding the sheet in the air or using the backing paper to stop the character coming away.*

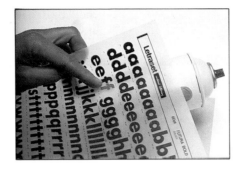

▲ *The character is ready to press onto your artwork or presentation once it has gone paler in colour than the characters next to it.*

▲ *Place the backing sheet over the character once it is in position and burnish it again to secure it.*

Dry transfer lettering

Dry transfer lettering is lettering that you buy on a plastic sheet and rub down when preparing artwork or mock-ups. There are several major companies producing large ranges of typefaces, as well as rules, borders, symbols and illustration images. Lettering comes in many sizes, and some sheets are available in colour. You will gradually build up a collection of sheets, which are most usefully stored in alphabetical order. Make sure that they do not get dirty or crumpled.

Dry transfer is applied by rubbing each character down with a soft pencil or a specially shaped burnisher, once it has been positioned correctly. Rub the letter gently at first until it begins to come away from its plastic sheet — you will see the letter go paler in colour as it is released. Sharp points such as hard pencils will distort the plastic sheet and break up the character. Once the character is released, secure it by burnishing again, but this time with the backing sheet or a piece of tracing paper over the letter to protect it. You can, if you choose, buy a can of protective aerosol spray that prevents the transfer image being scratched or damaged.

All dry transfer is supplied with a protective backing sheet. If you are working on a delicate surface that could mark, leave the backing sheet in position and rub very gently. This will partially pre-release the letter, so that when it is positioned on your work it needs only the slightest pressure to adhere. This backing sheet can also be used to protect your artwork while you apply the letters.

Although dry transfer is available in a wide range of typefaces, symbols and other textures designed to speed up artwork, do not always assume it is the answer to every job and use it automatically. Look at other solutions.

If you position a letter wrongly, remove it with a piece of masking or other sticky tape; but do it carefully so that you do not damage the surface of your work. If you find the letter is stubborn, a drop of lighter fuel (solvent) will help to lift it more easily. However, be careful in case the lighter fuel loosens other characters.

Letraset has small horizontal lines under each character which will help you to space the letters. If you prefer to space type visually, they are useful for keeping the type straight as you rub it down or for repairing the edge of a broken character.

Light box

A light box is essential in the studio for viewing transparencies, tracing through images or type and doing separations for artwork. It is quite easy to make your own, but you should use strip lights as ordinary bulbs do not give an even light source and get very hot. Transparent cutting mats are available so that you do not score the surface of the light box; these mats have a grid printed on the surface so that you can align your work.

Computer-aided design

The range of techniques and materials available to the designer has now been considerably enlarged by systems such as the Quantel Digital Paintbox, which was designed as a complete system for television art and graphics. This allows original designs to be created directly on the screen in virtually any style according to which mode is used. The 'paint' mode, for instance, gives a wide choice of media, including watercolours, chalk and airbrush, as well as an almost unlimited colour range, while the 'graphics' model has facilities for drawing straight lines, rectangles, circles and ellipses. The 'text' mode provides a large range of fonts with titling images or graphics, and all the modes can be combined if desired. Such systems dramatically increase the speed at which original graphics

▲ *The PMT machine is very versatile: it can reverse images from black to white, enlarge and reduce, make acetate overlays and screens and convert lettering and artwork to autotype. Most are automatic; you put in your requirements and the camera automatically adjusts itself. The machine and paper are expensive, but once bought will enable you to do practically everything yourself.*

can be produced, as well as facilitating the task of retouching. Since the Paintbox accepts video feeds, images can be altered or retouched directly on the screen without recourse to photographic methods.

The resolution quality of these systems is not of a particularly high standard and, therefore, they are best suited to presentation work. However, they are being improved and systems are becoming available that can be linked to digital scanners, thereby enabling the production of four-colour separated film.

Studio equipment should be looked after and kept clean. Before you begin work, clean everything you will be using with lighter fuel (solvent). Cultivating a meticulous approach to every aspect of your work can only help.

Photomechanical transfer machine

Photographic copying equipment — as distinct from photocopiers — using transparent or paper negatives, produces high-quality prints which can be used as successfully for reproduction as the original artwork, and, unlike cruder photocopies, can be made at any size within its maximum format.

One of the most popular systems, the PMT machine, produces an excellent quality of reproduction, is cheaper to use than conventional photographic systems, and some types do not require a darkroom for processing. A large variety of different screens is available, and halftones can be produced that, although not as fine as those made by photoengraving, are quite adequate for low-budget work or for reference prints.

The PMT machine can also be used to simulate colour in a design without having to go to the expense of a colour proof. First, the subject is printed onto a film base that is processed to give a colour simulation known as a colour key, and then a dye is used to develop the image in one of several stock colours.

Since both the colours and the film base itself are transparent, they can be superimposed to create the appearance of two or more colours printed in line or halftone. Duotones and even four-colour effects outside the standard printing colours can be simulated as well.

The colour key technique also enables a designer to make a single copy of a simulated colour image in the form of a self-adhesive dry transfer, which can be applied to presentation material such as package designs, to give a customer an impression of how the finished job will look. Recent technological developments in photocopying have increased the quality and capability of most machines, thus widening the areas of application, particularly in the design field.

Visualizer

Although they are rather large, visualizers (cameras lucida) are the easiest way to scale photographs, typography or, indeed, any image for artwork up or down. The handles adjust the size and the focus, and you trace the image off the top sheet of glass on tracing paper. Most enlargers have a light box fitted in the base for tracing off transparencies.

Photocopier

The most useful photocopying machine for the designer is one that will produce prints of the largest possible size — but will also give percentage reduction copies when required. There are two basic types of photocopier — thermal and electrostatic. In the former, a paper negative is used, which produces prints on the same special paper. The electrostatic copier needs no negative and will print onto any paper and even onto transparent film.

PMTs – a checklist

The most common use of the PMT camera is to produce copies of line artwork — either the same size, enlarged or reduced — to be used in the preparation of camera-ready artwork. Line artwork, or 'line copy', describes any image that consists solely of black line or areas of black and white, with no shades of grey, or mid-tones. Examples include dry transfer lettering and pen and ink drawings.

Whether you want to copy onto film or paper, the same basic procedure is followed:

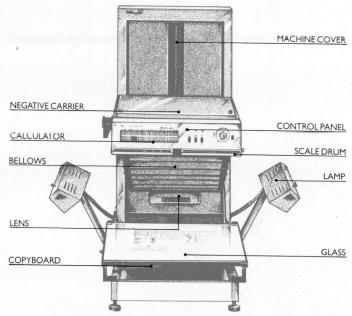

MACHINE COVER

NEGATIVE CARRIER

CONTROL PANEL

CALCULATOR

SCALE DRUM

BELLOWS

LAMP

LENS

GLASS

COPYBOARD

■ Switch on the electricity supply to the camera.
■ Switch on the darkroom safe-light.
■ Clean the glass cover to the copyboard and the image plate thoroughly with lighter fuel (solvent), or a special anti-static spray, to remove all greasy fingermarks and dust.
■ Check that your processor is filled with the correct developer.
■ Switch off ordinary room lights so that you are working in safe-light.
■ Place your original copy under the glass of the copyboard, ensuring that it is central and squarely positioned.
■ Set your camera to the required size of reproduction: same size = 100 per cent; double size = 200 per cent; half size = 50 per cent, and so on. Some cameras are automatic and some are manual, so the ease with which the desired size is achieved will depend on this.
■ With the lens fully open, check with an eye glass that the image on the focusing screen is sharp.
■ Mark the image area on the focusing screen with pieces of masking tape. This will help you position your negative paper and economize on materials.
■ Set the correct exposure time for your copy on the camera's timer and 'stop down' the lens to the required amount. You will have an established exposure scale which will give you all this information.
■ Turn off the camera's constant light.
■ Place the negative material on the image plate with the light-sensitive emulsion side facing the glass, and close the vacuum top. Activate the vacuum, and wait for the desired pressure to be reached.
■ Switch on the main lamps and wait for them to go off at the pre-set time. After exposure, open the vacuum top, remove the negative, contact it with the positive receiver paper, or film, and feed them through the processor. Wait for the recommended contact time. The result should be a clean sharp copy of the original. Complete the procedure by carefully washing and drying the print.
■ If the results are not satisfactory, check your developing fluid and lens aperture or f-stop. Problems are often due to the paper being faulty in the first place, or the paper not contacting properly as it passes through the processor.
■ The negative paper is light-sensitive, so must never be exposed to daylight. *Never open packs of light-sensitive paper or film except in safe-light, otherwise you will spoil the entire pack.*

One of the oldest copying systems, the dyeline process, has recently undergone a number of improvements — including substitution of the unpleasant smelling ammonia by another chemical. In this process, a transparent original is placed over sensitized paper and exposed to ultraviolet light. Dyeline is particularly suitable for copying engineering or architectural drawings, with a range of sizes extending up to A0.

A sophisticated version of the dyeline technique, the Safir SC process, enables the final appearance of a piece of artwork to be checked without going to the expense of getting it colour-proofed. Light passing through film-based images of the artwork — at its final size — activates a photo-sensitive coating on a white polyester base. Dye sticks to the exposed areas and successive layers of colour can be built up.

SKILLS AND TECHNIQUES

airbrush

colour mark-up

gouache

print preparation

correcting proofs

visualising

dry transfer

typography

A graphic designer is an orchestrator of words and images. Every designer will deal with typography, colour and composition in an individual manner, producing different results. To be a successful graphic designer requires an inherent aesthetic awareness and artistic flair — these are essential qualities. Developing these natural abilities requires practical training. The emphasis at most colleges is on self-motivation, and undoubtedly, a period spent exploring ideas and experimenting without the restrictions imposed by a commercial contract, is invaluable for the development of visual awareness. Few colleges, therefore, offer the working environment in which students can appreciate why they are learning certain skills. It is difficult to understand the importance of good copyfitting or artwork unless they are put in an appropriate context. The reason for learning how to cast-off, or how to mark up copy well, becomes clear very quickly when you begin working. If you are to succeed within this competitive industry, you must be equipped at the outset with a range of basic technical skills and a knowledge of design principles.

The career opportunities for a graphic designer are quite diverse, but you will find that similar kinds of visual and aesthetic judgements apply to most sectors of the commercial design industry. Your main objective is always to communicate information to your audience.

GETTING STARTED

The easiest element of working as a freelancer is actually doing the work once you have it. A client who is paying you money naturally expects you to give a good service. This will mean being available for meetings, talking through your ideas and basically keeping them happy. Much of your energy will go into becoming your own public relations officer. You must win the confidence of your client.

But how do you meet clients initially? Whom do you contact? The best form of introduction is recommendation. If you have worked successfully with one customer, they are likely to tell others about you, and so your reputation will grow. The reverse is also true, so remember this before you are late with a job or let anybody down. Success depends on your professional reputation.

Recommendation will come later in your career. Initially, contacts will be made by phoning people up, writing to them, then showing them your portfolio. This can be an extremely disheartening process at first, so brace yourself for the realization that it is not only very difficult to locate potential customers, but also you are going to have lots of refusals. Making contact with a company's marketing team on the telephone can be a major task, let alone persuading them to see your portfolio. You will learn to become persistent — skill in graphics does not qualify you in selling. This is something to consider before you decide on freelancing. Even when you are busy, make time to see new people, because there is no point in being hectic with work one week and then finding yourself unemployed the next. Planning plays a major role in the successful control of workload.

It is good policy to busy yourself seeing people, even if there are no immediate results. Art directors do keep records and may contact you several months, even a year, later — you can never tell. But you can be certain that if you do not make the effort to see potential clients, they will never contact you.

If you have already worked in one area of graphics, such as publishing, then that is the obvious starting point in your search for work. Draw up a list of all the publishers it is practical to visit. Business directories in the public library will give you a company's address, telephone number and a little general information. It will help you judge a company's size and possible design requirements. It is essential when writing to a company that you find out the name of the person to whom your letter should go. This can be found in a directory or by telephoning the company's switchboard and asking. If you have any problem, explain your purpose. Your local business telephone directory will help as well. Try to be logical about who you see, and when you speak to people on the telephone, assess their design requirements and the likelihood of

their needing designers — otherwise you may be wasting each other's time. Having said this, the most unlikely sources can often yield an unimaginable quality and quantity of work. So it really is down to trial and error and persistence. If your work is good you will find a market.

Your portfolio

Your work and its presentation are essential to your success. This cannot be stressed enough. When you walk into an office for the first time, your portfolio is an instant communication, not only of

▲ *When you prepare your portfolio ensure that the work displayed in it is relevant to the person you are seeing.*

Your portfolio is the first communication of your skill as a designer and should demonstrate that you are a professional.

your skill and talent as a designer, but also that you are a professional and you mean business.

The commercial world is a busy place, people are always in a hurry. Your work must be clearly presented if people are going to bother looking at it. An effective way of doing this is to display your samples flat, in a ring binder with transparent sleeves. This method not only protects your work, but also makes it easy to look through. You can mount your samples onto sheets of coloured paper (if in doubt, use black) and slip these into transparent sleeves.

Colour transparencies should be mounted in black window boards or plastic sleeves, so that they can be examined in groups. If you want a brochure to be handled, keep one mounted flat in its sleeve, and carry another with you at the back of the folder.

Keep your portfolio up to date with recent work, not what you have done over the last five years. But if you have litttle recent work available, put together some self-motivated ideas. It will demonstrate creativity and enthusiasm.

It's important that you don't try and show every single piece of work you've ever done. Be selective — people won't have time to see your total professional life flash before them — and think about who you are showing your work to, and, therefore, what would be relevant. You may have to change the contents of your portfolio for every interview.

Interviews

When you have arranged an interview, with an art director for example, never be late. Remember how important your personal presentation is. Many businesses are quite conservative and people do make judgements about personality based on appearance even though this is a foolish thing to do. But for the sake of getting work, present yourself in the best possible way and don't be late for the appointment. During the interview allow people time to look through your work at their own pace. Explain the contents of your folder as they go through it, but try not to talk incessantly — some art directors are happy to look quietly through a portfolio without a running commentary.

If you are unable to arrange an interview with a prospective client or employer you can always give them samples of your previous work. If your work is suitable for photocopying, make up a little package of photocopied specimens and leave them together with a business card and a *curriculum vitae* (résumé).

Freelancing

Many designers work as 'freelancers'. This means working for different clients on a job-by-job basis, usually from home or a separate rented studio. Most freelancers begin by working from home, because it is the most cost-effective and convenient way. You save on overheads and you can claim a proportion of your household expenses against tax. You should consider employing an accountant if you need advice about tax as a self-employed person.

Before you begin working from home, think carefully about practical considerations. It is all very well setting up a studio in the living room, but is working late into the night in order to meet a deadline going to upset others at home? Unless you have a separate

telephone number for your business, and this is unlikely, clients will be able to call you at any time, and they do. Will you mind?

Plan a studio in the home carefully. The space must be suitable for the job. Obviously, setting aside a separate room is the best way, but not always practical. Considerations such as clients visiting the home must be taken into account — if you are working in the top room of a house, clients will have to walk through the rest of your home to get there — do you mind this?

If you decide on renting a separate studio, the first consideration is whether you can afford it? One of the cheapest ways of separating your work life from your home life is to rent studio space or desk space in an existing studio. For a fairly small amount of money you can rent not only the area, but also facilities that you may not have, such as a PMT camera (stat camera) and darkroom, a photocopier or a fax. It may also be convenient for the studio to supply you with work, and this can be useful while you are building up your own contacts. However, take care to clarify any arrangement and commitments like this before you move in.

This arrangement has other advantages, too. Working with other people can be of a great benefit creatively; it provides an opportunity for discussing and exchanging ideas. Some clients will also be more impressed if you have a separate studio, which may lead to them trusting you with larger commissions.

Another way of lowering the cost incurred in renting a studio is to share one with other designers, or like-minded colleagues, on an equal footing. Working with other people is as difficult as living with other people, so think carefully about whom you share with — even if you are friends — and discuss any areas of possible discontent beforehand. You cannot expect colleagues to always fit into your plans — they may like a radio on while they work and you may prefer silence; they may be very tidy and you may not be. Look at fairly basic considerations like these before deciding to work together. Sometimes working with one or more colleagues means you can offer a wider range of complementary skills to customers, and working with illustrators or photographers can be of mutual benefit. Beware of working with direct competitors, unless you are both able to cope with one of you being busy while the other is not.

Another way of sharing the responsibilities of a design business is to form a partnership. This type of association is fraught with difficulties and should be considered very carefully. Do you offer each other benefits and different skills, and are you both going to inject equal effort into making the practice succeed. Remember that a partnership, like any relationship, will only flourish when aims and objectives are clarified and the direction of both partners remains the same. If you decide to go ahead, put an agreement in writing, whatever your relationship is, and make it legal. Partnerships only need this type of agreement if and when the association ends, but that is the very time when an agreement would make a difficult split easier.

The life of a freelancer can seem very glamorous, but it has many pitfalls. It can be demanding in terms of time, because you have to look for, and find, work. Sometimes you may be short of

work, at others, you may be hard pressed to meet deadlines. This is because you are entirely dependent on clients for your livelihood. It is untrue to say that a freelancer's life is more independent. It is important, however, that you learn basic business skills so that you can keep accounts, send letters and keep the business running.

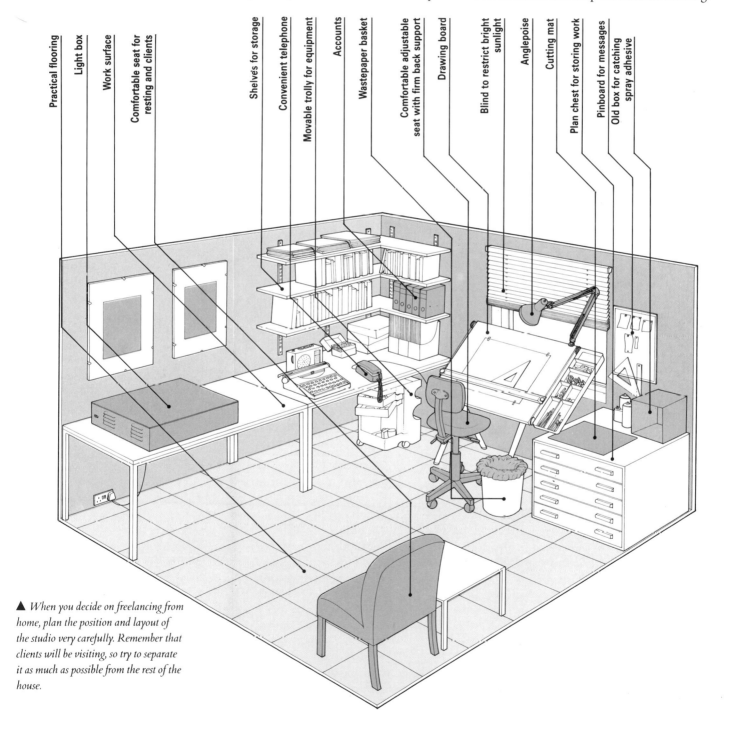

Practical flooring
Light box
Work surface
Comfortable seat for resting and clients
Shelves for storage
Convenient telephone
Movable trolly for equipment
Accounts
Wastepaper basket
Comfortable adjustable seat with firm back support
Drawing board
Blind to restrict bright sunlight
Anglepoise
Cutting mat
Plan chest for storing work
Pinboard for messages
Old box for catching spray adhesive

▲ *When you decide on freelancing from home, plan the position and layout of the studio very carefully. Remember that clients will be visiting, so try to separate it as much as possible from the rest of the house.*

THE DESIGN BRIEF

An important stage of any artist's work is the initial briefing from the client. This introductory section necessarily touches on the business aspects — time and money — rather than the creative.

Many graphic artists have learned the hard way that being businesslike is just as important as being able to wield a Magic Marker or use a PMT machine.

Whatever you are asked to do — whether it's a poster, a catalogue or point-of-sale material — it's up to you to find out what is involved and whether you can handle the work before committing yourself to the project. Being able to handle it doesn't just mean having the technical skills and a lively approach — it also requires you to work to a specific budget and schedule, and to feel confident that you can organize typesetting, photography, illustration work and printing as necessary.

Take some information during the initial contact on the phone, so that you go to a briefing meeting familiar with the subject of the brief. Some clients know very precisely what they want and are asking you to do a fairly mechanical assembly job; other will be expecting from you that extra input which they can't supply themselves. It is advisable to take along a few work samples; these could help you to convey the points you wish to make.

During the meeting, make as many notes as you want — it's embarrassing to have to phone the client later if you have forgotten a crucial detail, and bluffing it out risks the kind of glaring inaccuracy that will not enhance your reputation. Write down brand names and unfamiliar product titles, and be sure exactly who is directly commissioning you — is it an in-house designer or art director, the president or marketing manager? Keep a careful check on the deadline for the whole job, intermediate meetings and presentation dates for roughs and visuals. Be alert to strong preferences that may be aired during the discussion — on colour or style of imagery, for example.

Remember that you don't have to agree to take on the job at the first briefing nor does the client have to accept you. You may wish to settle the terms right away, or defer agreement until you have a chance to look into the time and expense involved. You may be asked to present samples or first roughs before a definite decision is made. It is your business to estimate a realistic fee in the first place and carry out the work efficiently within that set limit. Once established, the fee should not be altered unless the job description changes substantially. Include provision for a rejection fee, in case you can't agree the design approach after roughs have been submitted. When the terms are agreed, ask for a contract letter setting out the schedule and payment (and payment stages if appropriate). Have the job description set down in writing; you can do this yourself and give the client a job sheet for approval.

If you are working as a freelance graphic artist, check which side is supplying artwork, photography and so on. If you are expected to commission typesetting and illustration, find out whether these can be billed directly to the client. A graphic studio would be expected to bear interim costs and cover them from the overall fee.

Budgeting

To remain in business, you must be profitable. This applies whether you are a freelancer or running a studio that employs other people. You should base your fees on an hourly rate that takes into account

▼ This flow chart shows all the stages of the design process. The briefing session between designer and client is of paramount importance since it is there that the concept of the project is discussed and defined. The designer's task is then to produce the job to the demands of the brief, on time and on budget.

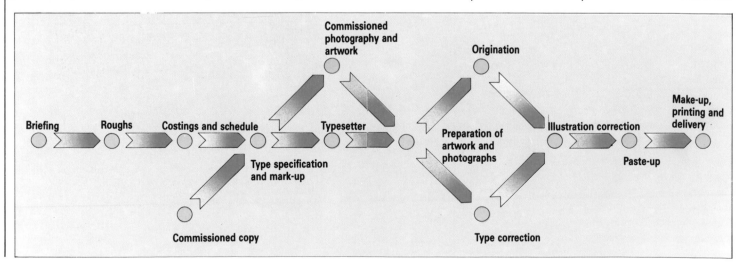

Briefing — Roughs — Costings and schedule — Type specification and mark-up — Commissioned copy — Typesetter — Commissioned photography and artwork — Preparation of artwork and photographs — Type correction — Origination — Illustration correction — Paste-up — Make-up, printing and delivery

Understanding the brief – a checklist

A list of general questions thought of in advance will provide a basic structure for discussion at the briefing.

■ **Client**   Make sure you know exactly who this is – and get the spelling of their name right!

■ **Date and time**   Make a note of when the first meeting takes place – if you are dealing with related products at separate meetings this will reduce the chance of confusion later.

■ **People present**   Write down the names of all the people present at the meeting and do not be afraid to ask how any unfamiliar ones are spelt. Just as important, find out what their role is and why they are at the meeting. It may well be that someone present who did not contribute much could be the person with whom you will mostly be working.

■ **Job description**   Agree on a name for the project or at least give it a working title.

■ **Market**   It is essential that you understand who the job is aimed at – to some extent the market will dictate the level of design. Establish, for instance, whether the job is to be aimed at a more sophisticated audience ('up-market'), or a less sophisticated one ('down-market'), and find out what the age group of the intended readership will be as this can influence design. Clients usually have a fairly clear picture of the type of people – their age-group, tastes and lifestyle – who comprise their market. It is up to you to ask for relevant information so the design can be tailored accordingly: sophisticated diagrams, for example, will not be appropriate for a readership of young children. No matter how well executed, a design should be produced with a particular audience in mind.

all your overheads. To achieve this hourly figure, total your annual expenses, work out a notional salary for yourself, add these up, and then increase that amount to cover times when you may not be working. Some of your time, for example, will be spent doing administration, which you cannot charge to any one client.

Designers are frequently asked to negotiate a fee. When doing this, aim to make a profit and yet remain competitive. It is important to remember that although design should always be viewed aesthetically, it is also a commodity that is bought and sold, like any other. Your prices must reflect the market rate. New clients need to be won, so you may have to accept a smaller profit on the early work you do for them. You must always be flexible with estimates, otherwise you can find yourself with no clients at all.

To do good business, you must organize and document each job carefully. This does not mean becoming a slave to paperwork, it simply means keeping accurate accounts of all time, meetings, expenses and materials relating to a particular job. This is essential so you are not only in a position to check that you are giving realistic estimates for work, but your invoicing of particular expenses will be much easier. If you do not have a logical system of keeping records, you will easily lose track of time and materials used – especially if several people are working together – and clients will not be charged for the full cost of a job.

A good solution is to create a job bag system. The job bag carries a job sheet, which can either be stuck or printed onto a large envelope. The envelope becomes a file for keeping all correspondence, photographs, small pieces of artwork, notes, etc relating to that job. The job sheet itself is used for recording all time, materials and services such as typesetting and photographic costs. This method keeps everying in one file.

When it comes to preparing a budget for submission to a potential client you will have to take at least the following items into consideration.

▲ *A job bag system keeps all the information for each job together. In addition, if you allocate each new job a job number, this becomes the invoice number as well and will make your records more efficient.*

Design fee   This is what you charge the client and the figure should be adhered to, provided the job specification does not change in any way.

Copywriting/text   The cost of this can be difficult to work out but it becomes easier with experience. You should make a rough estimate of how many words will have to be commissioned –

writers generally charge per 1,000 words (in the UK) or per word (in the USA).

Illustration/photography   To an extent the intended readership will dictate the degree of sophistication of imagery and therefore expenditure. If pictures have to be bought in from an agency of library, a picture researcher will probably have to be hired and copyright fees may have to be paid.

Printing   Designers handling a high volume of work usually have a constant, sometimes unwelcome, stream of printers knocking at the door offering print quotations – three is generally considered adequate. When choosing a printer cost must be balanced against quality. Not surprisingly, the aim of most designers is to achieve the highest possible standard – and maintain it overall – at the lowest possible price. Sometimes it is more expedient to ask a printer to quote for all related services such as typesetting and colour separations, but today these are usually handled by specialists and you should obtain independent quotations. Typesetters usually charge per 1,000 ens or by the number of keystrokes required to complete the job. There will be extra charges for complicated setting – for instance where words have to set or run around an irregular shape.

Originators of black-and-white and colour images will want to know not only the quantity, but also the size of each individual image and whether there will be silhouettes or other peculiarities. If a job involves a large quantity of separations, as in an illustrated book, some origination houses can be persuaded to estimate on a flat rate basis – that is, they will give a single price for each separation regardless of size.

Although final details may depend on the design solution, the printer will need to be given the following information before a price can be quoted: the run, extent, format, printings, paper quality, approximate number of halftones and the type of binding. The printer will also need to know whether final film or flat artwork will be supplied, or whether the job will require complete page make-up. If the latter is the case, the printer will need much more specific information, such as sample layouts showing the proportion of type to halftone illustrations, ruled lines and so on. It is usually necessary – and sensible – to obtain confirmation quotations from the printer of your choice once a design has been approved by the client.

When obtaining quotations it is important to remember that the fields in which printers work are as varied as those of the designers. A large, traditional book printer, for instance, may not be able to turn a rush job around quickly, while a trade printer who does general work of all kinds, though extremely quick, may be very expensive. Also, a small printer (sometimes called a 'jobbing printer') might not be able to bind a booklet and would therefore send the job outside, thus increasing the cost.

Schedules

In virtually all cases the client will tell the designer when the job should be completed and the designer should then give an immediate indication as to whether it can be done in the time. If it seems completely outside the bounds of possibility, the designer should say so straight away. How much time a job will take to do varies according to its complexity and the experience of the designer. Another important factor is how fast the designer and everyone else involved with the project normally works. Some people enjoy working under pressure but others do not and this can affect the quality of the work produced. Of all the elements involved in scheduling, only the more technical ones, such as printing, can be forecast with any degree of accuracy, and even these will be prone to a certain degree of flexibility.

Contracts

During the early stages of a design commission, some kind of written agreement should be drawn up between the client and the designer. In many cases the commission may not occur until after the presentation of an initial concept of a design idea, since the designer may be tendering for the job (competing with other designers). The extent of an agreement or contract will normally reflect the complexity of the work commissioned. Small jobs, such as a letterhead or a poster, may only require a letter, whereas jobs such as a complete corporate programme will require a proper contract or memorandum of agreement. Even before a contract is drawn up, a few guidelines should be observed:

Put everything in writing   No matter how seemingly insignificant, all points raised at a meeting – whether resolved or not – should be put in writing. This will reduce the chance of any misunderstanding arising in the future.

Agree the fee before starting work   It is sometimes difficult, if not impossible, to know exactly how much a job will cost at the outset, but a minimum and maximum limit should be

Budget considerations

Establish whether a budget has been set – usually it will have been, but sometimes clients are out of touch with current prices. Always agree to give the client a detailed breakdown of all costs, including your own time. It is a good idea to overestimate slightly when working out the budget so that the client is not presented with an unexpectedly inflated bill when the work is finished. In cases where the budget has already been determined, it is your responsibility to decide how the money should be apportioned within the job, although everybody on the project should be consulted.

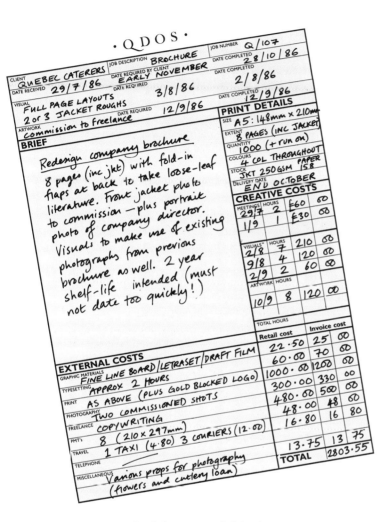

· QDOS ·

JOB NUMBER	Q/107
CLIENT QUEBEC CATERERS	
JOB DESCRIPTION BROCHURE	DATE COMPLETED 28/10/86
DATE RECEIVED 29/7/86	DATE REQUIRED BY CLIENT EARLY NOVEMBER
	DATE COMPLETED 2/8/86
DATE REQUIRED 3/8/86	
VISUAL FULL PAGE LAYOUTS 2 or 3 JACKET ROUGHS	DATE COMPLETED 12/9/86
ARTWORK Commission to freelance	DATE REQUIRED 12/9/86

BRIEF

Redesign company brochure 8 pages (inc jkt) with fold-in flaps at back to take loose-leaf literature. Front jacket photo to commission – plus portrait photo of company director. Visuals to make use of existing photographs from previous brochure as well. 2 year shelf-life intended (must not date too quickly!)

PRINT DETAILS

SIZE	A5: 148mm x 210mm
EXTENT	8 PAGES (INC JACKET)
QUANTITY	1000 (+ run on)
COLOURS	4 COL THROUGHOUT
STOCK	JKT 250GSM PAPER 158
DELIVERY DATE	END OCTOBER

CREATIVE COSTS

MEETINGS	HOURS		
29/7	1	£60	00
1/9	1	£30	00
VISUALS	HOURS		
2/8	7	210	00
9/8	4	120	00
2/9	2	60	00
ARTWORK	HOURS		
10/9	8	120	00
TOTAL HOURS			

EXTERNAL COSTS

		Retail cost	Invoice cost
GRAPHIC MATERIALS FINE LINE BOARD/LETRASET/DRAFT FILM		22·50	25 00
TYPESETTING APPROX 2 HOURS		60·00	70 00
PRINT AS ABOVE (PLUS GOLD BLOCKED LOGO)		1000·00	1200 00
PHOTOGRAPHY TWO COMMISSIONED SHOTS		300·00	330 00
FREELANCE COPYWRITING		480·00	500 00
PMT's 8 (210 x 297mm)		48·00	48 00
TRAVEL 1 TAXI (4·80) 3 COURIERS (12·00)		16·80	16 80
TELEPHONE		13·75	13 75
MISCELLANEOUS Various props for photography (flowers and cutlery loan)	TOTAL		2803·55

▲ *This is an example of a job sheet — it is very important to fill one of these in if you are working as a freelance graphic artist. Always give your client a detailed breakdown of these costs before you take on a job. It is a good idea to overestimate*

slightly when working out the budget so that the client is not presented with an unexpectedly inflated bill when the work is finished. If the budget has already been determined, then it is your job to apportion the costs.

given to the client before any work is undertaken. In any event, once a final presentation has been made, the fee must be agreed with the client. If possible, try to agree some sort of rejection or cancellation fee at this stage as well. A client may not accept a design solution for any number of reasons, but a job is much less likely to be rejected on a whim if a fee has already been agreed should it prove unacceptable. On the other hand, you cannot force a client to accept unsatisfactory work, so before the rejection fee is paid expect the client to ask for further solutions. If these are still not accepted, make sure you are paid for the work you have done.

Invoicing

When you agree budgets and costs with a client, you should also outline your own terms of business. Cash flow is a major problem for companies of all sizes, but in particular for individuals trading on their own. Graphic design is an industry that works at speed — clients often want every job yesterday. To trade successfully, you need to invoice promptly and then ensure that your clients pay you on time. If substantial sums of money are involved, you should ask for an advance.

Be straightforward when discussing terms of business and be wary if you are dealing with a client for the first time. The criteria for payments will depend on how long the job takes, and how much money you will have to pay out for typesetting, photography or other services. If you are particularly concerned, ask for a trade reference, and ask the client to agree terms in writing. On very large commissions you should agree stage payments — say three separate instalments; the first to be paid at the beginning of a job, the second on approval of the design, and the final instalment on completion of the job.

Invoicing when the work is completed is the most common method. Always itemize your invoice clearly, and if necessary enclose a separate sheet of expenses. If you are not paid on time, telephone your client and find out why. Be persistent in chasing invoices, otherwise you will all too easily run into financial difficulties.

However busy you are with work, it must never be at the expense of your administration. You must find time to invoice regularly, otherwise, whatever your system, it will be more difficult to calculate costs.

Commissioning

Few design jobs can be completed entirely by the designer's skills alone, and most involve the added expertise of specialists such as illustrators, photographers, writers, editors and so on. In many cases, such people may have already been commissioned for a particular job, but sometimes it is up to the designer to enlist the services of any extra necessary professional services that are required.

Text Commissioning text is normally the responsibility of an editor rather than the designer, but sometimes the designer will be called upon to commission as well. In ideal circumstances, the designer should specify the total number of words required and, if the design is sufficiently advanced, the number of lines and the measure (number of characters per line) to which they should be typed. This is by far the most efficient method, as it means that problems which arise if the copy has to be cut and reset can be avoided. However, a degree of rigidity may also be imposed on the design at a relatively early stage.

Sometimes, particularly in book publishing, the text supplied may be 'final': in other words, it cannot be changed or cut and so it is the crucial determining factor in the design. More frequently, the designer asks the person responsible for the words to cut, fill, add and even rewrite if the need arises.

If a designer is totally responsible for the text, and possibly required to commission a technical specialist, it is a good idea to involve a copy editor to ensure that the final text is of an acceptable standard. Whatever the job, the designer and editor or copywriter must collaborate; neither process can be carried out in isolation. This is especially important if captioning is involved, though this is normally done, particularly in book publishing, at a later stage.

The procedure involved in preparing and editing text varies, depending on how many people are required to read it and what form it takes. The 'raw', or first, copy will be read and then submitted for the client's approval. It will then be amended and

◀ Although photographers argue that there is little difference between the results produced by different colour films, the enlargements here clearly show the difference. This knowledge is particularly important to the designer, who will be frequently asking for original prints and transparencies to be enlarged. The Kodachrome 25 transparency remains clear and sharp; there is virtually no graininess. The colours are well-saturated, the reds and yellows being particularly true to life. The Ektrachrome 400 transparency is flatter and more grainy by comparison, with poorer colour saturation. This is partly caused by its extra speed. In addition, it is slightly bluer overall, which makes it more suitable for photographing tungsten-lit night scenes.

sent for typesetting. The typeset text should be read initially for literal errors (spelling mistakes) by the typesetter's own readers and then it is returned to the editor or designer, who will each check it in turn.

Photography   Photographers normally charge their time by the day, and rates vary depending on the premises and skills they offer. The daily rate does not usually include materials and any other extra expenses, so remember to get an estimate of these before a job begins.

If the job involves working with models or children, make sure that the photographer has the social ability to deal with the situation and also the facilities for the required shot. Always discuss the job thoroughly and agree on how much the work is going to cost. Remember that fees are negotiable, so if you want a particular photographer but your budget cannot accommodate him, be forthright and see if he will do the job for what you can afford. Most photographers are flexible and will lower their rates if they are gaining several days' work. Sometimes they can slot the job into a schedule to suit them which makes it economically viable.

If the job involves models, then you should make the ultimate decision who to use. Photographers often have models they like working with, who are relaxed in front of the camera, so although you should be guided by them, do not automatically assume that whoever they pick will be right.

When you begin to do the art direction during photographic sessions, you may feel inhibited. This may be because you have not worked with the photographer before, and do not feel confident to judge what the result will be like. Take advice from the photographer but be firm in achieving the results that *you* want. You will, of course, find it easier as you gain experience and work with people you know.

When you book time with a photographer arrange for the studio to be ready when you arrive, so that you do not have to wait while equipment is being set up. You may also need to employ a stylist who will organize the delivery of any props needed well in advance.

Always specify whether you want prints or transparencies, what format is required and whether you want alternative shots, so you have a choice of pictures. When the pictures arrive, take great care of them. They will have cost lots of money, so before you accept them examine every detail.

Picture libraries   Photographs can be borrowed from a picture library or agency. It is easier and cheaper to use a picture from a library than to commission afresh but it may not always be possible. Many libraries hold the work of particular photographers and some specialize in particular subjects; but most libraries have a general collection catalogued by subject matter.

The best way to use a picture library is to make an appointment to visit, having first specified exactly what you are looking for. They will have a selection of photographs ready for you when you arrive, and someone will help you if you need it. You can do all this by telephone and post, but you may specify a particular subject and eventually find what you are looking for in another category, so it

▶ *Picture libraries usually file their collections by subject matter.*

▼ *Some pictures cannot be re-commissioned so you are paying for their uniqueness. Picture libraries are often the quickest and most economical source for certain pictures.*

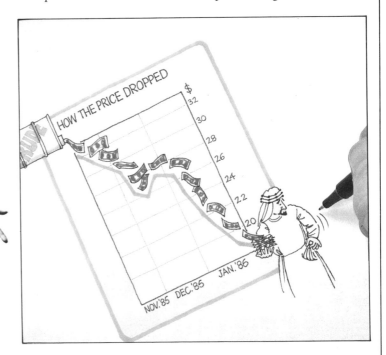

is better to go and look for yourself. If the library does all the work you will pay a fairly nominal fee for the service.

The agency loaning the pictures will want to know in what form and size the picture is being used, and in what countries the book, or magazine, is being published so that a reproduction fee can be calculated. They will also want to know the print run — that is, how many books are being printed. The fee is usually payable on publication and pictures should be returned as quickly as possible, otherwise a holding fee may also be charged. Reproduction fees vary from library to library, so before you use a picture make sure you have agreed terms.

Before you borrow pictures, check them very carefully; if they are already damaged and you don't make this clear, you may be charged a replacement fee, and this can be expensive. Check for quality too. It is quite usual to be supplied with duplicate transparencies which are never as sharp as the originals.

▲ *This is a pictogram, a combination of factual detail and illustration that conveys the message in a simple and visual way.*

Illustration   There are almost as many styles of illustration as there are illustrators. Each style adds a different quality to a commission, but being so subjective means that you must be sure about the function you want the illustration to perform. Clients, who perhaps are not used to looking at illustrations, may have

▲ *This is a highly finished Magic Marker visual.*

particular preferences for style. There are many illustrators' annuals available, and this is not only a good way of showing a range of styles to a client, but also a means of choosing one for the job in hand.

Establish a fee with the illustrator at the beginning of a commission. Illustrators usually estimate a job based on their own individual hourly rate, so prices can vary tremendously. You should also establish a rejection fee in case the work is not acceptable. The illustrator will need a full brief, including details of size, colours, overlays, etc, and deadlines for each stage of the job, allowing time for alterations.

There are other technical points to consider, too. Sometimes illustrators want their work reproduced at a particular size in order to enhance its style and character, so agree with the illustrator what size they should do the work to achieve the best results. At the same time, make sure that the illustrators you work with understand the mechanics of working in proportion, especially if they are fresh from college.

It is always a good policy to look at roughs of a job before finished artwork is produced. It ensures that both the designer and illustrator are thinking along the same lines and that the brief is being fulfilled. This is also the last opportunity for you to check with your printer if they require the work on a flexible surface so that it can be scanned.

Finally, remember to give illustrators sufficient copies of the printed job. They have a living to make as well, and their livelihoods depend on their portfolios, just as yours does.

Photographic retouching and special effects

Library transparencies and prints used in the graphics studio are frequently blemished and scratched. Retouching is normally done by a specialized studio, but it is quite usual for clients to expect

▲ *Although you can use almost any medium, a retouching paint box makes it easier to match image colour as well as image tone. Protect the surface with a sheet of white paper, so that your hand does not stick to the print, and use the edge of the protective paper to match the colour of the image. Use a brush that is very nearly dry to give maximum control.*

graphic artists to be able to retouch and combine photographs, and to combine photographs with artwork. Print retouching is a common task, because unlike negative retouching, it does not entail having to deal with a precious original.

One of the ground rules for retouching is to work with a print that is as large as possible, so that your handiwork is reduced in reproduction rather than enlarged. A size of 11 × 14in (280 × 355mm) is the largest that you can conveniently transport.

▲ *A hairline on a negative is much more difficult to remove than a spot. The first thing to do is to match the colour and tone of a given area of the hairline.*

Although the colour is unlikely to vary along the hairline, the tone may — this is where the paint box comes in handy.

▲ *Pencil retouching is suitable only for unglazed, paper-based prints. Most resin-coated papers will not accept pencil retouching unless sprayed with a varnish. Also, you will be unable to retouch any further on top of the protective fixing spray (used to prevent*

the retouching from rubbing off) unless you hold the print in front of the steam from a kettle to remove it.

◀ *It is very difficult to mix a pigment that can cover a black mark. The traditional way of lightening dark areas is by knifing as shown: either a scalpel (X-Acto knife) or a broken piece of a razor blade held in a pin vice may be used, but it must be very sharp, and even then there is a serious risk of scratching the emulsion.*

▲ *A brush can be used for bleaching small areas and spots. Simply touch a dampened brush to a crystal or tablet of*

potassium ferricyanide. Reserve the brush for bleaching only.

▲ *Whether you are working on a hairline or a larger area, use a dabbing action, applying the retouching medium*

in tiny flecks to break up the outline of the area. With very grainy prints, you can often emulate the grain successfully.

▲ Retouching negatives *For safety it is best to secure the red film mask onto a sheet of acetate and work on that. For blocking out you will need a chisel-ended brush. Nip off the end hairs of a watercolour brush with a scalpel (X-Acto knife). This makes the brush much less sensitive to variations in pressure, and makes it easier to control line thicknesses.*

▼ Slide sandwich *A slide sandwich is made by superimposing one slide on another. Both originals should be thin and light, and the patterns should be simple and dramatic or the result will be a jumbled, murky picture. Dark areas on one transparency will obscure parts of the other. This is the opposite of the approach for making a double exposure.*

◀ **Hand colouring** *Hand colouring is very similar to retouching. You need a fairly 'weak' print to begin with, although for specific colouring you can bleach selectively. A useful short-cut in hand colouring is shown opposite. Apply a waterproof Stabilo Boss pen to the shiny side of acetate or glass — anything that will not absorb the ink. Using a cotton swab, dip it into the ink and carefully apply to the print. You can see, on this album sleeve, that the results are very effective.*

▶ **Double exposure** *In a double exposure the dark areas on one transparency must be opposite the light areas on the other. To match the two elements, either mark the ground glass of the copying camera with a grease pencil or use a screen with a grid and make a scaled-up drawing showing the main shapes.*

▼ **Photomontage** *With photomontage you can achieve effects that have only been possible by illustration in the past. This example is created by a combination of the two top pictures, using very accurate masks to block out unwanted areas on the transparencies.*

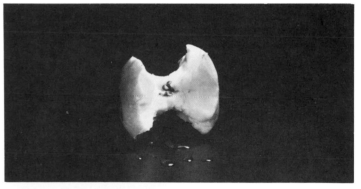

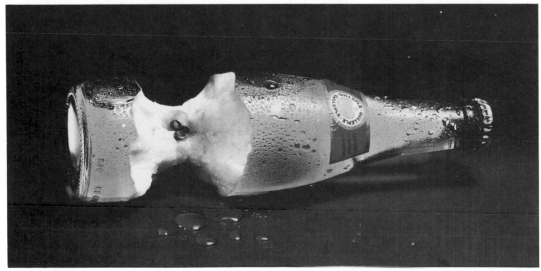

DESIGNING FOR PRINT

The visual

Once briefed, the next stage is for the designer to show the client a preliminary drawing, which is known variously as a rough, visual, scamp or tissue. This can take a variety of forms — from an outline rough, giving an indication of a basic idea, to a detailed, realistic facsimile of the final thing. Again, the level required varies according to the demands of the client or whoever is being given the presentation. A rough for an art director, say, need not necessarily be rendered as fully as one being prepared for a salesperson.

Although the medium in which the rough is executed must be sympathetic to the style of the design, pencil and felt-tipped pen are usual choices. The former is better for more detailed work, particularly if typography plays an important part in the design, whereas the latter is ideal for rendering rapid impressions of photographs or artwork.

▼ *Put all your initial ideas down as quick mini-roughs or thumbnail sketches. Picture areas and content can be quickly and efficiently indicated with Magic Markers.*

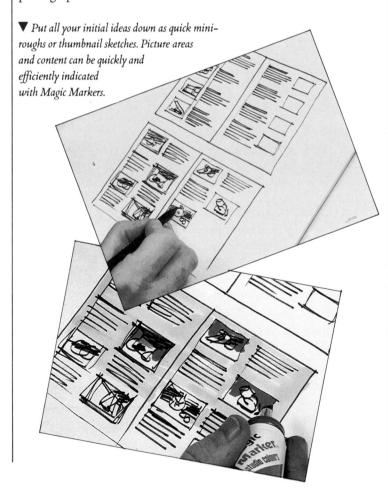

Always protect your work, whether it is a rough or finished art, with two overlays — a transparent one first, to note any changes at the rough stage or instructions to the printer on finished art, and an outer cover for extra protection. It is worth using attractive, coloured paper, as neatly presented work shows professionalism. It is also useful to have a form, with the name and date of the presentation and a space for the client to sign when the job has been approved. This saves any arguments at a later stage.

▶ *Always use two overlays, a transparent one to carry instructions and an outer paper to protect the work and give it a professional finish. Secure these together.*

▶ *Place the artwork or presentation face down on the transparent sheet. Cut the two top corners of the overlays at 45 degrees.*

▶ *Fold this flap over and secure it to the back of the work with double-sided tape.*

▶ *Trim off the excess paper from the other three sides. NB It is dangerous to do this without a steel cutting edge. Stick a compliments slip or label on the cover paper.*

One of the purposes of the preliminary rough is to create a talking point — it should never be inflexible. For instance, if the design incorporates pictures, at this stage you do not have to supply the actual transparencies that are going to be used. What is important is to establish what type of images are envisaged. Similarly, in a typographical design, there is no need to choose the exact fount to be used, but the rough should certainly show headings, subheadings and the area the text type is to occupy.

The designer may wish or may be asked to present two or three alternative versions of these first thoughts, and because this can be extremely time-consuming, the problems of time and cost-effectiveness should be considered yet again. Even if you are not completely satisfied with a piece of work, there is always a point at which you should stop making further changes to it. This is particularly the case when making a preliminary rough, which may well have to be altered several times. It is usually a good idea at the initial briefing to tell the client how many and what standard of roughs you plan to submit.

A 'finished' rough, on the other hand, must be an accurate facsimile of the final product. Although any images still need not be exact or final, they must give a very good impression of the final artwork or photographs; rough images should therefore be quite elaborate renderings, coloured if applicable. It is also sound practice to bring examples of the illustrator's or photographer's work to the approval meeting, so that the client has a clear idea of what style and standard the end product will eventually be.

What is finally presented should obviously be as attractive and professional as possible. In most cases the finished rough should be mounted on black card, protected with an acetate covering and given a black or coloured surround. Sometimes, all typesetting — headlines, text, captions and so on — must be 'live', or real, otherwise 'dummy', or false, type and dry-transferred headings can be used. If live copy is required the designer must establish an effective liaison with the writer, so that the illustrative treatment reflects the text and is ready when required. However, even if dummy type is being used, the headings should be live if possible.

Slick presentation – a checklist

Sometimes a client will want a visual that looks exactly like the final printed job to show his customer. This is quite a straightforward and enjoyable procedure, although daunting if you are doing it for the first time. Remember — the importance of the presentation is the impression it creates. It can be made up of real type and pictures, or mocked up. The better finished a presentation is, the more it will cost; watch your budget.

■ Produce black and white line artwork of all your text matter and any line illustrations. The text can either be typesetting which you have ordered or dry transfer dummy text, depending on whether the 'dummy' needs to be read or not. Real headlines should be used wherever possible; this helps to make the presentation more believable.

■ If the client has not supplied you with real copy to be typeset and you want to use a typeface which is not available in dry transfer, you can always have a random piece of text set and use that.

■ Draw picture areas on your artwork with a fine keyline, and remember to put in trim and fold marks.

■ Having pasted up your artwork, have a bromide or PMT copy (stat) made.

■ Paste in your pictures on the PMT (stat). These can be colour prints or pictures cut out of magazines.

■ Lay the PMT (stat) of your artwork on a lightbox, and carefully place the pictures over their keylined areas. The black line will be visible through the picture. This is a good method of cropping your pictures to the correct sizes.

■ The assembled presentation can either be mounted flat or stuck into a blank book or magazine, which a printer will make up for you. This is called a 'bulking dummy' and is used to show the size and thickness of a book or magazine using a specified weight of paper and cover material.

■ If you want a typographic headline in a specific colour, have a dry transfer or 'rub-down' made from your artwork in whatever colour you wish.

■ If you have your flat mock-up copied as a coloured print you will lose slightly on quality, but gain the impression of a finished printed page. Colour photocopies are less expensive and sometimes of acceptable quality.

■ If you want a glossy or 'laminated' surface, use a clear acetate overlay or a self-adhesive film covering. It is, however, difficult to put this down without creating air bubbles.

The materials are very expensive if you are producing only a single highly-finished presentation. They become more economical if you produce several. This process is very useful for consumer testing — you can simulate a package or book cover which, to an untrained eye, looks real. The colours on this type of presentation should be accurate. It is advisable to choose colours from a colour matching system so that they can be matched accurately by the printer.

Typography

Among the many considerations of typographic design, the two that require the greatest understanding are the varying width of alphabetical characters and the spaces between them. This understanding is essential in order to achieve the twin aims of aesthetic appeal and legibility.

The width of alphabetic characters or the space allotted to them depends largely on the equipment used to produce them. For instance, in order to maintain consistent letterspacing a manual typewriter uses exaggeratedly wide serifs on letters such as i and l. This gives a string of characters (words) an even appearance by reducing the amount of white space. Some electric typewriters are slightly more sophisticated with a system of three character widths, but phototypesetting machines use up to about 11 widths. On more advanced computer-controlled systems the number of character widths can be almost infinite. This greater flexibility of typesetting machines ensures optically even spacing between characters.

Point sizes

For many years, printing was an inexact science. No two printers could agree on a standard system of type measurement, which meant that type cast by one foundry could not be used with type cast by another. It was not until the 18th century that the pioneering French typographer Pierre Fournier successfully proposed a standard typesetting unit called the point. This was developed by another Frenchman, Firmin Didot, into a European standard. Even today, however, the process is not complete, since Britain and the USA base their system on one point measuring 0.013888in, the European equivalent being 0.0148in. The 12 point unit is a pica in the first system and a cicero in the second. The metric system, however, is now becoming the first universal standard. Right *The unit system used in typesetting for measurement and counting. Usually 18 units make up an em, the size of the unit varying with the type size. In the word Mot, the M is 18 units wide, the o 10 units wides an the t 6 units wide. The system enables spacing to be finely adjusted.*

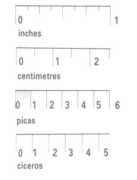

36pt em divided into 18 units

72pt em divided into 18 units

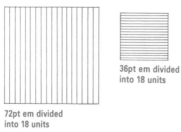

18 units   10 units   6 units

Perhaps the next most important consideration in typographic design is that of word spacing. The problem is made all the more difficult by a convention that was introduced in medieval times. Because they wanted to make facing pages in books symmetrical, scribes insisted that both the left- and righthand edges of text should be vertically aligned. The convention of vertically aligning edges of blocks of text was made possible by distributing approximately equal spaces between each of the words along a line. Today, this technique of ensuring that all the lines on a page are the same length is known as justified typesetting. Text with even work spacing is usually vertically aligned on the left (flush left), with the righthand margin set ragged (unjustified). With modern typesetting methods setting type justified is not necessary, and indeed can be undesirable since much research supports the theory that unjustified text, with even word spacing as opposed to justified setting with variable wordspacing, is more comfortable and easier to read.

Type measurement   Because the earliest type consisted of solid blocks (body) upon which the area to be printed (face) was punched, all measurements related to these three-dimensional objects. However even though most modern typesetting systems still use these measurements, they involve a two-dimensional system.

There are three type measurements with which the designer must be familiar: points, picas and units. These measurements can be confusing in that the Anglo-American is different from the European system, although both use the term 'point'.

Anglo-American system   This is based on the division of one inch into 72 parts, called points. Each point is 0.013888in, and 12 points make a pica (or pica em) and measure 0.166in. Although in the USA this system is still universal, in the UK it has been complicated by the introduction of metrification.

European system   The European or Didot point is 0.0148in and 12 of these form a unit measuring 0.1776in. This 12 point unit is called a *cicero* in France and Germany, a *riga tipografica* (riga) in Italy, and an *augustijn* (aug) in the Netherlands.

There is no relationship between the Anglo-American point and the Didot point, and neither of them relates to the metric system. Thus in Europe, including the UK, typographic measurements in points co-exist with metric, which are used in virtually every other allied trade. For this reason, type measurements are gradually being metricated and eventually all type sizes will be in millimetres.

Although many designers refer to a pica em simply as an 'em', technically this is incorrect — an em is the square of the body of a piece of type, regardless of its size (so called because the letter M originally occupied the full unit width of a piece of type). A 36 point em, for instance, measures 36 points, not 12. The most important measurement in controlling line length is that of each character width. This measurement is determined by dividing an

Gothic *These elaborate typefaces, also known as Blackletter, originated in Germany and were derived from manuscript calligraphy.*

Modern face *The thick uprights contrast with the thinner cross strokes. 'Modern' is rather misleading as these typefaces were introduced in the 18th century.*

Old style *There is little contrast between thick and thin strokes, and the wide-open characters and legibility account for their popularity today.*

Egyptian *The thickness of the serif matches that of the main letter, giving a uniform weight. Light and medium versions work very well as text*

Transitional
These fall between old and modern typefaces; examples such as Baskerville and Century are popular choices for book and magazine text.

Sans serif *This group of typefaces has no serifs and the letterforms, compared to other styles, are very uniform in character.*

em into vertical 'slices'. These are called set points or, more commonly in phototypesetting, units. The number of units in an em varies from one typesetting system to another, but probably the most popular is 18, and the more units there are in an em, the greater the possibility of refinement. Units control not only the width of characters, but also the spaces between them. Although the actual size of the unit varies according to the size of the type, because there are always the same number to the em, regardless of size, the proportions always remain the same.

In the design of typefaces, each character is given a fixed amount of space known as set-width or 'set', which is measured in units, as are the spaces in between each character or word. The set-width of a character controls the amount of space between itself and the next character and can be varied for special purposes — either increased to allow greater space or decreased. The latter is possible only in phototypesetting and electronic typesetting systems and is obviously limited as there comes a point when characters will lose their legibility.

Because different founts vary considerably in their characteristics, the set-widths of characters will also vary from typeface to typeface

so that a condensed typeface, for instance, will have a narrow set-width relative to its body size.

Typefaces Much to the bewilderment of the designer, there are many thousands of typefaces available today. But this is a relatively recent phenomenon — during the first 400 years of movable type the form it took depended upon the mechanical limitations of the printing processes of the day, and only in the 19th century did type design even begin to transcend the barriers of craft into art. Even then, typeface designs had to be translated by craftsmen using individual punches to cut the precise form desired. Only in the last few decades, with the advent of photographically reproduced typefaces, has type design proliferated to its present, seemingly saturated, state.

Typefaces can be classified in six basic groups.

Gothic Movable type was developed in Germany and the design of the type reflected the local handwriting, known as Gothic, Black Letter or Textura. The letterform itself was written in such a way that curved forms were difficult to reproduce and were thus kept to a minimum, which resulted in a distinctive typeface.

Old Style It was the introduction of printing to Italy that led to type design taking on the appearance it has today. Formal documents were handwritten in a style known as Chancery Italic, which is much lighter and more legible than Gothic. These Old Style letter-forms are characterized by a robust triangular serif (a small line used to complete the main stroke of a letter) and many forms, of which Bembo is a classic example, have been adapted for modern typesetting processes.

Transitional   Gradually, type design became more influenced by the refinement of printing processes — and its associated materials such as paper and ink — than by the conventions of handwriting, and printers' type began to assume its own separate identity. Transitional faces are identified by their generally lighter colour than Old Style, the emphasis of the curved strokes tending to be vertical rather than diagonal and the serifs more horizontal.

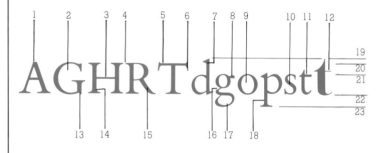

▲ *Each character in a line of type has its own individual characteristics. The terminology relating to different parts of a typeset character is extensive and a wide range of words are in common usage. Those illustrated here are apex (1), counter (2), bar (3), serif (4), arm (5), beak (6), ascender (7), ear (8), bowl (9), spine (10), cross-stroke (11), hairline (12), spur (13), bracket (14), tail (15), link (16), loop (17), descender (18), ascender line (19), capital line (20), x-height (mean line) (21), base line (22), descender line (23).*

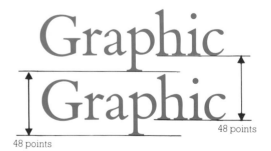

▲ *A typeface's point or body size is defined as the distance from the top of the ascender to the bottom of the descender. The amount of space varies from typeface to typeface. If there is no extra space between lines, the type can be measured from the base line to base line, the distance between the two being referred to as leading, or line feed in phototypesetting.*

Probably the best known example of a transitional face is that named after its English designer John Baskerville in the mid-18th century.

Modern   During the 18th century, developments became more rapid and in 1798 another style of type emerged. This was the work of an Italian printer named Giambattista Bodoni and became known as the Modern style. Bodoni, who was clearly influenced by the then current vogue for classical Greek and Roman artistic styles, gave his name to the design which most typified Modern faces, and had maximum contrast between thick and thin strokes, with fine horizontal hairline serifs, while the ascenders (the parts above the body such as in b and h) and descenders (the parts below the body as in g, p and y) are both extended.

Egyptian   The Industrial Revolution in the 19th century brought the introduction of mechanical typesetting and this combined with market demand — particularly in advertising — to produce yet more type forms. The advertising requirements at the time were for loud, bold designs which would stand out from their surroundings. This desire was fulfilled by a type design which was bold and black, and with serifs that carried as much weight as the rest of the letter. This form became known as Egyptian or Slab Serif. More exaggerated — and in some cases completely illegible — forms were called Flat Face.

Sans serif   The bolder a typeface becomes, the smaller its counters are, until a point is reached when it becomes illegible. The search for ever more striking designs led to serifs being abandoned altogether. These were called sans serif types and were initially used for posters, but before long they became used for general printing.

Using type   The evolution of type design does not rest solely on historical precedent, but also on the continuing development of production methods, with typefaces being designed, or redesigned, for specific technological innovations. With the introduction of Linotype and Monotype at the beginning of the 20th century — the first mechanical typesetting machines — existing typefaces were remodelled and adapted to the characteristics of the two systems. Linotype produces each complete line as a single piece of metal, whereas Monotype produces individual characters and spaces with which to form a line.

An important factor in type selection is the paper and printing process to be used. Earlier typefaces were designed to be printed by letterpress on handmade, cartridge or other uncoated papers. Thus, when printed on modern, smooth papers, they can often appear fragile and light. It is also the case that Modern faces, such as Bodoni and Walbaum, look more mellow and robust if printed by letterpress on uncoated paper. Similarly, the typesetting equipment can alter the appearance of a typeface — phototypesetting, for example, generally produces a lighter effect than the equivalent metal face.

◀◀ Estimating the number of characters and lines that a piece of copy will occupy in its typeset form is called casting-off. Always establish the layout before you mark up copy.

◀ Once you have calculated the number of characters in a piece of text, you are in a position to work out which typeface and type size is required. Many type manufacturers supply sets of tables to help you.

Drop-out type, that is white type on a black or coloured background, usually demands a heavier typeface, since faces with fine lines as an integral part of the design such as a Modern face or a light weight of type, are susceptible to the erosion of the image by surplus ink, and parts may well disappear as a result. Gravure printing can have the same detrimental effect upon the same range of typefaces.

Besides such practical considerations, type selection will be influenced by aesthetic demands. For example, sans serif faces, being simple, uncluttered and unpretentious, are sometimes more suitable for technical literature. They are also used extensively for children's books, the design of the letterforms such as the a and g more closely resembling today's handwriting. Serifed faces, on the other hand, are more suitable for text matter in books, particularly novels, and are also used by the majority of newspapers as they are usually easy to read.

Tables, indexes and bibliographies requiring complex typography, are best suited to a typeface with a wide range of weights and italic, such as Garamond or Bembo, while Times offers a particularly comprehensive range of symbols for setting mathematical formulae.

Colour and leading are the two other most important considerations when selecting typefaces. When set as text, each typeface produces its own tonal value, which is referred to by typographers as colour. This colour is influenced by the amount of space between each line, called leading — a name which derives from the days of handsetting, when fillets of metal, known as leads, were used to space the lines further apart. The equivalent term in photo- and computer composition is line feed, although leading is the term still in common usage, particularly among designers.

Some typefaces are what are known as 'large appearing', that is, when the overall height of the body of the lower case letterform (the x-height) is large in comparison with its ascenders and descenders. Conversely, typefaces with small x-heights and large ascenders and descenders are known as 'small appearing'.

Preparing the text

All copy, whatever typeface is chosen, has to be prepared before the typesetter starts work. It is difficult, if not impossible, to establish a clear typographic structure if the text is not typewritten, and it usually helps if it is typed to the approximate line length of the final, typeset form. The copy should be typed with double linespacing with ample margins at left and right for editorial comments, corrections and typesetting instructions. This can save considerable amounts of time and money, the latter being especially the case when the copy is to be filmset, since corrections with this process can be very costly. However, the tendency today is for copy to be entered directly onto a word-processing system — many of which are compatible with electronic typesetters and which typesetters themselves can use, which enables final corrections to be made even before the copy emerges as typeset text in any form. Retyping to the line length can also serve to confirm the typographic structure of a layout, and will allow the designer to make an accurate estimate of the number of lines, and thus pages, a manuscript will take up. At some stage, whether at the same time or after the text face has been determined, stylistic decisions must be taken on such things as size and position of headings, subheadings, crossheadings, references, footnotes and so on, even though additional copy editing may be needed later. This normally means that the designer must read the text before such decisions can be taken. Ideally, however, the designer should predetermine the typographic structure so that text can be written accordingly, especially where visual impact may be just as important as the content of the words themselves.

Casting-off Estimating the number of characters and lines that a piece of typed copy will occupy in its typeset form is called casting-off. This is an important process for the design of a book or any printed matter.

The methods by which the length of a manuscript can be calculated are at best only approximations. It is advisable when casting-off to round up any calculations and even to allow for a margin of error — about 5 or 10 per cent — to the calculations. This allowance should take into account the complexity of the manuscript and the number of words per line once it is set in type, although short lines, hyphenated words or exaggerated white spaces due to words being carried over to the next line will further complicate the estimate.

If typed on a fixed-spacing typewriter, casting-off the manuscript is made much easier because there are always the same number of characters per line, which can be measured with a ruler or typescale. If the manuscript is typed on a machine with a variable character width, the count must then be made manually. Manuscript paper is also extremely useful as it is pre-printed with pica measures on it, and this makes casting-off any type matter much easier.

First, an approximation must be made on an average line, each word space counting as a single character, and this is achieved by counting the number of characters in, say, 10 lines and then dividing the number of characters by 10 (the number of lines counted). This will give a fairly accurate average line count, which is then multiplied by the total number of lines of manuscript. Again, this can be measured by using a depth scale rather than by counting each individual line to give the total number of characters

involved. This figure can also be useful when estimating the cost of typesetting.

The next thing to establish is the amount of space the typeset manuscript will fill, and this will vary according to the typeface chosen. Normally, this is where cost considerations must be made; it is only very rarely that a designer is asked to increase the amount of space text may occupy, particularly in book work. More usually, the problem is to balance readability with fitting the text into a predetermined number of pages.

The way this is calculated is by referring to a sample alphabet, in the appropriate type size, provided by either the typesetter or the manufacturer of the equipment being used. Particular care should be taken to refer to a sample produced by the exact equipment that will be used for the job since the line length of the same typeface produced by different foundries may vary.

Many manufacturers produce a special set of tables covering their complete range of typefaces, which makes it easier to calculate text lengths. These can be presented in different forms; some will give the number of lower case letters per line for each face and size over a given length, while others may be given reference numbers which, when used in conjunction with a special copyfitting table, will give the number of characters per line. Others may give the

Casting-off copy

The number of words in a manuscript can only be calculated approximately, so it is advisable to round up any figures and even to allow for a margin of error of about 5 or 10 per cent. This will take into account short lines or hyphenated words once the manuscript has been set.

It saves considerable time and money if the text is well presented. Obviously this is not always going to be the case, but it is much easier to mark up for typesetting if it is typed out clearly, and much easier for the typesetter to read. If you decide not to cast off your copy you may have to have the whole job reset so that it fits the design. This is expensive and time consuming, so it pays to get it right first time.

Begin by estimating the number of characters in your typed manuscript — a character is a letter, a punctuation mark or a space between words. If you hold an imperial ruler under a line of typing, you will find that to every inch you will usually get 10 or 12 characters (depending on the typewriter). Count the number of characters in, say, 10 lines, divide that number by 10 and you have an average character count per line. Multiply this by the number of lines on the page to give you an estimate of the number of characters on that page.

If you are dealing with a large manuscript you can apply the

same process to working out an average character count per page. If you count the number of characters on, say, the first 10 pages (assuming they are fairly representative pages) and divide that total by 10, you arrive at an average. By multiplying that average by the number of pages in your manuscript you have a fairly good estimate of your total number of characters. This figure is also useful when estimating the cost of your typesetting.

The next step is to establish how much space the manuscript will fill when typeset. This will vary according to the typeface and the type size you have chosen. By measuring the length of the lower case alphabet, in a specimen book, in the appropriate face and size, you will discover that 26 characters take up, say, 30mm. If you measure the length of the line you wish to typeset to, in millimetres, divide by 30 and multiply by 26, that will give you the number of characters in that line. Measure the number of lines in your design with a depth scale (type rule), and you can calculate the number of typeset characters. This figure can be changed by altering your type size, typeface or length of line.

Many type manufacturers supply special sets of tables to make this process easier. Different typesetting systems produce different numbers of characters in a line. When copyfitting refer to the alphabets produced by the system you will be using.

▶ *Specifying type becomes much easier with experience. Always consider the function of the type so that you aim to achieve satisfying and effective results. A book set in centred type, for example, would be very difficult to read.*

Kabel centred type
Typefaces fall into two groups, those having serifs (that is, terminal projections on the stems of characters), and those without this feature, which are known as sans serif. In general, serif typefaces are easier to read for continuous text.

Bembo no leading
Typefaces fall into two groups, those having serifs (that is, terminal projections on the stems of characters), and those without this feature, which are known as sans serif. In general, serif typefaces are easier to read for continuous text.

Bembo 4 point leading
Typefaces fall into two groups, those having serifs (that is, terminal projections on the stems of characters), and those without this feature, which are known as sans serif. In general, serif typefaces are easier to read for continuous text.

Bembo justified type
Typefaces fall into two groups, those having serifs (that is, terminal projections on the stems of characters), and those without this feature, which are known as sans serif. In general, serif typefaces are easier to read for continuous text.

Helvetica ranged left
Typefaces fall into two groups, those having serifs (that is, terminal projections on the stems of characters), and those without this feature, which are known as sans serif. In feneral, serif typefaces are easier to read for continuous text.

Korinna ranged right
Typefaces fall into two groups, those having serifs (that is, terminal projections on the stems of characters), and those without this feature, which are known as sans serif. In generavl, serif typefaces are easier to read for continuous text.

number of characters per pica for every size of typeface. Because many type samples are not accompanied by copyfitting tables, a table can be used that gives the numbers of characters per pica for a variety of alphabet lengths.

Some type specimen sheets include a sample text set in a variety of different leadings, as well as a complete type synopsis. These sheets are worth collecting since it is through them that a designer can assess the appearance of what, on the surface, may seem to be insignificant minor amendments to a specification.

Marking up copy Once a manuscript has left the editor's hands, the designer marks on it a set of instructions so that the compositor or operator can typeset it. These instructions specify the founts required and the general style of the typography. They should always be attached to the manuscript for permanent reference. On the manuscript itself, the exact words, lines, headings or paragraphs to be capitalized, italicized, set in a bold face, small capitals or a different size must be clearly indicated. There may come a point when these instructions become too dense to follow clearly, and in such cases it is better to use a coding system based on

numerals or letters and keyed to a master style sheet. One reason for this is that typesetting can be extremely costly and a seemingly minor instructional error may involve massive resetting — so it pays to get it right first time.

It must be remembered that there may be more than one operator keying-in the copy and that a completely separate team — either within the typesetting company or completely outside — will be responsible for the page make-up. For this reason, it is wise to confine the type mark-up to the manuscript itself, and the layout instructions, such as the position of the text on the page, to the layouts themselves.

Proofs The first proof (or piece of typeset copy) provided by the typesetter is known as a galley proof. This is usually the last chance to get everything right, so it should be scrutinized with meticulous care. In the first instance this is generally done by the typesetter's own reader who will check it against the manuscript and mark any errors in red. All other corrections or alterations should be marked in a different colour — this ensures that typesetters do not charge for their own errors.

Next, the author or editor, or both, will be required to read the galley proof even though, in principle, all editorial alterations and corrections should have already been incorporated into the manuscript because of the cost of resetting type. In addition, the editor will need to check the text for such things as line lengths and 'widows' (single words set on a line at the end of a paragraph) and make adjustments accordingly. The designer should also check it for more aesthetic inconsistencies or anomalies such as wrong founts, erratic word spacing or 'rivers' (white lines running down a column of text caused by the coincidence of word spaces on different lines falling adjacent to each other).

It should be possible at this stage, with straightforward text, to return the corrected galleys to the typesetter for final galleys — for paste-up or for making into page film. However, it is quite usual for typesetters to supply second — and sometimes third and even fourth — proofs before final approval is given. The number of galleys supplied depends, of course, on the complexity of the job, and with very complicated setting such as timetables or mathematical formulae, it may be necessary to go to many proofs.

How may times proofs can be returned is usually determined by schedule limitations, rather than the need to achieve perfection.

DESIGNING THE PAGE

The style, or design, of a surface is a process of constant decision-making which evolves from an initial concept. While the finished, printed item may represent what appears to be a single and whole solution, it can only materialize as a result of making a constant string of decisions, usually spread over a protracted period of time. Even the most fastidious and accurate roughs will be subject to change during the evolution of a job.

Before any copy is sent for typesetting, the designer must first have determined the context which the job fits — whether the design is purely typographic or whether illustrations are also involved. The designer will need to determine the types of heading involved and to find a satisfactory way of displaying any required emphasis in the text, whether it be single words or complete paragraphs. There are several ways of achieving this; methods include capitalization, a change of size or weight, a change of fount, addition of colour, use of space or indentation, or any combination of these, although, of course, overemphasis may be counter-productive.

Naturally, the layout of text is determined by the number of lines that will fit within a page and this in turn is affected by the combination of type size and leading. The intended size, for instance, may be difficult to read when set solid (without space between lines), so additional line spacing may be added in the form of leading. This will result in reducing the number of lines on each page, which, in turn, will mean that more pages may be required in which to fit the text. It is also important to make allowances both aesthetically and practically for the blank spaces that may appear as the result of editorial or typographical constraints, such as subheadings and paragraphing, since, as well as the possibility of appearing ugly, such spaces will increase the number of lines.

The number of typeset lines can be counted by using a typescale or better still, a depth scale, or line counter — which gives a much greater number of increments. When using such equipment, always measure from base line to base line of each line of type.

When illustrations are to be included in a design, the problems are multiplied. Illustrations are usually accompanied by a caption, which needs to be as close as possible to it. Conversely, the captions for a group of illustrations on a page may be placed together, in which case the pictures to which they refer must be clearly identified. There are a number of ways of doing this; the most common is to use 'directionals' such as 'above' or 'top left', or alternatively to use numbers. Another method is to use graphic devices, or 'ornaments', but care should be taken when using these because the result can easily look messy or ambiguous. Illustrations should also be placed as near as possible to the relevant passage of main text, whether captions are used or not.

It is also important, when incorporating illustrations, to achieve a degree of consistency in the layout so that illustrations are not only balanced with each other, but with the text.

Grids

Almost all jobs that involve the integration of pictures with type should be designed on a purpose-made plan, or grid. The exceptions are those of the 'one-off' variety — those that involve few words or illustrations such as record covers and book jackets.

The purpose of a grid is two-fold; first, it ensures consistency, whether the job is a single broadsheet, whether it requires page turns or if it forms the basis of a series design such as product labels of a chain store. Second, it serves as a reference for all the various craftsmen involved in production.

The grid should show all the features common to all pages, such as column widths, text and illustration areas, positions of headings and folios (page numbers), trim size, folds, gutters, column depths, margins and so on. It is important that this information is as complete as possible, since designers, illustrators, photographers, editors and printers will all be working from it. The grid, however, should never be regarded as a straight-jacket; if an idea demands it, many of the dimensions can be ignored.

The way a printed grid is produced depends on the number of pages or folds involved and the type of printing process selected.

SKILLS AND TECHNIQUES

1 *Bleed*
2 *Position of chapter headings*
3 *Position of page headings and subdecks*
4 *Page trim*
5 *Trimmed size of page*
6 *Position of running head*
7 *Top line of text area (x-height of first line of type)*
8 *Text column*
9 *Caption column width*
10 *Position of folio number*
11 *Position of box rule*
12 *Maximum limit of illustration area*
13 *Special illustration (consistent on each page)*
14 *Number of text lines (from top)*
15 *Number of text lines (from bottom)*
16 *Base line of text area*

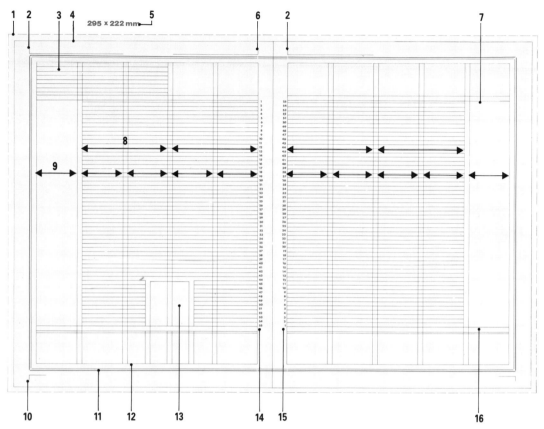

Printed grids are common in large jobs — books, for example — and their use helps minimize the amount of time required to prepare layouts, it also helps reduce any errors which might occur if each page was drawn up individually. Otherwise, pencil grids are adequate, but, in either case, accuracy is important.

The master drawing of the grid is best prepared on a transparent sheet, as this can then be used to check that originated proofs are the right size and that each double-page spread has been made up correctly. This is done by simply laying the grid over the proof. It is best to draw the grid on a material that is robust and dimensionally stable and that accepts fine lines in ink readily. Polyester draughting film is one of the most suitable.

If the grid is printed, it is advisable to have two versions prepared — one on semi-transparent layout paper and the other on thin board. The first can be used for tracing-off illustrations and for making rough layouts. However, it should not be used for checking the size of illustrations as layout paper is dimensionally unstable. The second is for more accurate paste-up purposes, whether 'camera-ready' (for photographically converting into page film) or otherwise. Grids are best printed in pale blue ink as this is not

▲ *Printed grids are an essential part of the design process, particularly in book and leaflet design. Their use helps to minimize the amount of time required to prepare drawings; they also help to reduce the errors which might otherwise occur if every double page was to be drawn up separately. The basic grid should include all the essential elements around which the designer must work — the column depths and type widths and text and illustration areas to margins and the positions of folios. When all this information is combined in permanent form, it serves as reference both for the designer and the various craftsmen involved in production. Frequently, two forms of grid are printed. The master drawing is often made on to a transparent sheet; the subsequent transparent grids can be used for rough paste-up, for tracing off illustrations and for checking the size and positioning of illustration proofs. Polyester film is frequently used. Board grids are used for final paste-up. Such grids are best printed in a pale blue ink, as this will not reproduce when the pasted-up text is photographed to produce final text film, as in camera-ready artwork.*

sensitive to photographic reproduction. Always remember to check the grid itself for accuracy, as soon as it is returned from the printer, since inaccurately printed grids, however slight the error, cannot be used.

GRADE 0

GRADE 1

GRADE 2

GRADE 3

GRADE 4

GRADE 5

▲ *When ordering black-and-white prints, it is vital to specify the paper they are to be printed on, since each paper has its own particular characteristics. The* *prints here show the effects of printing on Grade 0 paper through to Grade 5 paper. The softer the grade, the greater the amount of detail.*

Layouts

Having progressed through the preparatory stages, the designer can begin the task of assembling all the different elements — the photographs, artwork, text and so on, to be prepared for eventual printing.

This is done by drawing layouts — literally, laying out the various elements together on semi-transparent paper ('layout' or 'detail' paper). This serves two purposes; first, the designer can manipulate the images and type until a satisfactory result — both aesthetically and practically — is achieved. Second, it enables other people to carry out their part of the job, such as editors or authors who, once they know how much space is allocated and the position relative to the picture, can write captions.

Layouts can also be useful for the various people involved in production such as typesetters — especially if complicated setting is required — and origination houses, who sometimes need them for reference when making colour separations. Although layouts take

Grids

Grids are devised and used to enable designers to be consistent in their layouts. If you are designing a magazine, book or large catalogue, certain elements will be the same on every page, such as the position of page numbers or the width of margins.

Once you have styled a typical page of a book or magazine, you will have decided on page size, margins, position and size of text, column widths and number of columns. You may decide that on some pages you want two columns, but on others five.

Assess all the possible standard requirements and draw up a piece of line artwork with all this information on it. It is better to supply too much information than not enough. When drawing in the lines representing your text, you may want to number them so that if you are discussing text over the phone with an editor or author who has a copy of your layout, you can refer to specific lines on the page. A copy of the grid is also essential for illustrators, photographers, typesetters and printers who are working on the book.

If the job is a fairly small one, pencil grids will be sufficient, and you can draw these up by hand. However, the design of anything with a large number of pages necessitates using printed grids. Make sure the grid is accurate and point out to the printer that they must check reproduction size very carefully when making plates. It need only be very slightly inaccurate to be highly frustrating to use or, worse, useless.

When you have a grid printed, it is a good idea to have two sets prepared — one on transparent layout or tracing paper, and the other on artboard. The transparent one can be used for laying the book out and tracing in the illustrations, and the artboard version can be used for pasting up the camera-ready copy. You can use a transparent grid on an enlarger with ease when scaling illustrations. This then becomes an overlay and position guide for the pictures when presenting the camera-ready boards to the printer. When pasting-up the artwork onto the artboards, use the light box to position text rather than the parallel motion. The sheer number of pages will demand this. By placing the grid on the light box you will be able to see the lines through the repro proofs. This enables you to position text quickly and accurately.

Have the grid sheets printed in pale blue (photographic blue) so that the grid lines will not be picked up when a negative is made from the finished artwork.

If you are ever asked to prepare very precise miniature flow-charts, you can reduce the grid to the required size. In this way you effectively design a book in miniature but very accurately, and you can judge exactly how many lines of text are required on every page.

You must always remember that a grid is only there to make your life easier. It should never be regarded as a design straitjacket and should be disregarded if an idea demands it.

the form of a working 'blue-print', which may contain much technical information, in many cases, particularly small jobs of a one-off nature, the layout may simply be a photocopy or duplicate of a presentation visual. All relevant instructions to artists and craftsmen can be added to the photocopy.

Layouts should contain as much information as possible. Headings should be written in (or drawn as a facsimile of the relevant typeface, so that the length can be assessed); areas of text and captions should be accurately indicated with their exact number of lines; and illustrations drawn in (with a code number which matches that on the artwork, photograph or transparency. whether it is to appear in full-colour, black-and-white or other colours, and to whom the credit is to be given). The page numbers, whether they are four-colour pages or otherwise and so on should also be given. Layouts should always be photocopied before they are sent out, and the originals should remain with the designer.

Layouts are frequently made before illustrations and, although less often, photographs are commissioned. For this reason, layouts involving artwork should be drawn to a high level of accuracy, since the artist will need to know the *exact* dimensions of an illustration, especially if it is to occupy a free shape (one that has a loosely defined perimeter). If the illustration is to contain specific information, say of a technical nature, as in maps, charts and diagrams, the layout must be fully worked out — even to the extent of writing in any labelling (annotation), so that the artist has a precise visual guide to what is required.

Selecting photographs

The use and selection of photographs takes many forms, these being mainly determined by the requirements of the job in hand. For instance, a photograph for an advertisement may have been taken by referring to an accurate layout by the designer, in which case selection will be restricted to mostly technical considerations such as exposure, sharpness and colour. The photographer should always supply more than one alternative. On the other hand, photograph selection for an illustrated book may be from material supplied by picture libraries, which may range from the excellent to the barely discernible, in which case the overall effect of a design will depend as much on aesthetic as technical judgements.

Photographs exist in two forms: either as flat prints — whether colour or black-and-white — or as transparencies, which are always in colour. Although colour prints can be made to a very high quality, these are considered less suitable for reproduction purposes than transparencies. This is because light has to be reflected from a print, thereby losing its strength (it starts to become grey), whereas light is passed directly through a transparency, thus retaining its full strength and consequently optimum colour saturation (the degree to which white, grey or black is eliminated).

▲ *When selecting transparencies always check them with a special magnifying glass on a light box.*

This will reveal any flaws or scratches on the transparency that you may otherwise not notice.

▲ *One method of scaling an illustration is to square the image up on an overlay.*

▲ *On the layout, define the image area to be filled and then draw a diagonal line across it.*

▲ *Position the squared-up overlay on the layout and extend the diagonal.*

▲ *Having established how the picture is to be cropped, mark the dimensions.*

Photographers, to be on the safe side, usually supply bracketed shots — that is, photographs of the same subject, but shot using a variety of slightly different exposures and camera angles. It is important, therefore, to know which density will reproduce best, though the only real guide to this is experience. Generally, however, the picture that *looks* best invariably reproduces to a better standard, simply because the best looking picture is most likely to be the one at the correct exposure — the exposure which is at right level of density for reproduction. For instance, a red object photographed on a white background will give an exaggeratedly bright (fully saturated) and perhaps desirable red if slightly underexposed, but the background will reproduce as an undesirable grey. On the other hand, a slightly overexposed shot may give a perfect white background but with a slightly washed-out red subject.

Colour transparencies should be viewed on a colour-corrected light box, that is, a light box which has had its light source balanced to give the correct type of light (colour temperature) required for viewing colour film.

Many photographers, particularly in situations where colour is of paramount importance, such as in the reproduction of fine art, will include in the transparency some sort of colour scale. This will be outside the area of the transparency to be used. This scale, called colour control patches, gives highly accurate reproductions of each of the three layers of film emulsion — cyan, magenta and yellow. In addition, there are patches of black and combinations of the three emulsion colours. These patches indicate any bias there may be in a transparency, whether as a result of the lighting conditions in which the picture was taken or because of natural fading of the transparency over a period of time. Apart from being useful during the processing of the film, colour control patches are helpful to colour origination houses when making separations.

Sometimes the designer is faced with the problem of having to produce a colourful result, but only having black-and-white photographs to use, particularly when the subject is of an historical nature. The way round this is, from the black-and-white original,

to use combinations of colours from the four-colour process to produce duotones, tri-tones, three, two and one-colour tints and so on. This is done by the colour origination house. Use of four colours naturally means that the combinations of colour must fall within the limits of the process, and one of the most popular combinations is black plus one other colour.

Although not immediately apparent, good reproduction of black-and-white photographs can be difficult to achieve, so care must be taken in selecting a suitable original., In reproduction, the image is broken into tiny dots, so solid blacks lose their density,

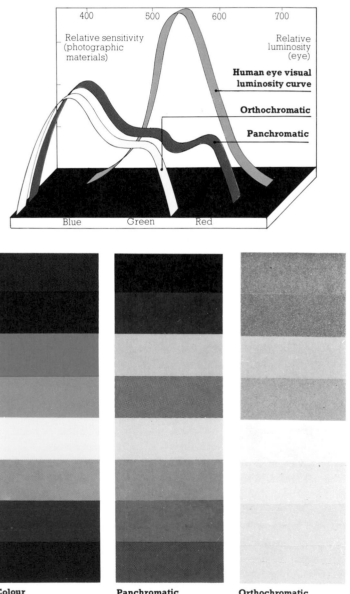

▶ *All designers should have a basic understanding of the nature of black-and-white film and how it works when faced with the problem of recording colour. When black-and-white film is used in this way, there are obvious anomalies in the way the various types react. The graph shows some of these variations by contrasting the colour sensitivity of film to that of the human eye. Although the eye reacts most strongly to green, for instance, film, in comparison, over-reacts to the blue end of the colour spectrum. Orthochromatic film does not respond at all to red, as the graph shows, while modern panchromatic film covers the full range of visual colours. This point is emphasized in the bar diagram (right) where the response of various black-and-white films to colour is clearly demonstrated. Again, panchromatic is on the whole the most faithful.*

Colour   Panchromatic   Orthochromatic

whereas lighter tones suffer from loss of detail and whites become grey. This means that the ideal black-and-white original is one that has maximum contrast from black to white and yet retains all the detail and subtle shades of the mid-tones.

Photographs and transparencies should be carefully checked with a magnifying glass for sharpness and for blemishes, such as scratches. Damaged pictures frequently need retouching and this is normally done by a specialized studio. If this is decided to be necessary, and the picture is from a library or museum, permission must be obtained first, or a duplicate made. Retouching can be taken to greater extremes if portions of the photographs are considered undesirable or if alterations or substitutions are required.

Sizing pictures

The first step when marking up pictures for reproduction is to determine which portion of the original if any needs to be cropped (excluded from the printed image), although, of course, the designer will already have a rough impression of this from the initial layout. This is done by a procedure known as scaling. First, the picture area of the original is traced to square it up on a transparent overlay. Then the tracing is placed on top of the corresponding picture area on the layout, with one corner of each matching. Next, a diagonal line is drawn from this corner to the opposite corner of the picture area on the layout, the line being extended to meet an edge of the area of the original. Where the diagonal lines meet this edge is the corner of the final image, the remainder being cropped. The tracing, with the area to be cropped clearly marked, should be attached to the original picture and both the dimensions of the image as it will finally appear should be clearly added as well.

The next step is to calculate the reduction — or enlargement — percentage. This is because the dimension controls of reproduction cameras and scanners are calibrated in percentages, rather than sizes. However, it is still necessary to indicate linear dimensions because the edges of the image at its final size will have to be cleaned up, or masked. Same size reproduction is 100 per cent, while pictures to be reduced in size are less than 100 per cent and those to be enlarged are greater. For instance, a reduction in size from 60mm to 40mm would mean a reduction of 66 per cent, while an enlargement from 40mm to 60mm gives an enlargement of 150 per cent. Only one dimension each of the final size and of the original size, though of the same axis, is necessary to make this calculation. The mathematical formula for calculating the enlargement or reduction percentage is: (size of final image ÷ size of original) × 100. Knowing the percentage of reduction or enlargement is also useful in that it is possible to group pictures of the same, or very similar, ratio together, thus saving money because they can be scanned at the same time.

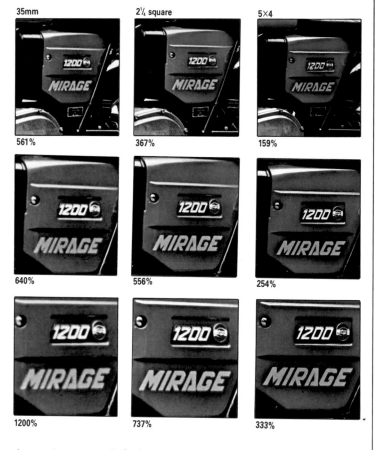

35mm   2¼ square   5×4

561%   367%   159%

640%   556%   254%

1200%   737%   333%

▲ Most design work calls for the enlargement of photographs, so take into account what effects this will have on the qualities of the original pictures. The greater the enlargement the more detail that will be lost and the more grainy the printed image. The strips here show the same image photographed in different formats — 35mm, 2¼in square and 5 × 4 — and the effects of varying degrees of enlargement. It is clear that the larger the original format, the more it can be enlarged, while preserving clarity and detail.

◄ Calculate the percentage enlargement or reduction of an image with a reproduction computer or calculator. The numbers on the outer ring of the reproduction computer signify the required size and those on the inner ring the actual size. Turn the two rings until the appropriate figures meet and give the percentage.

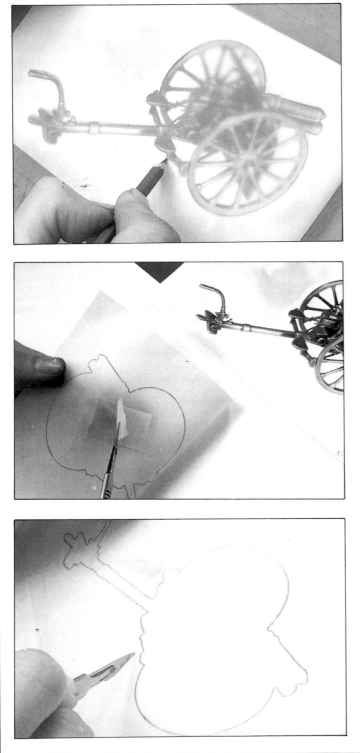

To help the client visualize how effective a cut-out can be, it is best to make a mask. Using white paint, follow the outline of the image and fill in any gaps, such as between the wheel spokes in this example.

Place a sheet of tracing paper over the image and pencil in the outside outline.

Remove the trace and secure it in the centre with double-sided tape onto a sheet of cartridge paper. Leaving ⅛in (0.3175mm) from the pencil line, follow the trace with a scalpel, cutting through both sheets. Always take great care when handling scalpels, but if you should be unlucky and cut a bit of finger off, put it in a clean plastic bag packed with ice and take it to the hospital with you.

Lift out the image area and you now have a mask, which is placed over the original image.

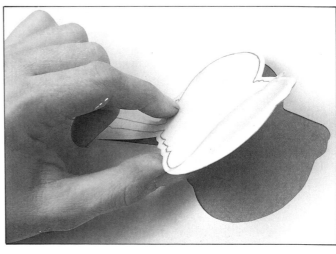

Black and white cut-out.

Black and white cut-out on 10-percent yellow.

Black and white cut out printed in cyan.

◄ *Use black-and-white photographs creatively but always ensure that however you want them to print, your instructions are clear. Mistakes in printing are expensive to rectify.*

It should also be specified on the overlay whether the image is to be squared up, cut out, or cut into another image. A squared-up image sits on a page with its edges square, while a silhouette picture is one that has a free shape, its background having been removed. With transparencies, it is best to select those in which a subject with a fairly simple outline is set against a white or pale background, otherwise the resulting image may have dark or messy edges. With black-and-white originals, unwanted areas should be painted out with opaque white paint. 'Cut into' means that a picture overlaps, or sits completely within, another. The origination house should be given very clear instructions, specifying which picture is to be cut into which, plus a layout showing their positions with all the dimensions marked.

Other essential information to include on the picture overlay is a code number. Each picture in a job should have its number recorded on the layouts. This is in case the origination house has any queries about a specific picture or needs to be given any special instructions, such as whether it is to appear as a duotone, or if a colour original is to be reproduced as a black-and-white. Origination houses always assume that if a colour original is supplied, then colour separation is required and, similarly, if black-and-white is supplied it is to appear as black-and-white.

The paste-up

The stage at which proofs of type and pictures are assembled together on a page is called paste-up. This term usually refers to the final state of paste-up as given to the typesetter or printer, but it is preceded by a preliminary stage, or rough paste-up, in which galley proofs and picture proofs are assembled together on layout sheets so that everything can be checked for size before the final paste-up begins.

Final paste-up takes two forms, depending on what the typesetter or printer is contracted to supply. Many typesetting systems now incorporate a facility whereby the copy, having been keyed-in and issued with various typeface instructions, can be

arranged in page position on a special screen and produced as page film from the typesetting machine. In such cases, the paste-up will consist of galleys and pictures pasted up accurately together on the same piece of board, with everything that is to appear in print — body text, captions, headlines, folios and rules — clearly marked up for any special requirements such as colour and the thicknesses and length of rules. Accuracy is obviously extremely important.

The other form of paste-up is that which is placed directly under the camera and photographed to produce final text film.

► *Cutting out an unwanted background is a frequently used design procedure. This is much easier to accomplish with a light background, since the image area can be more clearly defined than with a dark one. In this instance, it is important to shade out the areas that are not to reproduce, to define the outline of the figure. Dimensions should be clearly marked on the overlay.*

▲ *Always mark printing instructions for a picture clearly on an overlay. Indicate dimensions and any areas not to be printed.*

This is called camera-ready paste-up, or mechanicals. With this method, only type and rules should appear, because, if illustrations were incorporated onto the same surface, they would have to be masked out for final film to be made. The most expedient way of producing camera-ready paste-up is to paste the picture proofs onto the printed grid baseboard, with all type, rules and other matter to be photographed being positioned accurately on a draughting film overlay. Any areas to print as a tint should be marked clearly on the baseboard, whereas type or rules to print in a different colour should be marked on a tracing paper overlay, which also serves as a protective covering. Typesetting proofs used for camera-ready paste-up are generally called reproduction pulls (repro), but more specifically bromides or PMTs (for film or phototypesetting). Repro should not lift or curl at the corners, so it must be securely stuck with an adhesive that is reliable, but also one that permits the designer to remove or reposition it without damage. There are several proprietary brands of spray adhesive, adhesive wax and rubber solutions suitable for this purpose. Small pieces of repro — such as individual words — can be secured with double-sided adhesive tape, but this is difficult to remove.

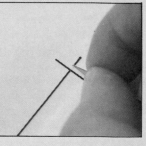

These three pictures show how to achieve a neat square edge when drawing a box rule by extending the lines beyond the point at which they meet, then scraping the overlap back with a scalpel.

PREPARING ARTWORK

If artwork to be reproduced is flat (with no additional 'bits' — usually overlays — to be incorporated) and in four colour, the marking-up procedure is the same as that for transparencies. Complications arise however, if other elements are to be incorporated into the final image. These elements appear on the artwork in the form of overlays of draughting film taped over the base artwork. Registration marks are added to show how each overlay fits together with the base artwork, and type is pasted down and any lines drawn onto the film. Each separate overlay fulfills a different function; a map, for instance, with a base drawn in four-colour may have the following overlays:

1 Type and other line work to appear in black.
2 Type and other line work to reverse out of colour.
3 Type and line work to appear in cyan.
4 Type and line work to appear in magenta.
5 Areas to appear as cyan tint.
6 Areas to appear as magenta tint.

A map is an extreme example in that there could be almost any number of overlays, each one representing a different combination of line printings and almost limitless tint combinations. It is most common to have only one overlay on a four-colour piece of artwork, this being for type.

Black-and-white artwork can be made to appear in four-colour

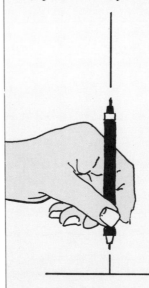

A technical pen is essential for all line work as it produces lines of an even and continuous width. The nib is simply a straight, hollow, metal tube with a flat, open end. This means that the pen has to be held completely upright, allowing the open nib to touch the paper on all sides, thereby containing and restricting the ink flow. Unfortunately they can be temperamental, especially when the ink starts to dry out and clog them up. This can be avoided by always storing them with the nib down. If this rule has not been followed it is usually cured by keeping the cap on and tapping the opposite end to the nib sharply on a hard surface. This shocks them into action. Because of the differences in hand pressure that occur naturally when moving in different directions, slightly different line widths may result. The best way to prevent this is to turn the artwork around, which enables the artist to draw all the lines in the same direction.

This artwork is to be reproduced in four colours as shown (lower right).

The black line work is drawn on the base board and the different areas of colour that are to be made up out of the four process colours — black, magenta, yellow and cyan — are drawn separately on overlays.

An alternative method is to supply only one overlay on which the various colours are indicated; the printer or origination house will then separate these colours at film stage. This method is more time consuming for the printer and therefore more expensive.

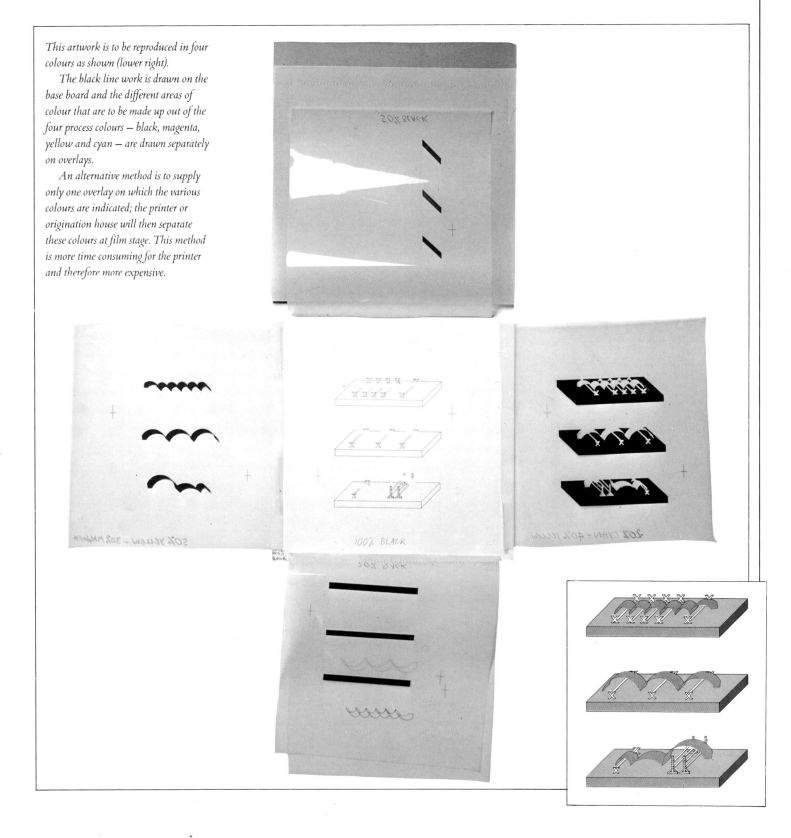

by the use of mechanical tints which are laid by the printer or origination house. These can be selected from a process colour tint chart or they can be specified as combinations of specially mixed colours.

Areas to print as tints can be prepared in one of two ways. The first is to use one overlay with key lines defining each area to be tinted — in other words, only one overlay is required to show all the various colours. the second is to use a different overlay for each combination of tints, although this can get very cumbersome if many colours are to be used. The former, therefore, is more convenient but can be more expensive since it involves a considerable amount of hand-work (as opposed to photographic) by the lithographic planners — the people who lay tints in an origination house.

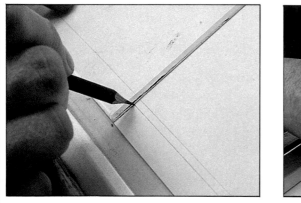

◄◄ *Rule up the areas of your artwork lightly in pencil as accurately as possible. Always double-check sizes before inking in any lines.*

◄ *When using a technical pen, hold it completely upright so that the lines you draw are of an even consistency. Technical pens are temperamental and have a tendency to dry and clog. Keep them clean and use them regularly.*

◄◄ *Start by trimming the repro squarely when pasting up typesetting, and it will be much easier to paste up accurately.*

◄ *The positioning of headlines is critical. Although you must check your artwork for mechanical accuracy, the good positioning of large type also requires visual judgement.*

Electronic page planning

Recent developments in scanners have produced machines that can scan, store the separation information on disk in digital form, and then use this information to create the image of a complete page containing several transparencies, output onto film, in position, so that the page film consists of one complete piece of film for each colour. In addition, these machines can be used to lay tints, produce shapes and cut-outs, airbrushing and other artistic work and carry out colour correction. Most of them have a colour monitor, so the operator can visually assess the layout and colour values before they are committed to film. Some page planners can include type as well as pictures in the layout, and can even alter typefaces and type sizes at layout stage.

The capital cost of these machines is very high, but their sophistication means that complex publications such as mail-order catalogues can be produced more cheaply and to a higher standard. Makes include Hell, Dai Nippon, Crosfield and Scitex. This is a rapidly developing field, with new machines coming out every few months. The newer systems can go direct to offset plate or gravure cylinder without having to use film.

◀◀ *Descenders of type sometimes have to drop below the cap height of the line beneath in order to look right. Cut around the descender as closely as possible.*

◀ *You may want to adjust the letter spacing of the typesetting. Cut as vertically as possible between the characters and adjust the spacing as required — the vertical cuts will make it easier to re-position.*

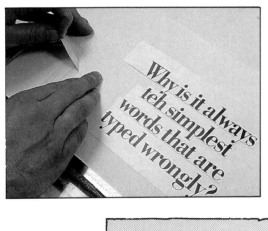

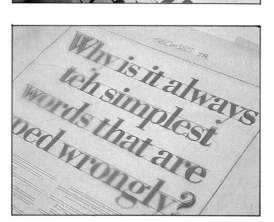

◀◀ *Clean and check the artwork and then have a PMT made. Ensure that the PMT is clean and sharp. Wet any small specks slightly with water and scrape them away gently with a scalpel (X-Acto knife).*

◀ *Position the PMT on the board, place a sheet of tracing paper over the artwork to protect it and give the whole area a final burnish. The overlay can be used to carry instructions for printing.*

◀ *When working with repeat layouts, to save time and avoid having to measure each one individually, mark up your drawing board. Attach the layout to the board and with a T-square and set-square (triangle) extend the lines past the edges onto the board. Mark the corners, then remove the layout, replacing it with your clean sheet. Draw the layout onto this by simply following the lines on the board.*

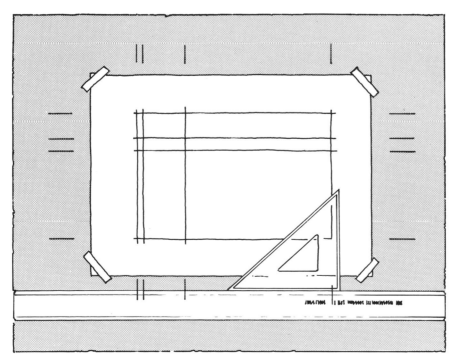

Preparing artwork – a checklist

Once your design has been approved by the client, you have to prepare camera-ready artwork, or mechanicals, which will be sent to the reproduction house to be proofed. Producing good artwork requires meticulous attention to detail. It is frustrating to look at a printed piece of work that you have designed and see badly spaced typography or a carelessly drawn rule. Errors on artwork which get into print can be disastrous and very expensive to correct.

■ Camera-ready artwork is always prepared flat, in black and white and on line board.

■ Before starting a piece of artwork, make sure that your hands are clean.

■ Fix the line board squarely to your drawing board with masking tape and rule up the areas of your design lightly with a hard pencil or blue pencil. Blue has the advantage of not being picked up on line film when the artwork is photographed during the reproduction process.

■ Your marks must be very accurate, so check all dimensions several times.

■ If your design is very complicated, you can work to a larger scale and then reduce it photographically. As long as your artwork is directly in proportion to its final printed size, you can work to whatever scale you find comfortable. If you work larger, very slight imperfections in the quality of line will be reduced visually as the artwork is reduced.

■ Always keep your equipment and instruments clean. Lighter fuel (solvent) is very good for this. It is also wise to wipe lighter fuel lightly over your ruled-up board with a tissue or piece of absorbent paper to remove the grease and dirt that will inevitably collect there.

■ A soft brush is useful for dusting your artwork. Remember, any imperfections or specks of dirt will be picked up by the camera during colour separation and will, in turn, be reproduced in the printing.

■ You should always rule in any lines that are to be printed with a technical pen before you begin pasting down typesetting. Once you get adhesive onto the surface of the line board, it is difficult to clean off and will affect the quality of line you draw. Remember to check that your pen is flowing freely before ruling any lines.

■ You can also use tape rules, dry transfer rules (format rules) or rules supplied by your typesetter.

■ Typesetting should be stuck down in position with rubber solution (rubber cement), adhesive sprays or warm wax. They all have advantages and disadvantages, so experiment.

■ Check that text and captions are pasted down in the correct order.

■ Do not discard spare typesetting. You or your client may find last-minute typographic errors.

■ Dry transfer lettering can be applied directly to the line board, or rubbed down onto a separate piece of paper and stuck down in position on your main board. If you apply dry transfer lettering directly onto artwork, be extra careful not to damage the transfer.

■ You should now clean your artwork again with lighter fuel (solvent) to remove excess glue and dirt. Be careful not to smudge inked rules or disturb dry transfer type.

■ Halftones do not reproduce well when pasted down as artwork. The size and position of halftones should be clearly marked on the artwork but they should be reproduced separately. All such information and any further instructions should be written on a tracing paper overlay. If you have any doubts about how to present your artwork to a printer or colour reproduction house, call them. It could save you time and money.

■ If you are preparing two-colour artwork, your second colour should be pasted up on a film overlay. This is not always essential because the printer can sometimes separate the two colours on film, but it will be more expensive. Always separate any parts of two-colour artwork onto different overlays which, when printed, will overlap.

Curved headlines and circles

Take the strip of setting and apply adhesive to the back as it is going to be cut several times and so will need to stay secure. Cut down between each letter, leaving them joined at the bottom edge. Move the strip onto the board and attach an overlay with the drawn curve, which will act as the guide over the board. The bottom edge is cut through as each letter is teased into position. When complete a PMT can be made for the finished art.

In the preparation of camera-ready artwork always follow this sequence of assembly. First, separate all the individual components (below). Secure the layout guide over the board (far below). Position all the larger and most straightforward components first (top right). Drop in the illustrations (centre right). Finally, add the small details (below right).

HAND LETTERING

In a world so full of technology it is understandable that an artist specializing in lettering might be assumed to be something of a dinosaur. However, even though a resident lettering artist is not necessarily a permanent member of a studio team, he or she still plays a very important role. With an ever-increasing choice of dry transfer lettering and phototypesetting it is not always necessary to hand draw all the larger scale work used for headlines, posters and advertising material. Expertise is essential, though, when original and distinctive lettering, such as an individual logo, needs to be created.

There is still some confusion as to the difference between calligraphy and hand-drawn lettering. The word calligraphy is derived from the Greek work *Kaligraphia*, meaning beautiful writing, whereas hand lettering is the construction of letter forms. Artists often like to make use of calligraphy's fluid spontaneity when designing letter forms, by using it as a basis, rather like a thumbnail sketch.

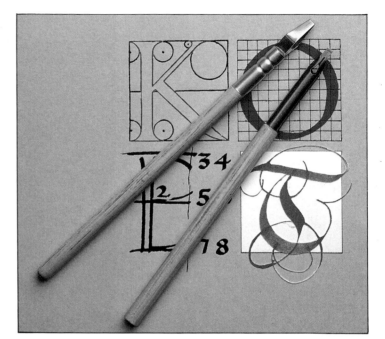

Certain styles of letter forms create optical illusions that have to be compensated for in their construction. Hand lettering is nearly always constructed between parallel lines, which give the initial cap height. In the example above we can see how the letter occupies this basic height, but the letters with points, such as A and V, must extend beyond the guideline or they will look too short. The same principle should be applied to the letters that have curved forms, or they too will look squat and too small.

There is a wide range of calligraphic pens available which enable the artist to create certain effects instantaneously. The strokes are alway made from top to bottom, allowing for greater control and even pressure.

◄ *This is a very clever adaption of existing type. The letters UFO were drawn and the flash was created by cutting out the centre of the letters and finishing the zigzag by hand.*

▶ **Reversed-out white** *Of course, the ideal way to reverse lettering out of a coloured background is simply to use white Letraset, but if this is not available in the chosen face black can be used.*

Lay the characters down and burnish them with the flat edge of a nib or any other blunt instrument.

Next apply the colour. If the paper has a coated background, apply a water-based paint with a wad of absorbent cotton — this will create a flat continuous tone and eliminate any brush marks. Do not use a spirit-based medium, since this will dissolve dry transfer lettering. Use a hair dryer to speed up the drying process.

When the paint is dry, remove the letters one at a time from the surface with masking tape, which will not lift the surface of the paper.

Any remaining specks of lettering or background colour that has seeped under the transfer and distorted the letter outline can be scratched away gently with a scalpel (X-Acto knife).

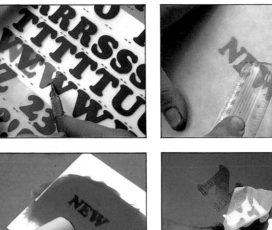

When you are designing letterforms and logos for packaging check which printing process is being used. For example, flexography can print six colours on some machines but the quality of the fine detail colour work is not high — this will affect your design. Also, the letterforms and logos must be designed within the limitations of the shape of the package. Look at some well-known drinks cans and bottles to see how the shapes themselves have been used to their best advantage.

◀ *From the close-up it is possible to see how the lettering was achieved for the artwork. The lettering was masked while the surround was stippled with a coarse spatter cap fitted to an airbrush. The double effect for the New York Dolls logo was created by reversing out a second version of the lettering.*

◀ **Outline lettering** *To produce outline lettering from a solid typeface, fill a ruling pen with process white and follow the inside of the letter forms. Then fill in with a sable brush, leaving the required outline width. It is always best to use sable brushes, since they retain their shape and springiness even when wet.*

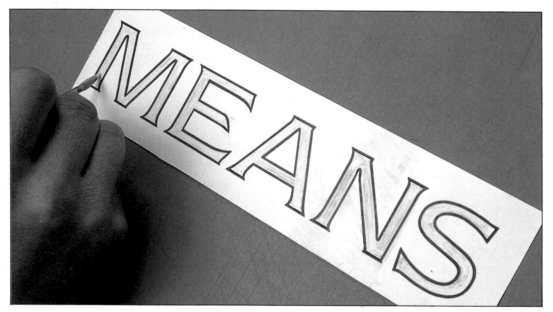

CUSTOMIZED LETTER FORMS

▲ **Customized letterforms**
A quick way to create instant yet original letter forms is to adapt dry transfer lettering in an already existing face. Cut and shape the letters with a scalpel (X-Acto knife) while they are still on the backing sheet and just rub down the required parts.

UNDERSTANDING COLOUR

Understanding colour is an integral part of being a designer. It is virtually impossible to be objective about colour because we all use colour in a subjective way. A basic knowledge of colour theory is, of course, useful, but time spent experimenting with colour is more rewarding. Colour theory shows why it works as it does, but not how to use it to create harmonious or shocking effects, for example. New types of colour, such as dayglo, neon and laser colour, in addition to the natural tones we are familiar with, have had a profound effect on the use of colour in design.

Daylight, or 'white light', is a tiny component of electromagnetic radiation and can be split up into seven different colours: violet, indigo, blue, green, yellow, orange and red — the colours of the spectrum. The colour of an object depends on how much of each of these colours is absorbed or reflected by the surface of that object. The three primary colours are red, yellow and blue. They cannot be mixed from a combination of any other colours, but all other colours can be made up from them. The three secondary colours are made from mixing any two of the primaries together — green (blue and yellow), violet (red and blue) and orange (yellow and red). The shade of a secondary colour will vary depending on the proportions of each primary mixed. Those primary and secondary colours which contrast with each other most strongly are known as complementary colours — orange and blue, yellow and violet, red and green. Complementary colours do not have a common primary colour.

For a designer, working with colour will mean choosing colours which are made up out of the four basic colours used in colour printing. These are yellow, magenta (red), cyan (blue) and black. These four colours can be mixed together in different proportions to achieve nearly all colours. It is important to remember that colour is modified by light. This is particularly important to a designer when specifying colours to a printer. The quality and density of a colour will change if you look at it in two different types of light, so it is best when choosing colours to look at them in daylight.

Colour correction

Proofs can be returned for colour correction from the origination house in one of two forms and the designer should ask for whichever is preferred. Either the illustrations are proofed in the exact position that they will be in when finally printed, or they are proofed — at the correct size — in random order. The latter are called scatter proofs — they are much cheaper to produce than

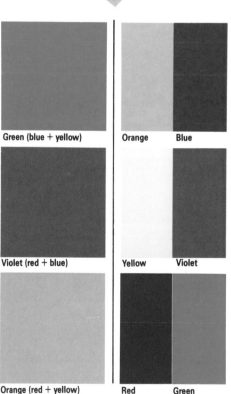

▶ *White light is made up of red, orange, yellow, green, blue, indigo and violet — the colours of the spectrum. These can be seen when white light passes through a glass prism.*

Red	**Green (blue + yellow)**	**Orange** **Blue**
Yellow	**Violet (red + blue)**	**Yellow** **Violet**
Blue	**Orange (red + yellow)**	**Red** **Green**

▲ *The three primary colours are red, yellow and blue and they cannot be mixed from other colours.*

▲ *The three secondary colours are green (blue and yellow), violet (red and blue) and orange (red and yellow) and are each made by mixing any two of the primaries together.*

▲ *The three sets of complementary colours are orange and blue, yellow and violet, and red and green. These are the colours that contrast with each other the most.*

▶ *Colour is subjective and there are no absolute rules as to how it should be used. The imaginative use of the four printing colours is a vital element in full-colour printing, and an awareness and willingness to explore colour are vital to you as a designer. The combinations illustrated here show just a few of the possibilities. On the chart Y = yellow, M = magenta, C = cyan, B = black; Tint values are specified as a percentage.*

Yellow

Magenta

Cyan

Black

Full colour magnification

▲ *The colours used in full-colour reproduction are yellow, magenta, cyan and black. They can be mixed together in varying proportions to reproduce most colours. Magnification of any printed full-colour picture will reveal these four colours.*

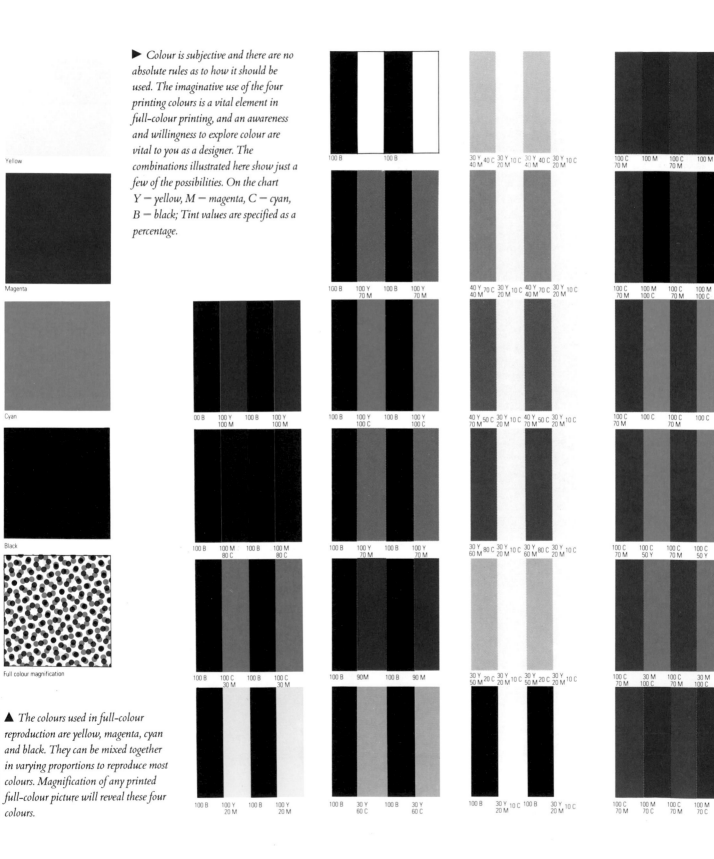

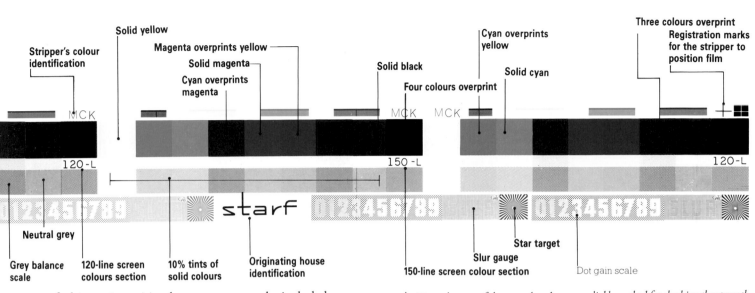

Stripper's colour identification

Solid yellow

Magenta overprints yellow

Solid magenta

Cyan overprints magenta

Solid black

Four colours overprint

Cyan overprints yellow

Solid cyan

Three colours overprint

Registration marks for the stripper to position film

MCK

120 -L

150 -L

MCK MCK

120 -L

Neutral grey

Grey balance scale

120-line screen colours section

10% tints of solid colours

Originating house identification

150-line screen colour section

Slur gauge

Star target

Dot gain scale

proofs that are in position because more can be included on a proofing plate.

An alternative to press proofing using ink and paper is the use of photographic/electrostatic methods such as Dupont Cromalin or 3M Colour Key. These are accurate for colour values, and this form of proofing is much cheaper when just one or two proofs are required. Also, these methods are being developed so that soon it will be possible using proofing systems such as Kodak Signature to have multiple proofs produced photographically on the actual job paper.

The most crucial task is to check the colour closely against the original. If there is a discrepancy, ask the origination house to correct it. In order to know the extent to which colour can be corrected, it is important to understand how colour separation works. Any increase or decrease in the amount of colour is achieved not by altering the amount of ink on the plate, but by enlarging or reducing the size of the halftone dots on the separation film. A colour is strengthened by reducing ('etching') the dot size on the *negative* film which, in turn, means that the dots are larger when converted to positive film. To reduce a colour, dots are etched on the *positive* film.

However, sometimes a proof has too much or too little of one colour which can only be accurately corrected by adjusting the proportions of one or two of the other colours. To increase the amount of magenta, say, it may be necessary to decrease the amount of cyan and possibly yellow.

There is a limit to which a dot size can be altered without having to reoriginate the subject. This limit is usually about 5 per cent, although it may sometimes be possible to achieve a 10 per cent variation. Because the dots are etched by a hand process (ferrocyanide applied with a brush), there comes a point when exaggerated corrections will begin to show on the proof — either as

▲ *Most colour proofs have a colour bar included on them. This is totally independent of the actual image and is used by the origination house, the designer and the printer to check the quality of the colours on the proofs. The bar shows the process colours in various forms. The amount of ink the printer should lay down is indicated by the solid colours. Colour bars provide a fast and* reliable method for checking the strength of colour. If there is not enough room beside a proof for a complete bar, a smaller quality control (QC) strip can be shown instead.

▼ *These symbols are widely used to mark corrections on proofs. Always write instructions neatly and make any expansion to the marks clear.*

Instruction	Marginal mark
Passed for press	✓
Reproof	⊿
Reduce contrast	☐
Increase contrast	■
Improve detail or modelling	◨
Too hard, make softer	U
Too soft, make sharper	∧
Rectify uneven tint	◑
Repair broken type, rule or tint	✕
Improve register	⧉
Correct slur	✗

Process colour	Increase	Reduce
Yellow	Y+	Y—
Magenta	M+	M—
Cyan	C+	C—
Black	B+	B—

▶ *Although the colours are identical on these two pages, the checks look totally different on a white base. By replacing the white with black the colours appear much more intense.*

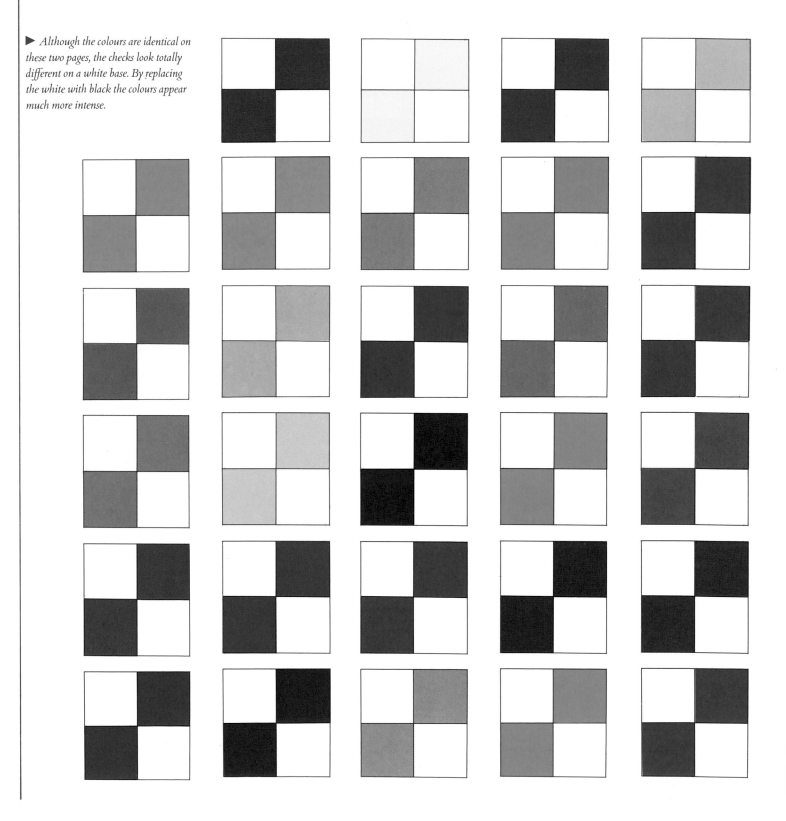

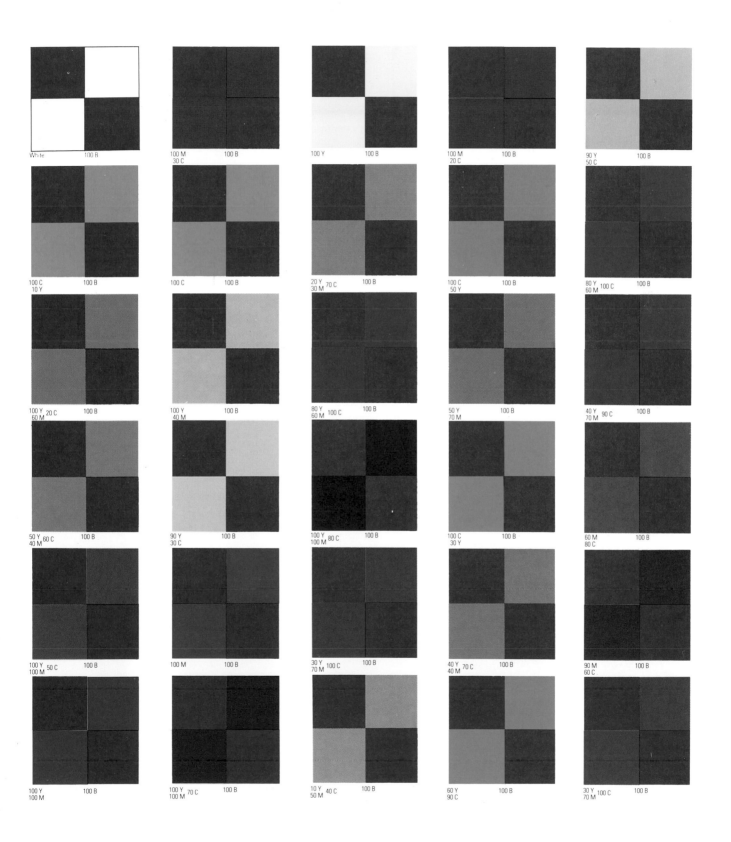

White | 100 B
100 M 30 C | 100 B
100 Y | 100 B
100 M 20 C | 100 B
90 Y 50 C | 100 B

100 C 10 Y | 100 B
100 C | 100 B
20 Y 30 M 70 C | 100 B
100 C 50 Y | 100 B
80 Y 60 M 100 C | 100 B

100 Y 60 M 20 C | 100 B
100 Y 40 M | 100 B
80 Y 60 M 100 C | 100 B
50 Y 70 M | 100 B
40 Y 70 M 90 C | 100 B

50 Y 40 M 60 C | 100 B
90 Y 30 C | 100 B
100 Y 100 M 80 C | 100 B
100 C 30 Y | 100 B
60 M 80 C | 100 B

100 Y 100 M 50 C | 100 B
100 M | 100 B
30 Y 70 M 100 C | 100 B
40 Y 40 M 70 C | 100 B
90 M 60 C | 100 B

100 Y 100 M | 100 B
100 Y 100 M 70 C | 100 B
10 Y 50 M 40 C | 100 B
60 Y 90 C | 100 B
30 Y 70 M 100 C | 100 B

Yellow printer

Magenta printer

Cyan printer

Black printer

Yellow proof

Magenta proof

Cyan proof

Black proof

Yellow proof

Yellow + magenta

Yellow, magenta + cyan

Yellow, magenta, cyan + black

LESS MAGENTA OVERALL (ESPECIALLY AROUND EYES)

IMPROVE HIGHLIGHTS

CLEAN UP HIGHLIGHTS

Y–!

▲ *In four-colour printing the image is photographed four times, once through each colour filter, to produce the separation negatives. When the four negatives are proofed in the individual colours and combined they result in a full-colour image.*

▶ *When you are working in full colour the printer will provide you with colour proofs. These must be checked carefully to ensure that there are no blemishes or spots, that they are the right size and fit, that they are in register and that the colour is right. Use the proof correction marks illustrated on page 61. A subject*

marked for reproofing normally requires reorigination unless the whole sheet is unacceptable. A request to improve detail and modelling refers to highlights and details that need enhancing. Hardness and softness refer to subjects in which edges of colour, shape or tone are too hard or too soft. An out-of-register subject is one in which the film for each colour has been wrongly stripped. Its edges should be in register; if they are not, the film was positioned incorrectly on the plate. Slur is a proofing defect that elongates halftone dots. These proofs (right) of the same subject show some of the things that can go wrong.

The correct version (**1**)

Too much contrast (**3**)

Not enough contrast (**4**)

Loss of detail (**5**)

Detail too hard or sharp (**6**)

Detail too soft (**7**)

Too much yellow

Too much cyan

Too much magenta

Too little yellow

Too little cyan

Too little magenta

◀ *If you magnify a full-colour printed image you will clearly see the pattern of overlapping dots that together make up the reproduction.*

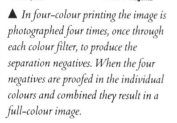

uneven patches or with defined edges to the etched portion. To see whether the proof has been incorrectly inked on the proofing press, check the colour control bar on the edge of the sheet.

Proofs should also be checked for register, blemishes, scratches, acid stains and broken screens. Use a magnifying glass to see whether the screen is damaged. If it has been it may be necessary to remake the subject, although highly skilled retouchers can sometimes work wonders. A subject that is out of register is one that has two or more colours appearing 'out of sync' with the others, although the edges of the illustration are clean and in perfect register with each other. If the edges are also out of register, then the film has merely been incorrectly stripped together for proofing purposes and can easily be adjusted.

Finally, it is vital to check that the pictures are the correct size, and that they are the right way round and not reversed. If the latter happens, the picture has to be 'flopped'. This is not just a simple case of turning the separated film upside down; a new contact film has to be made so that the emulsion is on the correct side of the film, as the emulsion, whether on negative or positive film has to come into contact with the surface of the plate or block.

When marking corrections on proofs it is best to be explicit as possible. If you do not know how to achieve the desired end result, tell the origination house what effect is required – they will know what needs to be done. Colour correction symbols are particularly useful if there is a language barrier – as when the origination house is abroad, which is frequently the case.

PRINTING

The next stage is for the text film to be matched with the illustration film. This can be done by the typesetter, origination house or printer, depending on how film is supplied or who has been contracted to do the job. (For instance, the typesetter will produce final page film of the text – working from the designer's past-up – and receive illustration film from the origination house.) The two are assembled together. The origination house, on the other hand, may have made film separations in page position and will then receive either page film from the typesetter or camera-ready paste-up from the designer. The process of assembling film in page position is usually called stripping or planning. Each individual piece of illustration film is stripped in position onto a much larger support film. This will eventually be photographically converted by way of contact print into a single, flat piece of film.

Before the final film is made, a proof is made from the stripped-together film. This proof is called a dyeline or ozalid (brown line or blue line). Text and illustration can now be seen in the positions that they will be printed. This is the last stage at which any corrections can reasonably be made. Once the printing plates have been made, making corrections is a costly process. In some cases, especially in commercial work, pages are proofed up after the ozalid stage and before machine plates are made.

The main purpose of the blueprint is to serve as a positional check for the designer, since illustrations can easily be repositioned even at this stage as they are individually taped to the carrier film. Textural changes can also be made, although the printer will have to cut up the film manually to position new type – or reposition old. The ozalid should also be read to ensure that the film is free from marks and that no broken type needs to be repaired. Ozalids of four-colour jobs usually consist of film of the black printer plus illustration film of one – sometimes two – of the other colours.

After the return of the ozalids, final, 'clean' film is produced and this is used to make plates. Any machine proofs after the ozalid stage are checked to see that each piece of colour film has been correctly assembled, the alterations carried out and that the film has not been damaged prior to platemaking.

Ideally, when printing starts, the designer should be there to view the illustrations, particularly if colour is involved. Even at this stage, colour can be corrected through manual alteration of the inking process. This is done by regulating the ducts which control the amount of ink passing from the ink reservoirs onto the rollers and thence the plates. Colour can only be corrected in strips parallel to the direction the sheets of paper come off the machine, and great care must be exercised to make sure that, by adjusting the colour on one section of the sheet, the balance of colour in another part is not upset, especially where two halves of the same illustration appear in opposite corners of the sheet. In any case, the printer will be on hand to offer advice although, once the running sheets have been adjusted and pasted, more formal approval will be required, usually the designer's signature on the printed sheet. This is quite normal, and while it absolves the printer from any recriminations by a dissatisfied customer, it puts all the responsibility firmly and squarely on the designer's shoulders. An added difficulty for the designer is that any decision about whether colour needs adjusting must be made almost instantly; presses print extremely quickly and stopping one is very expensive. The production of a book varies according to its type and how it is to be printed. For instance, producing a book that consists entirely of text – such as a novel – is relatively simple. However, the moment pictures are introduced, the procedure becomes much more complicated. The most difficult type of book to produce is probably an illustrated reference book but there are a few procedures that are applicable to all book production, and some of these are discussed on pages 92-7.

THE TECHNOLOGY

In many respects, it is curious that the term graphic design is given to a profession in which the time spent on actual design represents such a small proportion of the whole job. In practice, the designer acts as a coordinator, his or her knowledge having to incorporate extensive aspects of every ancillary reproduction process from typesetting systems to complete magazine or book printing. This knowledge permits the designer to make aesthetic decisions with the maximum amount of flexibility within each technical parameter, and indeed such aesthetic awareness must be used to police the standards of technological advancement. It is important, therefore, that the designer is totally familiar with every aspect of the design process in order that he or she may tackle with confidence and assurance the most important part of their involvement — that of design itself.

TYPESETTING

Methods of typesetting fall into two groups — direct and indirect. In the former, the image or impression of the letterform is created directly from the pieces of type that have been assembled, or, in the most basic example — typewriters — as the result of keys being struck. The oldest method of direct typesetting is where individually cast, or punched, pieces of type were assembled by hand and subsequently printed.

The indirect method involves keying matter into some kind of storage system from which it is subsequently converted — either by metal, photographically or by digitized computer — into an image. The storage system can be either punched paper tape or, for instance, in the case of computer-controlled phototypesetting or digitized image-formation, on magnetic disks.

Strike-on systems and typewriters

The cheapest way of producing typeset matter is with what amounts to nothing more than a sophisticated electric typewriter. These typewriters, for instance the IBM Composer, are used with interchangeable typing heads, each being a different typeface. Unlike the ordinary typewriter, which has fixed character spacing, these machines produce variable character spacing with up to four different widths. However, the quality of output of these strike-on systems can be inconsistent and does not match that of metal or photocomposition. Nevertheless, with jobs in which minimal costs are more important than typographic quality, most typewriters can produce acceptable results — and can even be used to dramatic effect where appropriate — as long as they are used with aesthetic sensitivity.

Hot metal

When type composition was mechanized at the beginning of this century it became known as hot metal composition because the type for each job was freshly cast from molten metal. The principal manufacturers are Monotype, Linotype, Ludlow and Intertype. With Monotype machines, text is converted into a punched paper tape from a keyboard. This is then used to control a casting machine which holds a matrix case of up to seven alphabets. The type is cast in lines of individual pieces of type. Linotype machines combine keyboard and caster and produce each line of typeset matter as one piece of metal.

Although still in use, hot metal machines are becoming increasingly rare, not least because of certain typographic limitations, such as their inability to reduce inter-character or inter-line spacing, even though combinations of certain characters have been designed to kern.

Photo-composition

Although having reached a high degree of technical sophistication, photocomposition is, in some ways, still in a state of infancy, with technology being developed at a rate almost too rapid for the designer to keep up with. Another problem is that because many

Every designer should have a basic knowledge of the common types of paper and their suitability or lack of suitability for various jobs. Good quality halftones, for instance, should be printed on a coated art paper to reproduce to best effect. Conversely, rough surface antique papers, though they reproduce text well, are not suitable for halftones. The chart here gives a selection of common paper types and a guide to their best uses.

Paper	Comments	Uses
Antique	Subdivided into two types — antique laid, if mould marks show, otherwise antique wove	Text books. Not suitable for halftone reproduction or large line plates
Art	Coated with china clay to give it smoothness. In imitation art, the clay is mixed with the wood pulp. Often polished, though some are matt	Halftones, especially four-colour printing. Frequently used for offset lithography. Reproduces up to 150 line screen; imitation art to 120 line screen
Art boards	Boards covered with lining paper on both sides	Packaging
Cartridge	Tough wove, similar to Antique, although smoother. Offset cartridge specially designed for offset lithography	Booklets, brochures, drawings. Print litho well. Reproduce letterpress halftones to 85 screen
Cast-coated	Very smooth, highly polished	Packaging, labels, booklet covers
Chromo	Very smooth, usually matt and coated on one side	Proofing four-colour halftones. Reproduction proofs
Cloth-lined board	One side lined with linen or cloth for strength. Depending on quality of paper, cloth can be sandwiched between lining papers	Covers
Cover-papers	Strong, fold and wear well. Available in plain and embossed finishes. Usually coloured	Book and pamphlet covers
Mechanical	Made from mechanical woodpulp. If polished, subdivided into super-calendered (SC), machine-finished (MF) and machine-glazed (MG), depending on how polishing is done	Cheap leaflets, booklets, magazines. SCs print tones up to 100 screen; MFs to 85 screen
Newsprint	Made from mechanical woodpulp. Cheap, discolours rapidly	Newspapers, cheap leaflets, proofing
Woodfree	Does not contain woodpulp. Strong, with good colour. Bulks well.	General and magazine printing. Lithography if hard-sized

phototypesetting systems can now be operated by people with little or no typographic knowledge, the designer must keep an eye on the quality of typeset matter. This means that designers today require a much greater understanding of the technological aspects of typesetting than ever before.

Technical experts often talk of phototypesetting systems as being grouped in 'generations' — first, second, third, fourth and, recently, fifth generations are referred to. It is more appropriate to regard phototypesetters as being grouped according to their method of image-formation. Of these there are three: photomechanical, digitized cathode ray tube (CRT) and digitized laser. The photomechanical method produces typeset matter ('output') by light being shone through a film negative of the typeform onto photographic film or paper. Digitized CRT produces output either by a contact process or by optical transmission of the tube beams directly onto photographic film or paper. Digitized lasers, as the name suggests, use a laser instead of a CRT to produce the image. Each group has its own advantages — from the hard-edged high-quality (but somewhat variable character spacing and alignment) letterform of photomechanical typesetters to the phenomenal speed of digital lasers.

All three categories of image-formation relate only to one stage in the phototypesetting process, since most systems involve three main components — keyboard, computer and (for image formation) phototypesetting unit. Because copy goes into the system by keying it in at one end ('input') and comes out at the other as typeset matter ('output'), the first and last parts of the whole system are referred to as 'front-end' and 'back-end'.

Some systems can incorporate more complex arrangements including, for instance, a page make-up (or area composition) facility, while other may be a single unit combining all three components ('direct entry'). Systems in which the various components are interconnected are referred to as being 'on-line'.

The keyboard is used to input the matter to be set, with the copy being recorded on a punched paper or magnetic tape, or on a disk, depending on the system. This can subsequently be used either for editing or setting type or it can be stored for later use. Floppy disks or 'diskettes' — similar in size to a 45rpm record — are becoming the most popular type of storage system as they hold more information than paper or magnetic tape, and, more importantly, they have the facility of 'random access'. This means it is possible to go instantly to any part of the keyed matter, as opposed to having to play the whole length of a tape through. This makes correcting and editing much easier.

Apart from the facility of controlling character spacing, word spacing, kerning and other typographic subtleties, the most important aspect of software is the degree of sophistication of its automatic wordbreak program. There are a variety of program

Loose
The form typography is to take
Normal
The form typography is to take
Tight
The form typography is to take
Very tight
The form typography is to take
Overlapping
The form typography is to take

▲ *Letterspacing defines the space between letters, which can be adjusted depending on the designer's requirements. The type of spacing required is normally specified as normal, loose, tight and very tight. In photo-typesetting, these instructions are translated into units or half units, depending on the system. The results are extremely flexible — up to a fraction of a millimetre.*

levels by which wordbreaks are controlled, the simplest being 'hyphenless' — one that will not break words at all, with its consequently poor effect on character and word spacing.

The typeset matter, or output, is provided by the phototypesetting unit. In the photomechanical group these are units that carry a fount — or founts — in the form of negative images

VAULT VAULT

AT	AY	AV	AW	Ay	Av	Aw
FA	TO	TA	Ta	Te	To	Ti
Tr	Tu	Ty	Tw	Ts	Tc	LT
LY	LV	LW	Ly	PA	VA	Va
Ve	Vo	Vi	Vr	Vu	Vy	RT
RV	RW	RY	Ry	WA	Wa	We
Wo	Wi	Wr	Wu	Wy	YA	Ya
Ye	Yo	Yi	Yp	Yq	Yu	Yv

▲ *When the spacing between specified characters is deliberately reduced, leaving the rest of the setting the same, the result is called kerning. The technique is frequently used with certain letter combinations, such as Yo, Te, LY and la. When these are set, there is often too much space between them, compared to the rest of the setting. Kerning solves this problem. If used properly, it can greatly improve letter-fit, legibility and the evenness of a line of typesetting — it is particularly useful with large display type.*

Desktop publishing

The term desktop publishing describes a major innovation that enables publications to be created completely in-house without recourse to outside typesetters or printers. All the equipment required will, literally, fit on a desktop.

Equipment   The equipment required consists of a personal computer and a laser printer. For more sophisticated work a larger, high-resolution screen and a scanner for reproducing pictures can be added to the basic equipment.

The computer will require software that can convert input in the form of word processor files, computer graphics, spreadsheet and database files into digital signals that drive the laser printer and produce a typeset page with graphics. These elements are brought together on the screen, and the page layout is created by selecting the typeface and size, the number and width of columns and by bringing in pictures and other elements such as rules and tint boxes.

When the designer is happy with the page, it is then printed on the laser printer. Short runs are produced completely on the laser printer. For longer runs the laser printed page is used as an original for conventional offset printing or high-speed photocopying. Current models of laser printer have a speed of 10 copies per minute and a resolution of 300 lines per inch.

Simple drawings or graphs can be created on the computer screen and stored as a file before being incorporated in the page layout. To reproduce existing artwork or photographs requires a digital scanner, which converts the image into digital form, which can then be sized and positioned in the page layout.

Applications   The system is versatile and allows a large number of different publishing applications ranging from a simple two-page newsletter to a complex manual containing graphs, tables and photographs.

The essence of the process is the ability to produce typesetting and reproduce pictures in-house without the cost and time required in using outside suppliers for these operations.

It is expected in the near future that the resolution of the laser printer will increase from 300 lines per inch to 750 lines per inch, which is getting near to the 1,000 lines per inch of the conventional digital typesetting systems. At the same time, prices are expected to come down to the level which even the smallest business can afford. The improved resolution will mean that publications such as books and magazines, which presently require the high resolution of typesetting rather than laser printing, will be able to be originated by desktop publishing. The incorporation of colour is further off but will come eventually.

This process represents both a threat and a challenge to the designer. The threat is that some publications that are at present professionally designed will be 'designed' by untrained staff with varying results. The challenge is for designers to have this equipment themselves and both retain and enlarge their traditional area of operations. The process is, after all, only a tool that still requires the designer's skill to produce a good result.

through which light is shone onto photographic film or paper which, in turn, is later passed through a processor to develop the image. The way in which the image is exposed varies from system to system. For instance, the fount may move while the light source remains stationary, or vice versa.

The founts themselves come in a variety of forms, each one being incompatible with the others. They can be in film strips, disks or segments of disks, and most will carry more than one fount, enabling typefaces or weights to be mixed — light, light italic, medium and bold, for instance — without changing founts. Some units carry more than one disk or film strip, so giving greater flexibility in typeface selection. The type of fount dictates the number of characters, which in turn determines the extent of its range — small caps, ligatures, foreign accents and so on. The range of type sizes also depends on the system being used — one may use a master to set from 5 to 10 point and another master for 11 to 36 point, while a different system may use one master to set all sizes.

Most digital CRT and laser typesetters generate characters that have been electronically stored in the computer's memory, although some recreate a photographic image on the tube by a process of scanning. CRT typesetters are now producing a more acceptable image resolution and, in addition to high-speed output, they have the added advantage of being able to store a vast number — as many as 1,200 — digitized typefaces in their memory.

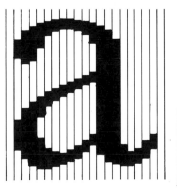

▶ *This character was set on a CRT (cathode ray tube) typesetter. These work in one of two ways. In the first, data are stored in the computer and the type generated electronically from a digital fount onto the video tube. From there, it is transferred to photosensitive paper or film. In the second, a photographic fount is scanned by the machine to recreate the characters. In both, the characters are made up of dots or lines.*

The CRT character itself is generated either as lines or, though more rarely, as linked-together dots — both methods being imperceptible to the eye at small sizes.

Unlike conventional galley pulls from metal typesetting, which are made on sheets of paper of uniform size, photocomposed output is made on a continuous roll of paper or film and it can be awkward to handle as repro because of its inconsistent lengths. However, galley proofs of photocomposed matter can be made by photocopying onto uniformly sized paper.

The cost of photocomposing systems can be massive, and for this reason, typesetting companies frequently concentrate their

Page make-up systems

Variously called area composition, video layout, and composition and layout systems, page make-up systems are basically sophisticated input terminals, although raw copy will normally have already been input through a photocomposing keyboard or a word processor. Its function is to manipulate matter into the position it will finally appear as a complete page before anything has actually been output, thus eliminating the process of manual make-up or paste-up.

As with photocomposing systems, the variety and scope of page make-up systems is wide, their capabilities being related almost directly to their cost. A major limiting factor is the cost of manufacturing video screens large enough to display entire large-format pages or double page spreads. Some are operated by keyboard controls, some by a graphics tablet and some by a combination of both of these.

A simple, low-cost system will merely enable the operator to position copy that has already been issued with a formatting code, displaying it on a video screen in a uniform face, size and weight regardless of its final appearance. Conversely, a high-cost system will allow the operator to edit copy and to alter any of its variables — typeface, size, weight, line length and so on — and some can display the matter in a simulated near-facsimile of the final result. Rules of any thickness and shape — even circular — can also be 'drawn' in. Proofs can be produced on a line-printer and final page film is output from a phototypesetting unit.

Although having mostly been used for jobs requiring less sensitive typographic treatment, such as directories and small ads, page make-up systems are now available that will enable the graphic designer to produce tight, sensitive layouts on-line, thus eliminating the sometimes cumbersome and time-consuming procedure of manipulating typographic elements of the paste-up process by hand.

investment onto whichever end of the system is most important for the predominant type of work they produce. A company typesetting mostly for advertising, for instance, will tend to have a more sophisticated back-end to their system, whereas those producing high-volume work will concentrate on the front-end of their system.

The quality of typesetting depends not only on the system being used, but also on the designer's knowledge of it. While the lens system, accuracy of the machine and software programs account for a large part of the quality of output, the difference between typefaces designed for conventional metal setting which are then converted for photographic use can be considerable. The tendency is for photoset type to be set comparatively closer than their metal equivalents, but there are some faces, such as Univers, which have been specially designed to set with wider-spaced letters and consequently tend to read better when set as the designer intended.

Another facility of photocomposition is the ability to distort the appearance of type by introducing prisms into the light path. Depending on the nature of the prism, type can be condensed, expanded or inclined to form an italic as required, although the appearance of type set by this method may be less acceptable than faces specifically designed for each purpose.

PRINTING

There are four principal ways by which ink can be transferred onto a surface in order to duplicate an image — by relief, planographic, intaglio or stencil printing.

In the relief method, paper is pressed onto raised areas of wood or metal, the surface of which has been inked. Commercially, this process is called letterpress printing. Planographic printing, or lithography, works on the principle that grease and water do not mix — image areas are made to attract ink and non-image areas to repel it. Intaglio printing employs a process of transferring ink onto the paper from very small cells of different depths that are recessed into the printing surface. Gravure is the commercial process using the intaglio principle. Printing from stencils is possibly the earliest known form of duplication — ink is simply passed through the remaining apertures of a cut-out shape. These shapes are held by a fine mesh, or screen, and consequently the process is called screen printing.

Letterpress

A letterpress printing surface may consist of just pieces of type or, alternatively, the type can be used in conjunction with photoengraved plates. These plates are used if a line or halftone

◄ *Study and understand the four basic methods of printing an image so that you can choose the most suitable. Take into account the number of copies you require and the quality.*

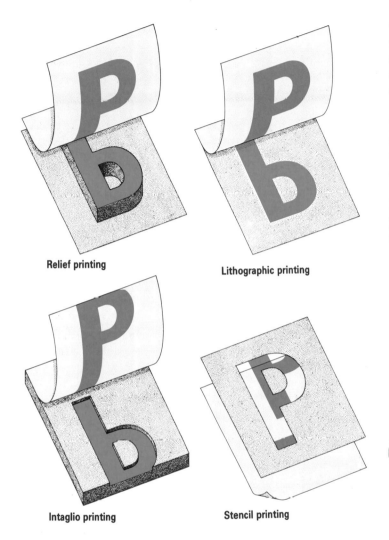

Relief printing

Lithographic printing

Intaglio printing

Stencil printing

photographic negative of the original subject. The areas of coating struck by the light become hard and will not dissolve in acid, which is subsequently used to etch away the non-image areas. The coated areas are left in relief so that the plate image is formed.

To make halftone plates, the photographic image is screened to break the subject up into a pattern of dots which vary in size, thus producing a range of different tones. Plates can be duplicated by making a mould, or plates made of a thermoplastic material —

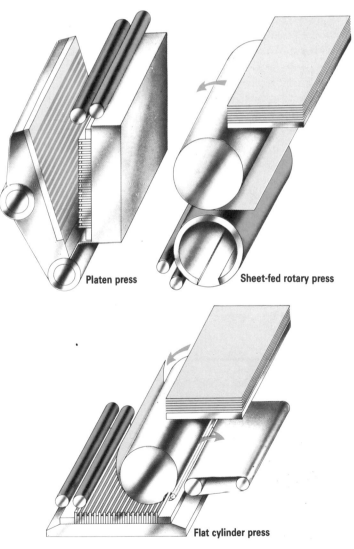

Platen press

Sheet-fed rotary press

Flat cylinder press

illustration is to be included. They are usually produced by a specialist firm of platemakers, and, having been mounted onto a base material — the whole assembly being called a block — they are locked up together with the type in a framework called a forme.

A line plate is coated with a layer of light-sensitive material which, when dry, is exposed to a powerful light source through a

▶ *Letterpress printing methods vary; three are shown here. The platen press is the simplest letterpress machine. In it, the forme is held vertically. When the platen opens, the rollers ink the forme and, when it closes, the paper is pressed against the inked surface. The sheet-fed rotary press is a cylinder press with a curved printing surface, which can print single sheets of paper at high speed. The forme in the flat cylinder press lies on a flat bed, which travels under the inking rollers. The paper is pressed against the type by a rotating pressure cylinder.*

PVC, for instance — can be produced on a hydraulic press. The resulting plates are flexible and can be wrapped around a cylinder for rotary letterpress printing.

To print letterpress, the type of machine used is either platen, flat-bed or rotary. The platen press is the simplest machine which operates by bringing two flat surfaces together. The forme is secured in the bed of the press and is inked by rollers when the platen opens. The paper is held on another flat surface and when the platen is closed, it brings the paper into contact with the forme under pressure.

With the flat-bed press, the forme lies on a horizontal bed and travels under the inking rollers, the paper being pressed against the type by a rotating impression cylinder. Apart from being used for almost every quality of printing job, flat-bed presses are also used, with modifications, by carton manufacturers for cutting and creasing.

A two-colour flat-bed press carries two formes, two inking systems and two impression cylinders, the paper being passed automatically from one cylinder to the other. Flat-bed perfecting presses are similar to two-colour flat-bed presses, but the paper is turned over for the second printing. These machines are frequently used for printing books.

The rotary press, like the flat-bed press, employs an impression cylinder, but, because it is designed for high-speed work, it prints on every revolution of the cylinder from a curved forme on

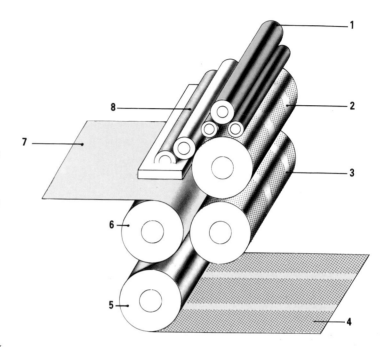

▲ *Offset lithography works on the same principles as planographic printing. The ink is offset from the plate to a rubber blanket and then transferred to the paper. Shown here are ink rollers (1),* *plate cylinder (2), blanket cylinder (3), printed image (4), sheet transfer cylinder (5), impression cylinder (6), paper (7) and dampening rollers (8).*

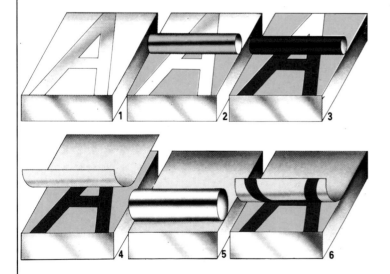

▲ *Lithography, or planographic printing, is based on the mutual repulsion of grease and water. The part of the plate to be printed is treated with a greasy medium (1) and rinsed. The plate* *is then dampened with rollers (2) and coated with ink (3), which sticks to the greasy image. Paper is positioned (4) and the plate run through the press (5) to produce the print (6).*

another cylinder, as opposed to every other revolution as with the flat-bed press.

Rotary presses can be sheet-fed or web-fed (that is, printing on both sides of a continuous web of paper passing from one cylinder to the other), and can produce a fine-register high-quality work at speeds making long runs extremely economical. Sheet-fed presses can produce up to 6,000 impressions per hour, while web-fed presses operate at speeds of more than 500 metres per minute.

From a design point of view, letterpress printing gives less control over the job because areas of text are positioned by the printer. Each letter is on its own little block of metal, so it is difficult and expensive to do very exciting things typographically, such as overlap letters. It is a process used chiefly for daily newspapers or quite small printing jobs such as simple business cards. A modern development of letterpress printing is the wrap-around rotary press, which prints from a one-piece shallow relief plate fastened around a press cylinder. It is ideal for general commercial printing, folding cartons, labels and business forms. Letterpress is gradually being replaced by lithography because better quality can be achieved.

THE TECHNOLOGY

Lithography

The most important and widely used printing process today is lithography, with applications ranging from small office duplicating presses to massive machines used to print magazines, books and newspapers. Unlike letterpress, the image areas on the printing surface do not stand up in relief. This is because the principle of lithography works on the basis that grease — on the image areas — attracts ink, while water — on the non-image areas — repels it. Thus, water plays as important a part as all the other elements in the lithographic process since the plate must first be dampened before it is inked.

Lithography (litho) presses use a rotary method of printing, with the printing plate — made of strong, thin sheet metal, plastic or even paper — being wrapped around a revolving cylinder. Although plates can be made from a great variety of materials, the most common are those made of aluminium — combining strength, lightness and excellent lithographic qualities with economy.

The printing image on all commercial litho plates is produced by photographic methods, the plate is first coated with a light-sensitive material. Although many printers and platemakers still sensitize their own plates, it is now more usual for them to use pre-sensitized plates.

To prepare a plate, a light-sensitive photographic medium is applied to the surface, usually in a 'whirler' — a machine that spins the plate to ensure that it is evenly coated. Next, the sensitized plate is placed in contact with a photographic film image and exposed to high-intensity light. The types of coating on a plate can be 'negative-working' or 'positive-working', depending on whether it is exposed to a negative or positive film image.

After exposure the plate is treated with an emulsion developer, which consists of lacquer and gum-etch in a solution of acid. After developing, the plate is thoroughly rinsed with water to leave a hard stencil image on the plate, which is then coated with a protective solution of gum arabic. The finished plate is mounted or wrapped around the plate cylinder of the press and clamped into place. In the press it comes into contact with two sets of rollers — one for dampening, the other for inking. The dampening rollers apply a solution of water, gum arabic and acid to the plate; this prepares the image to accept the ink when it comes into contact with the ink roller, and to repel it on the damp, non-image areas.

The plate then comes into contact with the 'blanket' cylinder, which, being made of rubber, prevents the delicate litho plate from being damaged through contact with an abrasive paper surface. The rubber responds to irregular surfaces, making it possible to print on a wide variety of papers — from newsprint to heavily textured papers to fine art papers. Because the printing plate does not come into actual contact with the paper, the process is widely known as 'offset' litho.

Offset litho printing relies as much on its chemical as on its physical properties. Therefore successful results depend not just on mechanics and on the skills of the printer, but on such things as conducive atmospheric conditions. As already mentioned, water is a vital part of the process, and too much of it in the air can easily affect the print quality. Excess dampening of the plates may give the printed sheet a 'flat' quality, so that the colours are lacking in density and 'lift' (the degree to which ink appears to lie on the surface of the paper, as opposed to being absorbed into it).

The speed at which machines run can also affect the final quality more in offset litho printing than in other processes. A relatively slow speed (5,500 sheets per hour as opposed to the maximum of 10,000) produces a good result in a country with very high humidity. Of course, ink and paper qualities are also important factors.

At the other extreme from four-colour, high-volume and high-quality lithographic printing presses are small offset duplicating machines, which are now common office equipment and are adequate for printing limited circulation material where sophisticated finished results are not essential. These machines are ideal for quick printing of price lists, forms, sales lists, wide circulation memos and so on.

Lithography offers a wide choice of print quality to the designer and most work that a designer handles will be printed this way. The designer provides camera-ready artwork, from which the printer makes film and then plates. Unlike letterpress, the designer has total control over the work because the printer follows the layout or artwork instructions exactly.

Gravure

Gravure is an intaglio printing process in which ink is drawn out from small cells sunk into the printing surface. This process can be used with equal success on papers of different qualities ranging from newsprint to coated art paper. Although used mostly for printing magazines and packaging, gravure is also used for such diverse applications as printing Cellophane, decorative laminates, wallpaper, postage stamps and reproductions of fine art pictures.

There are three main types of cell structure — conventional gravure, variable area direct transfer and variable area, variable depth. With conventional gravure, the surface size of the cells are equal although the depth of each varies, and this is used for high quality jobs of short runs. Variable area direct transfer cells are all of the same depth but with different surface sizes; this process is used widely for packaging and textile printing. With variable area, variable depth cells (or invert halftone gravure) the size as well as the depth of the cells varies, thus producing wider ranging, more durable tones, particularly suitable for printing colour periodicals in large quantities.

▶ *In intaglio printing, the image to be reproduced is etched or incised beneath the surface of the printing plate (1). Ink is applied with a roller and a thin, flexible steel blade, known as a 'doctor', is drawn across the plate to remove surplus ink from the non-printing areas* (2). *Paper is put on the plate (3) and pressure applied by a rubber-coated roller (4). This forces the paper into the recesses on the plate to pick up the image. The design is transferred and the finished print removed (5).*

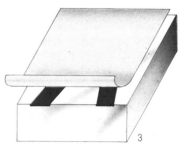

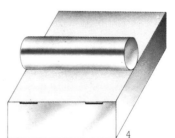

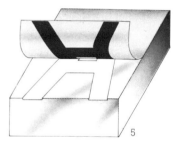

There are various methods of engraving a surface. In electro-mechanical engraving a scanning head 'reads' the image to be reproduced, from which signals are used to control a diamond engraving head which cuts out the cells. Another method uses a laser beam to break up a selected area according to the strength of signal received from the scanning head.

Gravure printing surfaces are usually made of a thin, highly polished copper skin which has been electroplated onto a solid steel cylinder. This skin may be chromium plated after engraving to protect it against hard wear during long print runs. If the surface is to be engraved by conventional methods rather than by scanning, the image is transferred from positives of both text and pictures by the use of a sensitized gelatine transfer medium called carbon tissue. This is exposed to bright light in contact with a gravure screen (comprising transparent lines surrounding opaque squares).

The positives are then exposed – in contact with the carbon tissue – to a diffused light, which passes freely through the positive where the tones are light. Consequently, the gelatine on the carbon tissue becomes harder on these areas. The tissue is mounted onto the cylinder and when the paper backing is removed it is

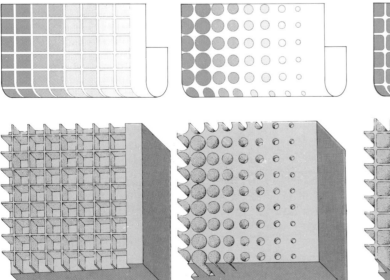

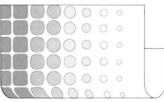

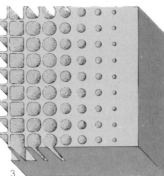

◀ *Gravure printing is particularly suited to the production of long runs because of the durability of the plates. On a conventional gravure plate (1), the cells vary in depth, but have the same surface areas. In variable surface, variable depth gravure (2), the size of the cells varies as well as the depth. This form of gravure is suitable for long-run periodical printing. Variable area direct transfer gravure (3) is widely used in the printing of packaging and textiles. As the image areas do not vary in depth, only limited tones are available. The enlarged details above each example show the effects of each method. They also demonstrate the gravure principle of printing in thousands of dots.*

THE TECHNOLOGY

▶ *Both sheet-fed rotary presses and web-fed presses are used for gravure printing. Sheet-fed presses are best suited to small runs, where the overriding aim is high quality, as in the printing of fine art illustrations. Web-fed presses are used for long runs, printed at high speed.*

They are particularly useful for the printing of packaging. Four or five units can be combined for high-speed colour printing, for which fast-drying inks are used. Impression cylinder (1), paper (2), paper roll (3), doctor (4), plate cylinder (5) and ink trough (6).

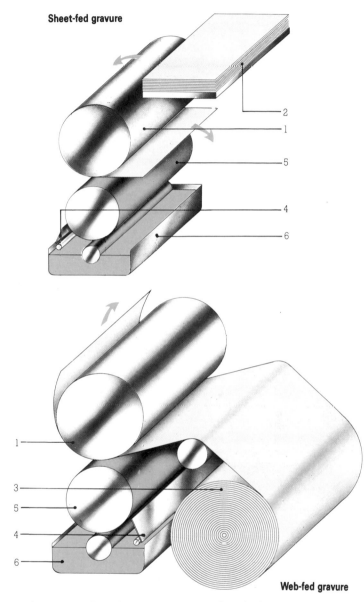

Sheet-fed gravure

Web-fed gravure

'developed' in warm water to wash away any unhardened gelatine, the remaining gelatine forming an acid resist.

The cylinder is etched in solutions of ferric chloride, the rate of penetration depending on the thickness of the gelatine resist. A graded etching is produced by using a series of solutions of progressively decreasing concentration. The process etches the image below the surface of the plate so that it will retain the ink. It is at this stage that a first proof is usually taken, and corrections to tone and colour can be made by rolling-up the cylinder with a stiff ink. This permits local etching, needed to achieve the desired finish.

The finished cylinder is mounted onto the rotogravure press and 'made ready' — positioned and locked in register below the impression cylinder. Register can be controlled automatically by using an electric eye, which ensures accurate colour reproduction. The printing surface is inked by rotating the cylinder through a trough of printing ink. Any excess ink is removed from its surface by a flexible 'doctor' blade so that non-image areas remain clear.

In web-fed gravure, the paper is fed through the press continuously, passing between the etched cylinder and the impression cylinder, which has a hard rubber surface. This applies considerable pressure, forcing ink from the etched recesses of the cylinder onto the paper, thus transferring the image. Sheet-fed gravure presses employ the same method as web-fed machines, each revolution of the cylinder printing a single sheet. Gravure is an expensive process and alterations are difficult to make, so it is only really economical for long print runs.

For the designer, gravure gives excellent results, but its use is rarely necessary, because lithography now usually offers adequate printing quality, and clients are not often prepared to pay the extra costs. The greatest disadvantage of gravure is the considerable cost of corrections once the plate has been made. Gravure is commonly used for magazine and high quality, long-run brochure and catalogue work.

Screen printing

One of the simplest and cheapest forms of printing is by using stencils. A stencil is held in position by placing it on a fine mesh or screen which is stretched very tightly over a wood or metal frame. Traditionally the screen was made from silk and the process was called silkscreen printing, but synthetic materials are now used in

preference to silk and so the process tends to be known as screen printing. Many screen printing presses are manually operated and consist of a simple frame hinged to a flat surface. The equipment can be very cheap and, as such, is often used by people printing at home.

In commercial screen printing, the most common method of producing stencils is by photographic means, although knife-cut stencils — cut directly from layouts — are still used occasionally. There are two methods of photographically preparing a stencil — direct and indirect. Direct stencils are made by exposing a screen mesh coated with light-sensitive emulsion to a film positive of the image by using ultraviolet light. The emulsion in the image areas is hardened by the light, leaving soluble emulsion in the image areas which is subsequently washed away with water. The same basic principle applies to indirect stencil making, the difference being that the stencil is exposed and washed out or developed before it is applied to the screen.

Once the screen has been prepared, it is scraped to remove any excess emulsion that may have built up. The paper to be printed is positioned accurately under the screen by aligning corresponding

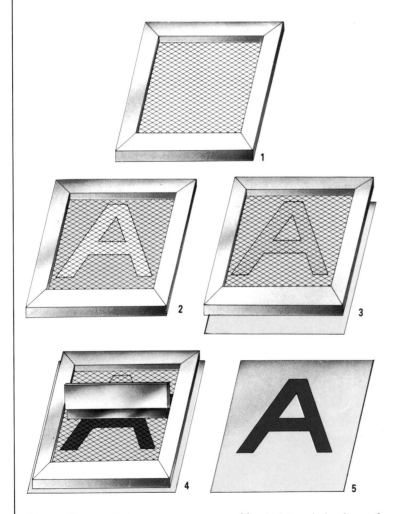

▲ *Basic silkscreen printing uses a simple stencil. The screen itself consists of a fine gauze stretched over a wooden frame (1). The design is cut into the stencil, which is then placed over the screen so that certain areas are masked off (2). The paper is positioned under the screen (3) and ink is applied to the top of the screen, using a squeegee (4). The ink passes through the unblocked areas to produce the image (5). Commercially, photostencils are used. These are produced either directly or indirectly from a film positive.*

register marks in the corners. When the screen and the paper have been assembled on the frame, the actual printing process, known as 'pulling' the print, can take place. Printing ink is drawn across the screen with a rubber squeegee. The action of the squeegee presses the screen into contact with the paper — onto which the ink is forced through the unmasked areas of the mesh.

One of the chief characteristics of screen printing is the thickness of the ink on the printed surface — sometimes up to 10 times as heavy as that of letterpress — although modern ink technology has reduced the ink film thickness considerably. Screen printing equipment can be used to print at relatively high speeds and can be specially designed to suit almost any requirement, but much of it is done on hand-operated presses.

From the designer's point of view, screen printing offers an interesting technique for certain work. Because the ink is applied relatively thickly and has a dense quality, it is very suitable for printing light colours onto dark surfaces. The texture of the screen is quite restrictive and the process is not suitable for reproducing fine halftones. The main advantage of screen printing is that it is versatile and can print on almost any surface, such as wood, glass, metal, plastic and fabrics. For these reasons it is a popular method of producing exhibition stands, point-of-sale displays, posters and PVC stickers.

Other printing processes

Collotype   Like lithography, collotype printing is a planographic process but it is not used on a large scale. However, this process is the only one which can produce high quality black-and-white or colour continuous tone prints without the use of a screen.

The image is carried by a film of gelatine which has been made light-sensitive with potassium or ammonium dichromate. The gelatine, carried by a thick sheet of plate glass, is placed in contact with a photographic negative and exposed to light. The gelatine hardens according to the amount of light reaching it — the harder the gelatine, the more capable it is of accepting ink.

As with lithography, the process depends on water repelling grease, and thus the unexposed parts of the gelatine are kept moist with water and glycerine so that they repel the ink. This gives a result rather like that of a photograph in that it achieves gradations from the deepest black to the lightest tones of grey.

The machines used for printing are special collotype presses, which are similar to litho machines, but they run at particularly slow speeds; it may take two days to produce 2,000 copies — the maximum that can be taken from one plate. Despite this, the process can produce extremely high quality results and is consequently used for printing small runs of fine art reproductions.

Flexography   This process is a derivative of letterpress using flexible plates and thin, fluid inks that dry by evaporation

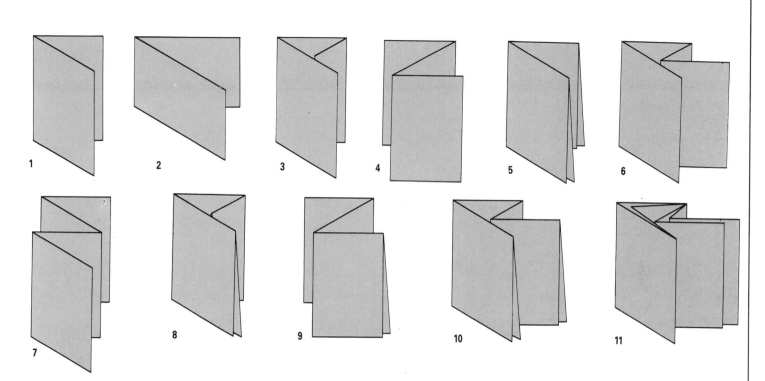

(sometimes assisted by heat). The plates are made from rubber or photopolymer and the image is raised as in conventional letterpress.

Most flexographic presses are web-fed and many machines are four-colour presses. Flexography's main use is for packaging — printing on Cellophane, plastics and metallic films; it can be used to print on virtually any material which will pass through the press. It is also used to produce newspapers and paperbacks, and here, the publications are filmset and use photopolymer plates.

Photopolymer plates are made from negatives, much in the same way as letterpress blocks. The plate material is given a light-sensitive coating that is exposed through the negative. The light hardens the image area, while the background (non-image) area remains soft and can be dissolved away to leave the image area in relief.

Thermography This process produces a glossy, raised image by using infra-red light. The image is first printed either by letterpress or litho using an adhesive ink which is coated with a fusible resin containing pigment or a metallic powder. When passed under infra-red light the coating is fused to give a hard image.

Die-stamping This process also gives a raised printed image, but has the added advantage that designs can be 'blind embossed' — so the image stands out in relief, but is not inked. The process works by using two dies — a female die of engraved steel, and a male 'force' of plastic or card which presses the paper onto the female die to produce a bas-relief effect.

▲ *A four-page folder is made by folding the paper once, either across the length (1) or width (2). Six pages are produced by making a double fold. Two types of parallel six-page folds are regular (3) and accordian (4). The eight-page folder is made by folding paper six times — either one parallel and one right angle fold (5), two parallel folds (6) or three accordian folds (7). Twelve pages are made with one parallel and two right-angle folds — regular (8) or accordian (9). The 16-page folder is one parallel and two right-angle folds (10) or three parallel folds (11).*

Foil blocking This is also sometimes known as hot-foil printing and hot-foil stamping. Bright durable foils are pressed onto paper with a heated die. The foils come in a wide range of colours, have a highly reflective quality, and when used sparingly can look very lavish. The process is most often seen on mass-market paperback covers.

IMPOSITION

Perhaps the most important aspect of print production to the designer is that of the position of the printed page on a sheet. The way in which pages can be 'imposed' (placed in position on a printing plate) vary considerably, and knowledge of how the printed sheets are to be folded is essential to ensure that the pages appear in the correct order.

PRACTICAL GRAPHIC DESIGN

▼ Imposition refers to how the pages are arranged on each side of a printed sheet, so that they read correctly in the right order when cut, folded and trimmed. The illustrations (below) show the commonest forms of imposition schemes.

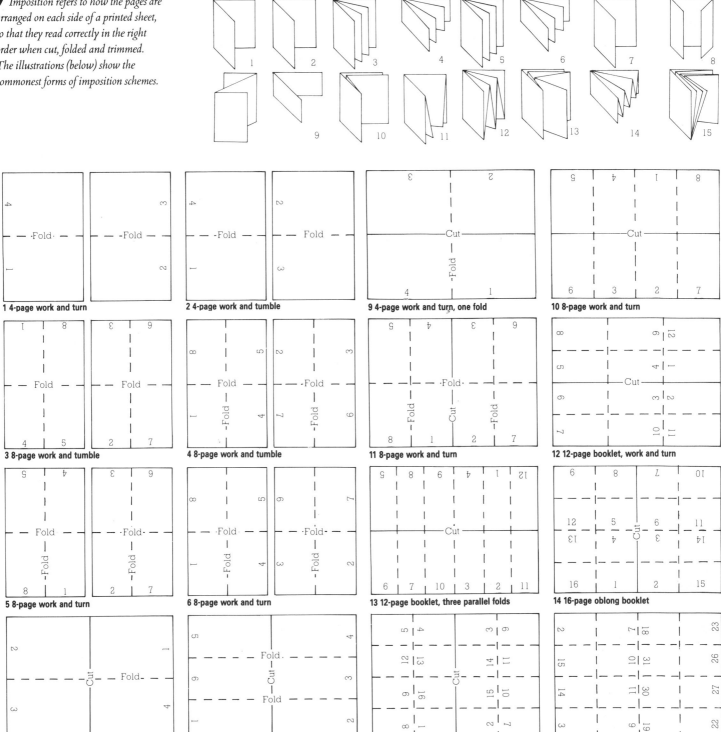

1 4-page work and turn

2 4-page work and tumble

9 4-page work and turn, one fold

10 8-page work and turn

3 8-page work and tumble

4 8-page work and tumble

11 8-page work and turn

12 12-page booklet, work and turn

5 8-page work and turn

6 8-page work and turn

13 12-page booklet, three parallel folds

14 16-page oblong booklet

7 4-page work and turn, one fold

8 6-page work and turn

15 16-page booklet

16 32-page section (16 to view)

This whole procedure can be particularly vexing to the designer, and before planning any job which involves complex colour fall — such as an uneven distribution of four-colour pages among single-colour pages — the printer should be consulted first, since the size of the machine to be used will dictate how many pages can be printed on a sheet.

If a job is to print evenly — such as four-colour throughout — then imposition need not necessarily concern the designer, but if, say, a job is to print 'four backed two' (4×2 — four-colour backing onto two-colour pages) the actual fall of the colour is paramount to the design of the piece. Knowledge of imposition will reveal to the designer that a seemingly rigid distribution of 4×2 in fact allows considerable flexibility as to where those four-colour pages actually occur. For instance, a publication of 192 pages printing 4×2 means that the designer has 96 pages of four-colour and 96 pages of two-colour to play with. If the book is to be printed on sheets of 32 pages (16 on each side, or '16 to view'), six sheets will be required to print the job. This means that the colour pages can be printed in a number of combinations with the two-colour. Three sheets, say, may be printed 4×4, leaving the remaining three to print 2×2, or, alternatively, one sheet may print 4×4, another 2×2 and the remaining 4×2.

Further flexibility is possible if the sheets are slit after printing, or if the job is printed as 'work and turn'. This is when all the pages are printed on one side of the sheet which is then turned over to print the other side. The number of pages on a sheet depends on the page size related to the sheet or machine size. While most printers print and bind in multiples of 16 pages, it is also common for them to work in multiples of 20 or 24.

Imposition not only affects the position of colour pages throughout a publication but also the degree to which colour can be corrected on machine. Balancing the colour of two halves of a double spread picture, for instance, can be extremely difficult if each half appears on opposite sides of the sheet and out of line from the direction the sheet comes off the machine. Colour correction is obviously easier to control if the two halves appear on a portion of the sheet passing through the same part of the inking process of the press.

FINISHING

Scoring and perforating

Scoring is done on board or thicker grades of paper to facilitate folding. In letterpress printing a scoring rule can be part of the printing forme on the press. In offset, perforating rules can be stuck around or across the cylinder or scoring wheels can be brought into the operation between the printing unit and delivery of the sheets or done on a scoring machine.

Perforating can be carried out similarly, using a perforating rule in the forme on a letterpress machine or a perforating rule or wheel on an offset machine. The same separate machine used for scoring will also perforate.

Folding

Thick paper should not be used for folders of more than eight pages and these should be planned with great care. If a book is to include a fold-out page, allowance must be made for the page to fold-in, which must be slightly smaller — at least 0.25mm — than the trim size; the fold must not project beyond the trim size otherwise it will be trimmed off.

Collating

As well as the gathering process used in bookbinding, there are also machines that assemble individual sheets to produce reports and manuals.

Embossing

This is normally carried out on letterpress printing machines or die-stamping machines. 'Blind-embossing', the creation of a raised image without ink, is often used for letterheads. Paper or board can also be embossed overall before or after printing on special roller-embossing machines.

Die cutting

This is known also as 'cutting and creasing'. A forme is made consisting of knives — blunt for creasing and sharp for cutting — and placed in the bed of a converted letterpress machine or a special cutting-and-creasing machine. The process is used mainly for cartons, where irregular shapes have to be cut out and the box corners scored.

Stitching

There are two principal methods of stitching — saddle-stitch and side-stitch (which is also called stab-stitch). Saddle-stitching is used for publications of up to $\frac{1}{10}$in (3mm) in bulk. Folded sections are positioned on a 'saddle' underneath a mechanical head and a wire staple or thread stitch is forced through the spine of the book. Although a cheap method of binding, saddle-stitched publications will lie flat when opened.

For books of greater bulk, side-stitching is used. The folded sheets are gathered (placed one on top of the other) and the stitches are forced through from first page to last. The stitching is about $\frac{1}{4}$in (6mm) from the spine, and will not permit the book to be opened flat.

BINDING

Of the many different types of binding available probably the most common is 'perfect', or threadless, binding. In this, the folded and gathered sections have the back fold trimmed off and the pages are glued by their back edges to the cover. An allowance of ¼in (6mm) must be made for the trim at the backs and for the gutter margins. The minimum thickness for a perfect bound book is about ¼in (6mm) — any less and the pages may fall apart.

Covers for perfect bound work should only be laminated or varnished on the outside — glue will not adhere to a gloss-coated surface, unless a strip of uncoated paper has been specially left for the glue. Publications which have covers consisting of the same paper as their insides are described as having 'self' covers. These may be the same size as the text pages ('cut flush') or may overlap them, and in either case they may require some reinforcement. This can be achieved by a French fold — double thickness paper, folded at the top — or as a 'wraparound' cover in which the paper is folded at the fore-edge and turned inwards. The latter may be given further support by wrapping the cover around a sheet of stiff card.

Case-bound work, in which the text pages are glued into covers made of boards wrapped in cloth, is used extensively for more expensive trade books. This method of binding can range from wholly-mechanized mass-produced publications to specialized hand-tooled work. A wide variety of finishes is available, from real leather to imitation cloth. Alternatively, a case-bound book may have a printed cover, known as a printed paper case, which is glued onto the boards instead of cloth, and this may sometimes eliminate the need for a dust jacket.

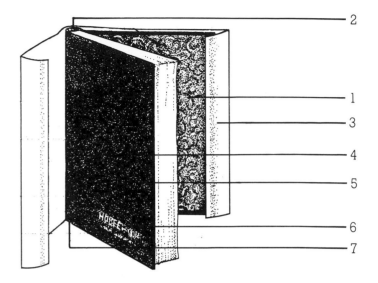

▲ *Bookbinding methods vary according to the nature of the job and the materials used. The various elements involved in the binding of a conventional jacketed hardback are endpapers (1), headbands (2), dust jacket (3), spine (4), case (5), metallic foil stamping (6) and tailbands (7). This form of binding is known as edition binding; paperbacks are perfect bound, a preprinted cover being glued to the spine.*

Varnishing

A gloss finish can be achieved by applying lacquer or varnish after printing. This can be done by printing a varnish on the normal printing machine or by 'spirit' varnishing' on a special machine. Very high gloss can be achieved by using an ultraviolet (UV) cured

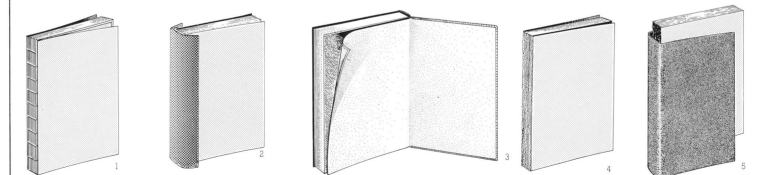

▲ *Edition binding and perfect binding are the conventional forms of binding for hardbacks and paperbacks respectively. In edition binding, the sheets are folded into 16- or 32-page signatures to be collated and sewn by machine. The edges are trimmed and the sewn-back edge coated with glue (1). This is then rounded and a strip of gauze glued to the backbone to overlap on both sides (2). Finally, book and cloth cover (3) are placed on a casing-in machine, which pastes the endpapers and fits the cover. In perfect binding, the folded and collated pages have the spine edge roughened, so that the binding glue adheres strongly (4). A lining is placed over the backbone and the cover glued firmly in place (5).*

◀ *Quarter-binding and half-binding are more luxurious versions of edition binding. In both, leather — or a similar substitute — is used to strengthen the spine; in half-binding patches are also used to reinforce the corners.*

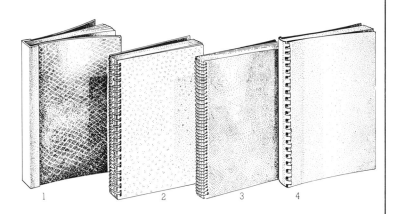

▲ *In one version of mechanical binding, a plastic gripper is fitted tightly over the spine to hold the pages together (1). In open-flat mechanical binding, holes are drilled through covers and pages, which are then bound together with a wire or plastic coil. Examples include the Wire-0 (2), spiral (3) and plastic comb (4) methods. Because the pages lie flat when the book is opened with these three forms of binding, they are ideal for reference manuals or notebooks.*

lacquer. In this process, the lacquer is applied by a roller and then dried with UV lamps. Most paperback books and many cartons have this finish.

Blocking

The case of most books is impressed either with its title or a design, or both. This may be done by blocking (stamping) the case with a metal die forced into the cloth through gold or metallic foil. Metallic foils are available in a variety of finishes which are produced by vaporizing aluminium with coloured dyes. Black, white and other colours are also available — either in a matt or in a bright, polished finish.

The finesse of a blocked design largely depends on the material onto which it is being stamped. A coarse canvas cloth, for instance, will respond better to a simple, clearly defined image, whereas a smooth, paper-covered board will accept designs with a high degree of intricacy.

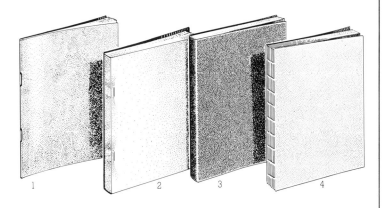

▲ *There are four main stitching methods. Saddle-stitch binding is the most common (1). In this, the book is opened over a 'saddle' and stapled along the back fold. In side-wire stitching (2), wire staples are inserted from the front, about 1/4in (6mm) from the back edge, and then clinched at the back. In thermoplastic binding, the gathered signatures are trimmed along the back edge and bound with a hot plastic glue (3). In sewn-thread binding (4), the gathered signatures are sewn individually, then sewn together again.*

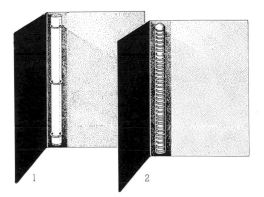

◀ *Ring binding allows a book to lie absolutely flat when it is opened. The loose-leaf post or ring binder (1) is based on two or four rings, riveted to a stiff cover. These springs open so that ready-drilled paper can be inserted. The multiple ring binder (2) works on exactly the same principle, but uses many more rings.*

▲ A screen is used to reproduce a halftone original. If this is enlarged, the halftone dots become clearly visible. The lightest areas are black dots on white, and the shaded parts are larger black dots.

A screen angled at 90°

A screen angled at 45°

55 lines per inch
(20 lines per centimetre)

65 lines per inch
(26 lines per centimetre)

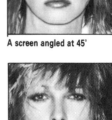

85 lines per inch
(35 lines per centimetre)

100 lines per inch
(40 lines per centimetre)

120 lines per inch
(48 lines per centimetre)

133 lines per inch
(54 lines per centimetre)

150 lines per inch
(60 lines per centimetre)

175 lines per inch
(70 lines per centimetre)

200 lines per inch
(80 lines per centimetre)

ONE- AND TWO-COLOUR PRINTING

We have briefly considered the various methods and techniques used to create a printed image. It is very important to understand each of them, what they are suitable for and the results they achieve. When you receive a commission to design a leaflet or brochure, for example, your choice of process will depend on your budget — you will not always be able to afford four-colour printing, nor will it always be the most suitable solution.

Single-colour printing usually means printing black ink onto white paper. However, always try to make the best use of one colour. Consider using tints as well, a range of greys for example, from light grey to solid black. Of course, the one colour you use for a single-colour job does not have to be black, nor does the paper have to be white. By using another colour of ink or paper, you can achieve a completely different result. When you specify a particular colour to a printer use the Pantone colour selector. This is an internationally recognized colour matching system. Using the selector, a designer can specify a colour to a printer working anywhere in the world, simply by quoting a reference number. The selector will show a wide range of colours printed on both matt and glossy papers. The more expensive selectors have little squares of the colour which you can tear off and attach to your artwork. The other Pantone products too, such as printed papers, films and markers, can be used when visualizing a job. This makes it easier to transfer the colours in a visual into print.

Two-colour printing can appear very colourful given the imaginative use of two colours. Always be positive about printing restrictions and use them to your advantage. The clever use of tints and overprinting can make two colours seem much more colourful.

When you are printing by letterpress, lithography or screen, ink is transferred to the surface to be printed in a layer of uniform density. This is fine for areas of solid colour, but if gradations of tone are required, such as in a photograph, the original must be broken up into a pattern of dots. Each dot varies in size to give the optical illusion of continuous tone when printed small enough not to be detected when viewed at a normal reading distance.

The conversion into dots is made by placing a screen between the original subject and the film negative. The screen itself can be one of two types: a conventional glass cross-line screen or a

◄ Halftone screens have to be placed at an angle of 45 degrees so that the pattern of dots cannot be detected by the eye. If the screen is placed at 90 degrees, the lines of dots form a noticeable pattern. Screens vary in coarseness, ranging from 55 lines per inch through to 300 lines per inch.

A duotone is a two-colour halftone which is created from a black-and-white photograph (although it can be achieved in numerous other ways). Two plates are needed for this process, one for the black and one for the colour; so the photo will have to be shot twice at different screen angles. The black plate holds the dark or shadow tones and the colour plate all the middle tones. When printed together the halftone dots from the two plates create a complete range of tones. Duotones can be particularly effective when colour is important to the design but when only black-and-white photographs are available.

vignetted contact screen. The cross-line screen is composed of two pieces of glass, each one having had parallel grooves etched into its surface, these being filled with opaque pigment. The two pieces are sealed together with the lines intersecting at right angles to create square windows in a lattice pattern of opaque lines. This is placed a few millimetres in front of the photographic film thus allowing incoming light to spread slightly behind the screen. The

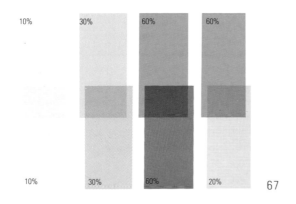

▲ *Tints of colour consist of tiny dots of varying density. The higher the density of dots, the darker the tint. By using tints imaginatively and overprinting different tints you can achieve a vast range of effects and colours.*

gap between film and screen is crucial since it is the spread of light – dictated by its intensity as reflected from the subject – which determines the final size of the dot. For instance, the highlights from a subject reflect the most light and the resulting image on the film – in negative – will be an opaque area with pinpricks of tiny windows which will eventually print – in positive – as small dots, the area surrounding them being predominantly white. The opposite happens in the dark areas of the original. The same principle applies to all the intermediate tones but in varying proportions; the illusion of different tones of grey in a printed subject is the result of the arrangement of different size dots, their centre points being exactly the same distance from each other.

Vignetted contact screens employ the same principle of converting the intensity of light into different sized dots but in a different way. Instead of a lattice pattern of lines the screen is comprised of dots – each one being vignetted (solid at its core, but fading away gradually towards its circumference until it disappears altogether). This screen is placed in direct contact with the film emulsion, the size of dot being determined by the intensity of light passing through each dot. In monochrome reproduction, the screens are positioned with the rows of dots running at 45 degrees to the page as this makes them less noticeable to the eye.

The distance at which dot centres occur between each other on a

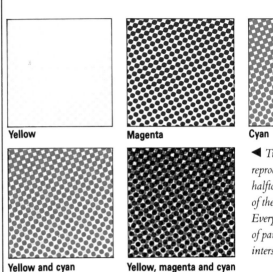

Yellow   **Magenta**   **Cyan**

Yellow and cyan   **Yellow, magenta and cyan**

◀ *Transparencies are reproduced using a halftone screen for each of the coloured inks. Every screen is made up of parallel lines which intersect to form rosettes.*

screen is measured in terms of their frequency per inch or centimetre. Thus a screen with 133 rows of dots (lines) to each inch (54 per centimetre) is referred to as a 133 screen (54 screen), but because of the wide use of both imperial and metric measurements it is usually safer to be specific. Screens are available in a variety of sizes ranging from 55 lines per inch (20 lines per centimetre) to 200 lines per inch (80 lines per centimetre). The finer the screen, the finer the detail in a printed subject.

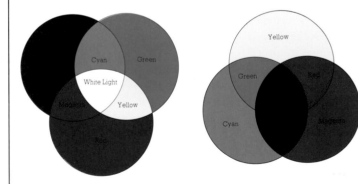

▲ *It is extremely important for the designer to be aware of the colour properties of light. Red, green and blue are known as additive primaries because they produce white light when they are added together. When two additive colours are combined, they create a third colour which is termed a subtractive colour. Thus red and green will make yellow; blue and green make cyan; and red and blue make magenta.*

▲ *In the same way that two additive primaries combined will produce a subtractive primary, two subtractive primaries mixed together will create an additive primary. In other words, cyan and yellow make green; yellow and magenta make red; and a mixture of cyan and magenta makes blue. Unlike the additives, which produce white light, when combined, the three subtractives together make black.*

The coarseness of a screen depends entirely upon the printing process and the porosity and smoothness of the paper to be used. Newsprint, for instance, with its high absorbency, is only suitable for coarser halftone screens of, say, 65 lines per inch (26 lines per centimetre), whereas very smooth coated art paper can produce a high quality reproduction with screens as fine as 200 lines per inch (80 lines per centimetre).

FOUR-COLOUR PRINTING

In its crudest sense, the term 'colour printing' can be applied to anything that is printed in more than one colour — and in some cases anything printed in any single colour except black. More often, however, it is used to denote the reproduction of full-colour originals. Because each colour in the printing process has to be applied by a separate printing surface, reproduction is achieved by the use of three process colours — yellow, magenta and cyan — with black also being used to add finer detail and greater density in dark areas. Consequently, any original that has been presented in colour first has to be separated into pieces of film, each one representing a different colour.

Originals for colour reproduction can be grouped into two main types — those consisting of solid areas of colour without intermediate tones (line originals) and those comprising a subject which appears as full-colour continuous tone. The latter can exist as any form of hand-created art — such as a watercolour painting — on a flat surface (called flat artwork or flat copy), as full-colour prints on photographic paper, or as colour transparencies. A flat original is reproduced by light being reflected from it, whereas light is shone through a transparency.

In printing, nearly all colours can be obtained by mixing yellow, magenta and cyan inks in their correct proportions, which are determined by the size of the halftone dots on each piece of film. Photographic colour originals produce more faithful reproduction since the same principle is employed, colour film emulsion being comprised of yellow, magenta and cyan dyes.

In some high quality reproduction work such as fine art paintings, the standard tri-chromatic process colours cannot achieve faithful results and need to be supplemented by one or two — and, though rarely, even more — additional colours because some colours — lemon yellow, for example — cannot be achieved with process colours alone.

The simplest use of colour printing is by reproducing line originals as solid colours. Depending on the limitations of the job specification, there need be no restriction on the number of colours used, since any number of inks — each applied by a separate plate or block — can be used to match the original. If the design is to be printed in a publication restricted to the process colours, overlapping solid colours can be used to create more than just yellow, magenta, cyan and black — yellow and cyan, for instance, can be used to produce green. Different shades of the solid colours can even be achieved by using screen tints.

The easiest way of presenting line artwork for colour reproduction is to produce a black representation of each respective colour on a transparent overlay. If the original is presented in full-colour, a separation process must be used. To separate a colour original into its process colour components, it is necessary to make a negative for each respective colour by photographing the original through a colour filter which has been matched to the standard inks and also to the respective parts of the colour spectrum.

To explain this, some understanding of the colour components of light is required. White light is formed by a combination of all of the colours of the spectrum, and these can be broken down into three main colour sectors — red, green and blue. Since these colours are added together or overlapped to create white light, they are known as 'additive' primaries. If a primary colour is taken away, a different colour is produced — the combination of red and green, without blue, makes yellow, whereas red and blue without green produces magenta, and green and blue without red give cyan. The colours made in this way — magenta, yellow and cyan — are known as 'subtractive' primaries.

Thus, related to colour separation, the negative for each of the process colours (subtractive primaries) requires the use of a filter of

1 White paper reflects every colour

2 Yellow paper absorbs blue and reflects red and green

3 Magenta absorbs green and reflects red and blue

4 Cyan absorbs red and reflects green and blue

5 Black absorbs all colours

▶ *In reproduction and printing, the colour of the paper used determines the colour that is eventually perceived by the human eye. This is because coloured paper absorbs or reflects light of other colours. When light falls on yellow paper (2), anything blue will be absorbed but red and green — the constituents of yellow — will pass through. The red and green are thus absorbed to give an impression of yellow. White paper (1) reflects any colour that falls on it while black (5) absorbs everything with the result that no colour is produced.*

Magenta (3) will absorb green light but reflect red and blue. Cyan (4) reflects green and blue but absorbs red.

▼ *Occasionally, when a halftone is photographed through a screen a moiré effect occurs. This give the image a* characteristic but undesirable chequered pattern. The reason moiré happens is because two halftone screens have been superimposed incorrectly at the wrong angle. The screens should be repositioned so that there is at least an angle of 15 degrees between them. If a moiré effect needs to be removed, this should be marked up on the colour proof when it is being corrected. The designer should also check that colours have not been transposed. This is normally detectable on progressive proofs, which show the progressive combinations of each process colour in printing sequence. Here (centre below) cyan is printing as magenta and vice versa. The corrected proof is (below).*

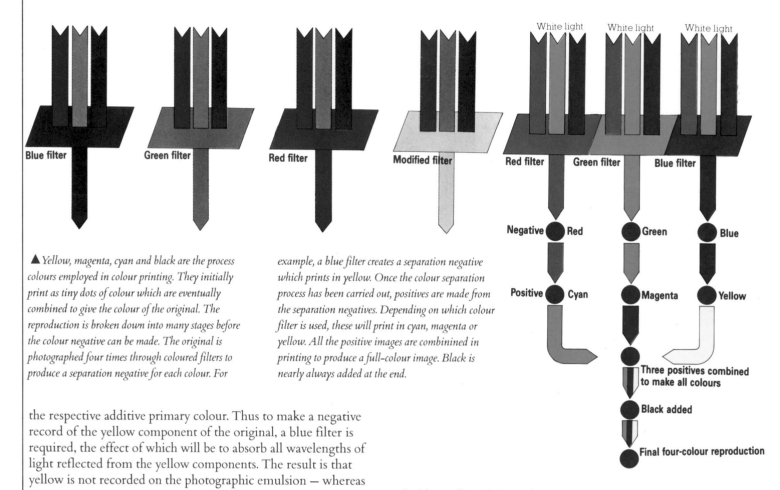

▲ *Yellow, magenta, cyan and black are the process colours employed in colour printing. They initially print as tiny dots of colour which are eventually combined to give the colour of the original. The reproduction is broken down into many stages before the colour negative can be made. The original is photographed four times through coloured filters to produce a separation negative for each colour. For* *example, a blue filter creates a separation negative which prints in yellow. Once the colour separation process has been carried out, positives are made from the separation negatives. Depending on which colour filter is used, these will print in cyan, magenta or yellow. All the positive images are combined in printing to produce a full-colour image. Black is nearly always added at the end.*

the respective additive primary colour. Thus to make a negative record of the yellow component of the original, a blue filter is required, the effect of which will be to absorb all wavelengths of light reflected from the yellow components. The result is that yellow is not recorded on the photographic emulsion — whereas

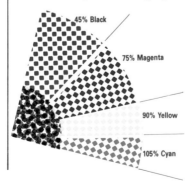

▼ *One of the most important aspects of printing is ensuring that all the screens have been positioned correctly otherwise moiré can easily occur. When an image is being printed in two-colours the black screen should be placed at an angle of 45*

45% Black

75% Magenta

90% Yellow

105% Cyan

degrees — the least visible angle — and the second-colour screen should be at 75 degrees. These two screens remain at the same angles for three-colour printing, but an additional screen (for the third colour) is placed at 105 degrees. In four-colour printing, the black screen is angled at 45 degrees, the magenta at 75 degrees, the cyan screen at 105 degrees and the yellow one at 90 degrees. This is the most visible angle and for this reason yellow — the lightest colour — is always positioned there. The illustration shows all the dots greatly enlarged, but they become invisible and impossible to distinguish when the picture is reproduced at the correct size.

the blue reflects light and *is* recorded. Similarly, a green filter is used to record magenta (in negative), and a red filter for cyan. To separate black, either a combination of all three filters is used, according to the colour bias of the original, or no filter at all.

To produce separated negatives for printing, a halftone screen must be introduced. There are various ways of doing this, but they are all referred to as being either indirect or direct. The indirect method involves a two-step process. An accurate continuous tone record of the primary colours is produced as a 'continuous tone separation negative' which is then used to make a positive image, the halftone screen having been introduced at this stage. In the direct method the halftone screen is introduced at the initial separation stage, without first making a continuous tone negative. Thus, the negative is already screened.

It is always extremely difficult, if not impossible, to produce perfect colour reproductions when printing the separated subjects. This is because pigmented printing inks are not pure in that they do not reflect or absorb all incidental light accurately. Thus the colour must be corrected by adjusting the negative or positive

THE TECHNOLOGY

Colour scanning

Colour scanning is rapidly superseding traditional camera methods of reproduction because it is speedier, more accurate and more flexible. In principle, the way it works is simple. Images are scanned by a high-intensity light or laser beam, which, via colour filters and a computer, converts them into individual screened films for each colour. These films can be either positive or negative, according to requirements.

Scanning transparencies   The first step is to tape the transparencies to the glass cylinder or drum of the scanner. Since the process is expensive, it is cost-effective for the transparencies to be batched so that the optimum number of whatever size can be fitted to the drum at the same time. Their densities, however, should also be similar, since the scanner will be set to average this out. In addition, the accuracy of a modern scanner means that the slightest flaw or scratch on a transparency will be picked up and magnified. This is a particular risk with 35mm transparencies and, for this reason, it is common for such transparencies to be floated in oil on the surface of the drum if an enlargement of more than 500 per cent is required.

The operator then keys in the percentage reductions or enlargements required on the scanner's computer. These are expressed in two dimensions, or factor numbers, which are calculated from the master chart supplied by the manufacturer. At the same time, the screen percentage is set. This dictates how many lines of dots appear per inch on the final film.

The drum is then fitted to the scanner and rotated at high speed. The light or laser passes through a system of lenses to be angled by a mirror set at 90 degrees to illuminate the images, which are then analysed as the scanning head moves along the surface of the drum. The signals are passed to the computer via the colour filters and the computer transmits this in digital form to the film. This is held in 20 × 16in (50 × 40cm) cassette form of which 19½ × 15½in (49 × 38cm) is the image area. The film used is hard-dot film. Its use means that, if the dots are slightly etched away in colour correction, their area remains the same, as opposed to soft dots, which become smaller.

The film is removed and processed by rapid access developing. This takes 90 seconds, as opposed to five minutes or more in traditional photolitho processing. Many operators can tell the accuracy of the colour by visual examination of the film even before proofing. Normally, very little correction is needed, though proofs are correctable up to between 5 per cent and 10 per cent on hard film (20 per cent on soft). The reason colour correction is still necessary — even with this sophisticated system — is simple. With the pigments currently available, it is impossible to produce a perfectly pure printing ink, since each ink absorbs some of the light it should reflect. Colour correction compensates for this absorption of colour by the inks.

Often, it is quicker and cheaper to re-run the images than correct. The entire process — from mounting the transparencies to proofing — can take as little as five hours, but the normal time is around 10 days.

Scanning artwork   The scanning of artwork is carried out in exactly the same way as the scanning of transparencies. However, it is important to remember that the scanner is even more sensitive, because of the amount of light artwork will reflect. Certain colours, too, are difficult or impossible to reproduce. These include turquoise — a slightly warmer colour than cyan — and orange-reds, while excessive amounts of process white tend to make the colour read-out, the basis for the computation, inaccurate.

When preparing artwork for the scanner, it is vital to use flexible board as the base, so the artwork can be wrapped around the drum without damaging it. If artwork is incorrectly presented, the operator may try to strip it off so that it can be mounted, with the consequent high risk of tearing. If paint is applied too thickly, it may also crack.

separation films. This is done either by photographic 'masking', skilled hand-retouching or, if an electronic colour scanner has been used, by programming corrections into the scanner.

To make colour halftone reproductions each colour negative or positive is photographed through the same screen. In order to avoid a screen clash, known as moiré, the screen lines are set at different angles to each other — usually about 30 degrees between each. This produces the desired 'rosette' pattern — imperceptible except under a magnifying glass — giving the appearance of a smooth variation in tones when viewed at a normal distance.

Most types of original can be used for colour halftone reproduction (though not colour negatives), and an unwanted colour bias — if slight — can usually be corrected at the filtration stage, especially if a scanner is being used. Contrast can also be improved although never up to the standard that a perfect original would produce. Generally, transparencies produce better results than reflective flat originals because the light path is direct, and does not suffer from the subsequent degradation suffered by reflected light. The best results are obtained from transparencies in which the density range is not too great, the details clear in both the shadows and highlights, definition good and, finally, the colour balance neutral, with no bias in any particular direction.

THE DESIGN BUSINESS

The design studio is where most graphic designers begin their careers. Studios vary tremendously. They can consist of any number of designers and work in specific design areas, such as three-dimensional display and corporate identity, or they can be totally non-specialist and tackle anything.

Most studios have senior designers who produce designs from a given brief. The brief may come directly from the client or via the art director or account executive. Senior designers will usually have assistants, such as typographers and artworkers, who help produce the work. In other studios which are not so departmentalized, the work is spread more generally. As a junior in a studio you will be expected to do what might seem like quite menial tasks at first. However, this early experience is essential to your development, and I would strongly recommend that you absorb as much information from those around you as possible. The pressure in a studio — assuming it is run efficiently — is due to the fact that design and production are final links in an often long chain of people. When clients decide to promote their products, for example, they will invariably be working towards a deadline. If any time is lost in the schedule of events before the job reaches the design studio, then that time has to be made up by the design team.

The full-time design members of a small general design studio might include the art director, a very experienced senior designer, a designer, a general assistant and a junior. The different roles are, to some degree, interchangeable, especially when more hands are needed to get the work done on time. This sort of studio would have the back-up support of freelancers, including perhaps one regular designer who might work in-house for part of the week, depending on the workload, and others from whom work would be commissioned as and when the need arose. Many studios do most of their own artwork because it gives control and continuity in the design process right through to the artwork stage. Slight adjustments and refinements which could not be expected of anyone else can then be done more easily.

The art director is usually responsible for dealing with clients and, in turn, briefs the designers. This gives the art director a first-hand insight into each brief and an opportunity to assess the client's exact requirements. It also inspires confidence in the clients, because they know that the art director is directly involved. If the art director is not designing the initial visuals, one of the team will be briefed, and then the two of them will probably work closely throughout all stages of the job's development. The art director is ultimately responsible for every job that leaves the studio.

ADVERTISING

An advertisement or promotion is produced on behalf of the advertisers by advertising agencies. This organized industry carries out market research within social groups, on spending power and consumer trends, then directs and organizes a campaign for a client, controlling its exposure through the media. Graphic design is an integral part of all advertising, and the advertising industry is one of the largest sources of work for designers.

The growth of the advertising industry over the last 100 years or so has been considerable. It plays a vital role in the era of mass production and mass consumption and has become an accepted part of modern life. Without advertising, many products would simply not exist. Industry has to involve itself in mass retailing in order to sell what it makes. It is very difficult to judge the success of advertising in helping to sell a product, because sales also depend on other elements such as product quality, availability, distribution, competition, fashion and, of course, price.

Many people say that advertising adds to the price of a product, but it can be argued that advertising keeps prices lower by stimulating competition. Customers also benefit by having a much wider choice of brands. Advertising is now seen as an essential part of a company's capital investment in its product, and most

▲ *Comedy is used very effectively in a series of advertisements for Holsten Pils lager. Comedian Griff Rhys-Jones appears in situations with Hollywood stars and their success depends on the marrying of old and new film footage.*

▶ *The Marlboro campaign has been running for 30 years and is now seen in most countries of the world; it has made the brand the largest selling cigarette in the world.*

companies advertise in one form or another.

When a company decides to promote a product or service, it will appoint an agency. Different agencies will usually compete or 'pitch' for the same account, although this is becoming less fashionable. 'Pitching' is usually speculative and involves convincing the client that one particular approach or another will succeed. An agency's experience in a certain area will sometimes be the deciding factor, or perhaps its known ability to handle a very big account efficiently. A large company may decide either to split its products between several agencies, or split the types of advertising, placing say, the press advertising with one agency and the television advertising with another. The company will not want to advertise one brand at the expense of another and this will also affect any decision to use several agencies. It is pointless merely switching sales without developing new customers.

It is important to point out at this stage that not all companies are Ford Motors, nor are all agencies Saatchi and Saatchi. Many highly creative and effective advertisements are produced by small agencies for small companies on low budgets. No two agencies are

▲ *Newspapers are heavily sectionalized and this enables advertisers to place their advertisements in the most appropriate section for their audience.*

identical in their structure and organization. Top agencies can offer a total service to their clients, but there are many other agencies and graphic design companies that offer a partial service and buy outside skills as a back-up.

Many graphic design companies will be asked to produce the occasional press advertisement and perhaps even organize its appearance in a paper or magazine, but they are fundamentally different from advertising agencies. The role of an agency is much more complex. A large agency will have the resources to develop marketing strategies, do market research, provide consumer information, administer the account, analyse audience data and schedule the campaign.

Once an agency has been appointed, it will be given an overall budget, which it has to decide how to utilize to the greatest advantage of the client. An advertising agency makes its money by charging its client 15 per cent of the money it spends on their behalf. This commission is usually paid back to the agency by the media in which the advertising is placed. This percentage varies and like most things is negotiable.

Choosing which media to advertise in will depend on the product, the target audience and the advertising budget. The main areas to choose from are newspapers, magazines, television, radio, posters and direct mail. Once the target audience has been identified the advertising strategy can be planned accordingly. For instance, the target audience for soap powder is unlikely to be the same as that for office equipment. Different advertisers want to reach different audiences, and it is important to know the characteristics of that audience — age, sex, class, income, purchasing habits and so on. The product can then be exposed through the medium which the agency believes will be most effective.

Once all the planning is done and the information collated, the agency begins to generate the creative ideas which will achieve the client's marketing objectives. The creative team usually comprises a copywriter and an art director. The responsibility for the creative approach lies jointly with these two people, although it is usual for copywriters to head the team.

When the ideas are agreed, they are presented to the client. The

▶ *Press advertisements make their point with both words and pictures. In this Heineken press advertisement the only copy is the long-running line 'Heineken refreshes the parts other beers cannot reach', and the picture has to do all the work.*

◀ *This stylish Persil poster shows how eye-catching and visible an image can be.*

HEINEKEN REFRESHES THE PARTIES
OTHER BEERS CANNOT REACH.

Some of the press advertisements that were produced for Metro, a chain of up-market fashion shops in Singapore. The shops are aimed at the 20–30 age group, and the models and accessories were chosen to emphasize the youthful but stylish appeal of the clothes.

campaign strategy is then planned in cooperation with the media team. They decide on the best use of the budget. Obviously the budget is one of the main criteria for deciding where to advertise. Advertising on television and in national newspapers is expensive so those options might be ruled out immediately in some cases. An advertiser may have specific regional requirements because its market-place is limited to one area of the country. This has to be considered when planning a campaign too.

Once the campaign has run its course, the results have to be measured. This is done by market research. By sampling the responses of a small number of people it is theoretically possible to determine the responses of a much larger group. Market research gauges — as accurately as it can — whether the advertised product or service was right, whether the campaign achieved its objectives and whether better results can be achieved next time.

PUBLISHING

Broadly speaking, publishing covers the production, distribution and marketing of books and magazines. These two areas have much in common, although there are some important differences as far as the designer is concerned.

Books
One of the major differences between book publishing and most other forms of design occurs at the earliest stage, where, as opposed to the rough, the design concept is normally presented in the form of a dummy book or bulking dummy. A blank book is ordered from the printer to show its proposed size, bulk (the thickness determined by the number of pages and the quality of

Magazine and book production – a checklist
■ Initial roughs of styling for discussion.
■ Produce finished 'dummy' presentation or flow-chart for sales purposes.
■ Agree production specifications.
■ Design and finalize jacket or cover – this is always one of the first things to be done, so it can be used to help sell the book or magazine.
■ Draw up the grid artwork and get grid sheets printed. Order one quantity on tracing paper for layout purposes, and another on artboard for the final camera-ready paste-up of the text.
■ Mark up the edited manuscript and send for typesetting.
■ Plan any commissioned illustration and photography as early as possible. Sometimes this can only be done after the layout is complete, but if you know this will be required, decide who to commission and book their time.
■ Galley proofs returned from the typesetter. One set will come to you for laying the book out, and others will go to the editor and author for checking.
■ Paste down the galleys onto the tracing paper grids and finalize the picture areas.
■ Once the required 'extent', or number of pages, has been successfully filled, pictures can be traced into their areas and any copy amendments needed in order for the text to fit precisely can be marked.
■ Layouts are sent to the editor for checking and writing captions. Caption positions should always be marked on the layouts so that directions such as 'above' or 'opposite' can be included in the caption if necessary.

■ Layouts, captions and edited galley proofs are returned to the designer.
■ Typographic style changes are marked on the edited set of galleys, the captions are marked up by the designer and returned to the typesetter. 'Folios', or page numbers, running-heads, contents and so on must have been marked up for setting.
■ A photocopy of the layout can be sent to an indexer at this stage. Indexing is a specialized skill and requires the alphabetical listing of all significant subjects and names and the page numbers they fall on.
■ Final galley proofs are returned. Again, one set goes to the editor for checking, and another to the designer for camera-ready paste-up.
■ The galley of the text is pasted onto the artboard grids, along with any black and white artwork.
■ Once this is done, the galleys on the tracing layouts can be removed. The tracing layouts — which have all the picture positions traced on them — can then be attached to the artboard as an overlay. This not only protects the artwork, but shows the size and position of the pictures in relation to the text.
■ The book can then be marked up for the colour reproduction house or printer. This should be done on the tracing grid overlay.
■ The book is now ready to go for colour separation. Check everything thoroughly.
■ Any last minute line changes in text can be pasted in as individual lines, called 'line strips'.
■ The responsibilities of the designer extend to checking the colour proofs.

paper) and binding. Inside this, a number of dummy pages are pasted, and these can either be 'live' (with real type and artwork), make-believe or a mixture of the two — real pictures with dummy text, for instance. In any case, these pages should show the style and level of the projected contents, such as the proportion of illustration to text.

Depending on the scale of the project, presentation spreads (two pages together) are sometimes made by preparing flat sheets mounted on board and protected by transparent acetate film to accompany the bulking dummy. Again, these can be dummy, live or a mixture.

A book can be the most complex job a designer has to put together — especially if it contains a large number of pages or if it involves the distribution of full-colour, two-colour and black-and-white pages — so it must be carefully planned in advance. This is done by drawing up a flat plan, showing the chapter breakdown, number of pages devoted to the end matter and preliminary pages, where colour pages fall and so on. The most complex flat plans are called flow charts, and these serve as a visual contents list, giving an idea of what will appear on every page of the book. Flow charts consist of pages drawn in miniature, showing text and illustration on every page, and they are often used more for sales rather than editorial purposes.

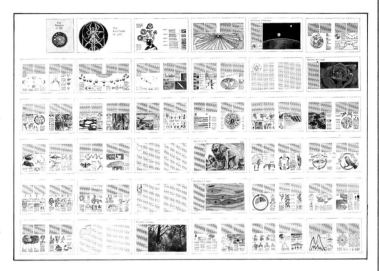

▲ *Flow charts are miniature layouts that enable a designer to see a book as a whole and plan where pictures and colour should fall.*

Paper bulk (after binding)	8	10	11	12	14	16	17	19	22mm
Spine width (with 3mm boards)	14	17	19	21	22	24	27	30	30mm

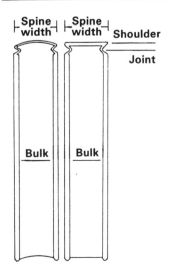

◀ *When designing a bookjacket, it is always preferable to work from an accurate bulking dummy to establish the spine width. This is because the paper bulks less when bound and, unless this is taken into consideration, the jacket will not fit properly. The thickness of the boards must also be taken into account. On book jackets, flaps should not be forgotten; they should normally be about 3in (75mm) wide. The most accurate way of assessing the size of jacket is to wrap paper around a bulking dummy and mark off where it folds round the foredges and spine of the case. It is essential that the dummy is made to the exact specification of the intended book, so check that the trim size, the number of pages, the thickness of the boards and the weight of the paper are all correct.*

Binding and budgetary considerations also have to be taken into account, especially when planning the colour distribution. If a book is to be bound in 16-page sections, the designer has to work in multiples of 16. That is, each block of 16 pages must be consistent within itself — either four-colour throughout ('four backed four') or four-colour spreads alternating with two- or one-colour spreads ('four backed two', 'four backed one'). It may be the case that, while a book is to be bound in 16s, it will be printed on sheets of 32 pages — 16 on one side and 16 on the other ('16 to view') — in which case each block of 16 pages of one treatment must be matched by an identical block of 16 elsewhere in the book. It does not matter if those blocks are not consecutive since the sheets can be cut ('slit') after they are printed. It is possible to divide a 16-page section in two — say eight pages of four-colour followed by eight pages of one-colour. In this instance, the printer uses a procedure known as 'work and turn', whereby both sides of the 16 pages appear on one plate which is used to print both sides of the sheet, thus printing two copies on one sheet.

Book jackets   The design of a book jacket is often thought just as important to the publisher as the inside of the book, because it not only has to convey its quality and content instantly to the prospective buyer, but also has to project this information boldly from the midst of a vast array of books on what may well be the same subject. The selection of jacket designs is usually made by several people representing the sales, marketing, editorial and managing aspects of a publishing house. In many instances the final decision will be compromise since a combination of opinions tends to rule out intuitive judgements. For this reason, it is a mistake for the designer to consider a book jacket merely as a design exercise. It is not. Certainly, the designer always starts with the premise that the solution that looks aesthetically pleasing is the one most likely to appeal to the prospective buyer, but what may appeal to the designer may not appeal to the market at which the book is directed, and vice versa.

Market research is rarely, if ever, carried out on a book or book jacket prior to its publication, and any reasons a publisher may have for preferring one jacket design over another are very often based on precedent — if particular types of jacket have worked for a particular audience in the past, then further designs on that subject are likely to fall within those parameters already known. These precedents will often extend to such things as preference for one colour, and even these preferences will vary from publisher to publisher — for instance, one may have had considerable success with predominantly black jackets, while another may not.

Individual taste is another important factor in book jacket design whether it is based on precedent or not. A designer who is familiar with the likes and dislikes of the personalities involved in decision-making is more likely to find a design accepted.

As with most design jobs, the level to which a rough jacket design is drawn depends largely on the criteria for making final decisions — an in-house designer, for instance, may only have to satisfy an art director, in which case a fairly rudimentary visual showing the intent rather than the final effect, will suffice. In any other circumstances, however, the only way to put across the total impact of a design is to present a full-scale mock-up, complete with actual photographs or illustrations and type, covered with self-adhesive film laminate to give the impression of proper lamination and wrapped around a bulking dummy.

1	2	3	4	5	6	7	8	9	10	11	12	13	14	15	16
17	18	19	20	21	22	23	24	25	26	27	28	29	30	31	32
33	34	35	36	37	38	39	40	41	42	43	44	45	46	47	48
49	50	51	52	53	54	55	56	57	58	59	60	61	62	63	64
65	66	67	68	69	70	71	72	73	74	75	76	77	78	79	80
81	82	83	84	85	86	87	88	89	90	91	92	93	94	95	96
97	98	99	100	101	102	103	104	015	106	107	108	109	110	111	112
113	114	115	116	117	118	119	120	121	122	123	124	125	126	127	128

1	2	3	4	5	6	7	8	9	10	11	12	13	14	15	16	
17	18	19	20	21	22	23	24	25	26	27	28	29	30	31	32	A
33	34	35	36	37	38	39	40	41	42	43	44	45	46	47	48	B
49	50	51	52	53	54	55	56	57	58	59	60	61	62	63	64	B
65	66	67	68	69	70	71	72	73	74	75	76	77	78	79	80	C
81	82	83	84	85	86	87	88	89	90	91	92	93	94	95	96	C
97	98	99	100	101	102	103	104	105	106	107	108	109	110	111	112	A
113	114	115	116	117	118	119	120	121	122	123	124	125	126	127	128	D
																D

Magazines

Editorial procedures in magazine production roughly parallel those of book production although on a much larger labour-intensive scale, depending on the frequency of the publication. Magazines are put together as a result of constant discussion between the editor, art editor and picture editor as well as various feature editors and staff writers. The largest single influence on the number of editorial pages available is that of the number of advertisements sold in any one issue, since most magazines rely on advertising for their profit.

Having decided what is to go into an issue, the pictures are obtained first, since most magazine features cannot be laid out without the pictures. Two or three main features will then be assembled as layouts and if any of them are disliked they are discarded at this stage. More features are prepared than are actually needed for a single issue just in case any are rejected. Those that are

acceptable may be held over for a subsequent issue. Magazines usually rely heavily on picture libraries for main features such as sporting events, and also for back-up material. Many articles will require specially commissioned photography. If this is to be done in

The method used for printing a magazine is a major factor in determining its design limitations, as is, of course, the market at which the magazine is aimed. If, for instance, a magazine is printed by offset lithography, roughly the same principles and limitations apply as those of book production. On the other hand, magazines printed by gravure require special considerations; design for gravure-printed magazines needs to be much bolder than for litho not least because everything — including type — is screened. This means that more delicate designs may start to break up or even disappear entirely. Also, subtle detail in pictures is much more

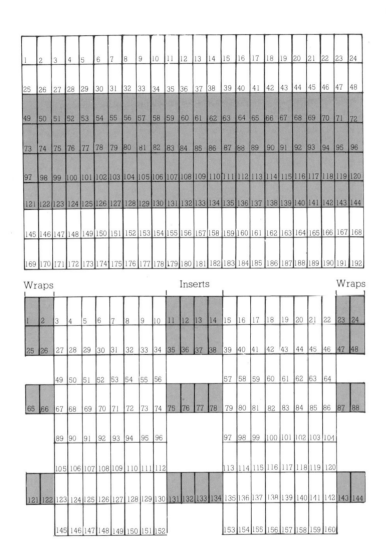

◄ *A flat plan is essential whenever printing in more than one colour combination. The plan ensures the combination works in terms of the number of pages to be printed in two passes through the press. The first three examples (opposite) show a 128-page job using four sheets of paper with 32 pages printing on each sheet. The pages are arranged in 16-page strips, since they will be bound in 16-page sections, or signatures. When planning the colour fall on a book specified to print with 64 pages of four-colour and 64 pages of single-colour, the simplest method of achieving even distribution throughout the book is to arrange the colour so that one side of the sheet prints in four-colour and the other in one-colour. The result is that every alternate double page spread is in four-colour (opposite above). The distribution can be varied by, say arranging four-colour to be printed in two blocks of 16 pages — 32 pages in each block — to make up the 64 pages available. These 32-page blocks can be located anywhere in the job, provided that each 16-page section matches up with another 16-page section, so that 32 pages always print complete (opposite centre). Another possible variation is 48 pages of four-colour, 32 pages of two colour and 48 pages of one-colour, remembering, again, to work in matching 16-page sections (opposite below). The basic determining factor is the number of pages on each side of the sheet and the binding requirements. Wraps and inserts are used when illustration is less evenly distributed than in the other examples shown here. Here (below left), a 160-page job is printing as 128 pages of single colour and the separate insert of 32 pages of four-colour can be wrapped around, or inserted into, each section in blocks of four pages. Wraps and inserts are frequently inserted when the sheets are folded and gathered.*

The reasons for using one printing method as opposed to the other rests solely with the quantity of magazines to be printed. While the quality of offset litho is much higher than that of gravure, litho plates will generally only print up to about 100,000 copies before the image quality becomes unacceptable and the plates need to be remade, whereas gravure cylinders can print an almost limitless number. Some weekly magazines may be printing up to four or five million copies.

Speed is another important factor when deciding which printing process to use — gravure machines run at much faster speeds than web offset. It is becoming increasingly common for some magazines to be printed by a mixture of gravure and litho, the latter normally being used for regional inserts. This enables advertisers to aim at selective, localized markets, without having to pay the considerably higher rates for national coverage.

Having obtained the material for a feature, the designer sets about making a rough scheme of the layout. The pictures are sized up and printed on black-and-white document paper straight from the transparency. Areas of type are indicated by using cut up text from previously printed issues; this is so that everyone working on the magazine knows exactly where the type is going to be and how much is required. Colour images are normally sent down to the printer about six weeks before the magazine is due to appear, the

difficult to control in gravure printing, and although very deep blacks can be achieved, any detail in dark areas will disappear. Even the degree of blackness in a picture can be variable — the result is just as likely to be very thin as it is to be very black. These limitations affect the size at which a picture can be satisfactorily reproduced — whereas an image to be reproduced by litho can retain a certain amount of detail at sizes of one inch (2.5cm) or even less, 2-3in (5-7.5cm) is probably the smallest size that gravure can handle before the readability of an image becomes difficult. Although the results achieved in gravure-printed magazines can be somewhat unpredictable, postage stamps — which require the highest standards of technical reproduction — are printed by the process, but at much slower speeds and on equipment that can produce much greater technical tolerance.

deadline for monochrome pictures being about four weeks before publication. It is possible for last-minute features — on a current, topical theme, for instance — to be put together within two or three hours and sent to the printer as late as one week before publication, but if it can be avoided this rarely happens because of the cost of printers' overtime.

The fall of colour pages throughout a magazine is determined by the printer in consultation with the production editor, but this is never so rigid that the designer is not permitted to make last minute changes provided, of course, that this does not affect the location of advertisements — the main criterion in deciding the colour imposition.

One or two days after the colour has been sent off, the text copy is marked up and headlines are specified. These are then typeset, assembled in position with the colour pictures by the printer and returned as black-and-white photoprinted page proofs. At this stage the position of colour pictures cannot be changed, but alterations can be made to the type. Correction marks are then made on the proofs and sent back to the printer, who makes the corrections and returns them. These latest proofs are called 'as to press' and it is extremely difficult to make any changes at all at this stage.

The as-to-press proofs are returned to the printer who then

makes colour proofs of the pages — but without any type appearing unless it is to be in colour. These colour proofs do not contain any monochrome pictures either — the next time they are seen is on 'running' copies (the actual printed copies of the magazine).

The proofs are then colour corrected and, when all the corrections have been done, the gravure cylinders are put onto machine and printing commences. Once the magazine is being run (printed), it is very difficult to make last minute colour adjustments

— not because of technical difficulties, but because any adjustment may affect the colour of an advertisement. Since it is the advertisers who provide the financial backing for producing most magazines, they must be satisfied with the quality of their advertisements. If they are unhappy with results, advertisers simply will not pay the bills, even though they will already have had the opportunity to reject any unsatisfactory proofs.

PACKAGING

Packaging a product is another specialist area of the design industry, and few graphic design studios have the real expertise to deal with the process fully. The designer's task when dealing with packaging is to produce an effective selling device.

The pack itself is often the only element of the product on display for shoppers to see, and the design is the only way that manufacturers can communicate their ideas to the customer. Packaging can serve as purely functional wrapping, or it can be attractive enough in itself to tempt the purchaser. Packaging can shout loudly, and, in its most prestigious form, totally seduce.

A can of oil and a box of cereal do not have to look the way they do — they have been designed.

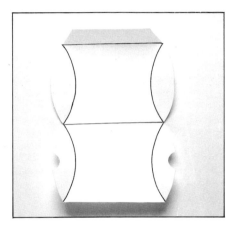

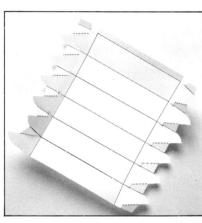

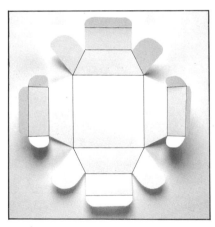

◀ Here are some examples of well-known package forms adopted by leading manufacturers. These designs have successfully created a unique visual identity without forgetting the practicalities of protecting the products and making them easily accessible.

▲ These are the flat patterns from which the packs shown (right) were constructed. It is worthwhile noting the basic simplicity of the mechanics and how they were all created from a single sheet without any separate components.

◀ Designing for packaging can involve using a wide range of skills, and it requires a knowledge of what kind of print and reproduction methods can be used on different materials.

New packaging approaches are continually sought for long-established products. Packaging can also make a product easier to transport, more practical to display and more convenient to use.

Packaging has developed alongside mass production and the evolution of retail selling. Supermarkets are designed for shoppers to select items themselves, without the help of assistants, and the ranges of products on the shelves are packaged to sell themselves. The shopper often depends on the pack to reveal its contents. The pack not only creates brand identity and appeal but has to fulfil statutory requirements such as listing accurate details of contents, quantities and nutritional values.

Manufacturers readily appreciate the selling power of good package design and consistently invest time and money in this sophisticated market. The designer cannot control how a package will be handled or displayed once it has left the manufacturer, but must take these aspects into account in the design. A pack is a three-dimensional object which is handled. It is placed alongside competing packages for the shopper to choose, it may be viewed from several angles and it should be bought by the customer. The packaging designer must be concerned with the graphics and also with the material, its construction, sealing and manufacture.

TELEVISION

Superficially, graphic design for television resembles graphic design for print. The image is two-dimensional and its composition — a grid of coloured dots — resembles a printed image created using a halftone screen. However, that collection of electronically activated dots offers the graphic designer opportunities which are unique.

Consider the infinite permutations of design possible using photographic, illustrative and abstract ingredients of form, line and texture. Then multiply these permutations by the infinite variations of movement, light and sound.

All media impose technical constraints or have characteristics which will influence the conception and execution of a project. Happily, the technology of television is so advanced that such constraints are few. The format of the screen is a 4:3 ratio and this is, of course, fixed. Apart from a need to avoid excessively saturated colours or type forms which are too small or fragile in their design, television will cope with virtually any kind of image. The only limitations are those faced in any commercially controlled medium: time, money, talent.

Transmitted television is the end product of a very sophisticated technology. There is a tendency to regard the graphic designers working in television either as artistic boffins, or to assume that a knowledge of advanced imaging systems is essential before they

can tackle the creative aspect of the job. Familiarity with the technical aspects of production will obviously improve designers' confidence in the medium, but the quality of the televised graphic image will depend ultimately on design talent.

How does the design get from the drawing board onto the screen? At the most primitive level, a caption card can be placed in front of a video camera. At the most advanced level it can mean a lengthy, expensive process involving powerful computers or a whole film studio.

Movement is the magic ingredient which separates television graphics from its print-based counterparts. At the primitive caption-card level, movement can be applied at the control desk by a vision mixer or video editor. At the touch of a button, zooms, wipes, fades and flip-over, can be activated. Ideally these should be controlled by the graphic designer, but for practical reasons they are often controlled by the editor, director or producer. This accounts, to some extent, for the predictable character of such instant effects. Only when a designer is given total responsibility for a whole sequence can the style, movement and sequential structure of the graphics be fully controlled.

Although film technology is increasingly giving ground to videotape, its distinctive character and accessibility at the editing stage will guarantee its use for some time. The film set-up most commonly used by graphic designers involves a 35mm or 16mm movie camera designed, or adapted, to expose single frames. It is mounted to shoot and move vertically at right-angles to a table carrying the artwork. This table is also capable of lateral and rotational movements. The set-up is known as a Rostrum Camera Stand or an Animation Stand. The combination of these camera and table movements, as well as fades and dissolves, can be controlled to a specific number of frames. Increasingly, such equipment is linked to a computer, giving greater control over the recording of elaborate movements or multiple exposures. Computer-controlled camera effects should not be confused with computer-generated graphics.

In place of the film camera, a Rostrum Stand can hold a video camera. The advantage of being able to record and instantly play back pictures is obvious, but this must be offset against the inability to record multiple superimposed images.

Movement can be built into the artwork itself by creating a series of sequential pictures, that is, by drawn animation. The cartoon animation industry tends to follow methods and styles developed by the American cartoon studios, in particular the work of Walt Disney; but there has been a great deal of innovation in the field in recent years.

Computer animation, sometimes mistakenly regarded as a threat to traditional cartoon methods, has quite different characteristics and potential. The computer can tirelessly generate

▶ One of the newest areas for the designer are videos. The commission here was for a video that could be shown in banks to advertise Barclays Home Mortgage scheme, and one of the main features to be emphasized was the fact that the scheme was available for all types of domestic property. Building bricks became the main theme for the video, and they were used to build images. The visual effect of the video was important because, although there was a soundtrack, the pictures had to stand on their own as a silent sequence.

▲ The advertising industry has increasingly called on the talents of television graphic designers. Computer-generated graphics provide glossy images, and so 'high-tech' graphics frequently feature in commercials. At the other end of the scale, raw, casual innovative animation — often simulated by art students' experimental work — gives advertisers a link with the valuable youth market. The electronic paintbox is a computer capable of amending pre-recorded pictures, creating information graphics, and achieving many other effects without artwork. This new technology is becoming daily more sophisticated, but is only as imaginative as the operator controlling it.

series of almost identical images of complex three-dimensional objects, and so it can tackle the movement of such objects in space with a degree of refinement that a human animator would never consider. Unfortunately, flexible articulation of humanoid forms is only possible if a disproportionate amount of data are prepared *for* the computer or if complex, expensive programs are specially written.

The dimension of movement can also be achieved by the more direct traditional means of filming three-dimensional objects, using methods developed for stop-frame puppet animation or conventional live-action. Any of these techniques can be used exclusively or can be combined at a final editing stage.

The introduction of computers revolutionized not only the means of animation, but also the generating of static individual images. Computer-based imaging systems, commonly referred to as electronic paintboxes, were developed for news and current affairs programmes which require graphic material at extremely short notice. Much of this material deals with repeatable or predictable imagery such as maps, charts and stock photographs. The electronic paintbox can be used to call up certain standard

▼ *The brilliant British TV character Max Headroom was created by Annabel Jankel and Rocky Norton in 1985 to be the host of a TV video show. Film frames of the talking head - in fact an actor in Latex make-up — are shuffled and repeated under computer control to give a jerky effect, and the swirling background is computer-generated.*

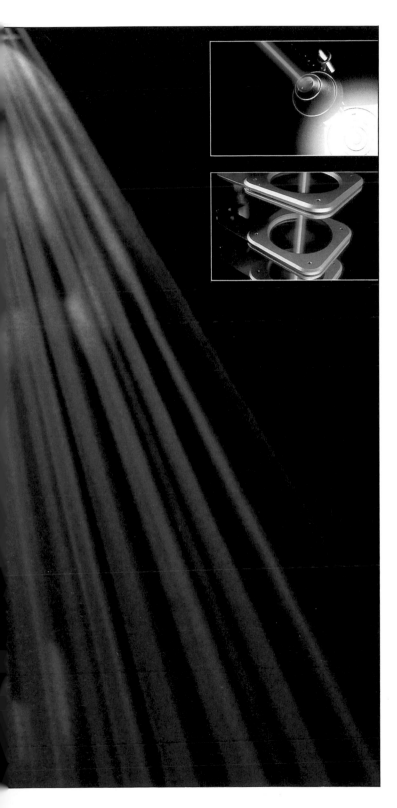

pre-recorded pictures and make additions or amendments instantly. The designer 'draws' directly with an electronic pen and can choose from a 'menu' of colours, pen widths, textures, rules and boxes, for example. Smooth gradations of tone — the electronic equivalent of airbrushing — can be achieved without the skills normally required for airbrush work.

All of these images and combinations are achieved without artwork. Existing pictures can be input from videotape and modified or combined with graphic elements. Considered initially as a convenient means of imitating conventional artwork, electronically generated pictures have developed a style that has dominated the industry.

Typography, probably the most common graphic element, is not dealt with kindly by television. Unlike print technology, which gives the designer complete control over the final product, electronic typography is modified by the brightness, contrast and colour saturation of the domestic television receiver. Initially, and to some extent today, type is set using traditional metal or photosetting systems and then televised directly by a video camera or scanned from transparencies. The introduction of the character generator has simplified and revolutionized the means of displaying type on the screen. Because each character is composed as a collection of electronic pixels, almost any typeface, whatever its weight or character, can be generated. Legibility, a factor governed by the 4:3 ratio and a limited display time, remains a major consideration. Similar to a word processor, text correction, character and line-spacing are controlled from a keyboard.

Despite a certain amount of specialization, most designers, working either as freelancers or staff in television companies, find their talents stretched across a wide range of programmes. The versatility demanded of a television graphic designer can be best demonstrated by examining some of the different categories of programme production — news/current affairs, drama, light entertainment, educational, promotion and presentation.

The design and production process will obviously vary from project to project, but in broad terms this method has a common structure. The designer is briefed, considers the possible solutions, then puts these ideas into some visible form — usually a storyboard — which is presented to the 'client'. If the concept is approved, then the cost of production will be estimated and, once the budget is approved, will go into production.

◀ *A title sequence for Channel 4's Equinox was commissioned — the brief requiring that it be 'charged with mystery and atmosphere' but that it would also be sufficiently general to suit a wide variety of programme material. The face, which evolves from a beam of light, creates an image that is both mysterious and haunting. The insets show the 'light factory' that harnessed the sun's energy was specially constructed to appear man-made.*

THE COMMISSIONS

So far in this book we have looked at the basic skills and techniques that are needed by today's graphic artists. On the pages that follow are descriptions of 10 actual projects that used many of the techniques already described. These projects reflect the wide range of application of graphic skills and give some indication of the variety of work that is involved. In addition to the brief, each project gives detailed information — often in the form of step- by-step instructions — on how the commission was carried out. There are also useful professional tips and shortcuts gleaned from years of practical experience.

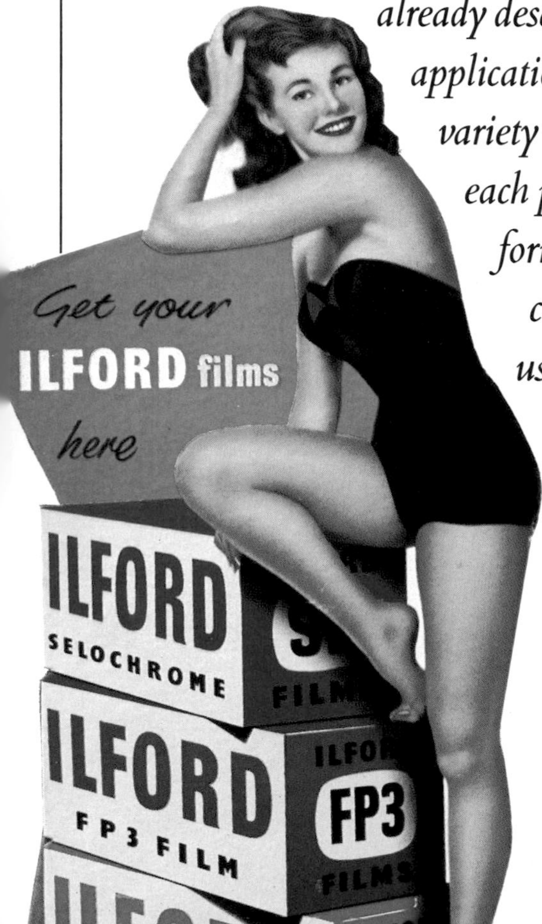

Album Sleeve
Book Jacket
Brochure
Corporate Identity
Film Promotion Poster
In-flight Magazine
Packaging
Point-of-sale Packaging
Press Advertisement
Television Storyboard

Get your
ILFORD films
here

ILFORD
SELOCHROME
FILM

ILFORD
FP3 FILM

ILFORD
HP3 FILM

ILFORD
S
FILM

ILFORD
FP3
FILMS

ILFOR
HP

N° C.C.45 PRINTED IN ENGLAND

ALBUM SLEEVE

The brief was to design a 7in (18cm) and a 12in (30cm) sleeve for the single *So Good Now*, which was to be released on Chrysalis Records. The single was recorded live on an American tour, and the client wanted this to be made clear. The size and card stock were standard for this kind of work.

The music industry is highly competitive, with record companies all vying for rack space in stores, particularly in the busy pre-Christmas period. Record sleeve design is regarded as being one of the fastest moving areas of graphic design, and, depending on the urgency of a release date, a sleeve can take anything from an hour to several weeks to complete. Most of the

▶ *Record sleeves are produced to various standard formats, and designers therefore have to work particularly hard using fashion and applied graphics to sell the product.*

▲ ▶ *The original roughs were prepared very quickly, together with colourways and a type mark-up.*

records produced by Chrysalis are planned several weeks or months in advance of release, but occasionally it is necessary to rush-release a record to order to coincide with an unexpected appearance.

Pop music is a slave to fashion trends, so inevitably many of the products have visual parallels with fast food. Recording artists are also involved in the packaging of their projects, and designers usually have to work closely with recording artists, managers, marketing directors and retail people, and ideas and proposals are discussed thoroughly at the briefing stage. The company policy for design is to resolve as many of the creative problems as possible at the rough stage.

Good design and packaging generates interest in a product and persuades the potential customer into parting with money. This first rule of marketing is especially true in the entertainments industry, where competition is fierce and the market is very transient.

Record distribution houses cannot stockpile vast quantities of paper and plastic, so often a record and its cover will be

▶ It is a good idea to keep ideas for colours in a notebook. This advertisement was part of the promotional material, and although the copy is different from the record sleeve, it retains the changing colour style of the type.

◀ The letterspacing in the typography was essential for this project. It is not always done so well by the typesetter as here.

▲ Flat proofs of the 7-inch (18cm) sleeve. The reverse side of some standard white stock board proved to be just as good as the original suggestion of a special textured card.

▶ A finished copy of the 12-inch (30cm) sleeve. Most record sleeves are laminated, but this one is not as the lamination would have destroyed the tactile qualities of the board.

manufacturered at the last minute, depending on a chart position and retail orders. An hour spent on corrections can affect an important delivery by anything up to a week. Deadlines and delivery dates are established with print production as soon as roughs are approved.

Expertise in all areas of print and mass-production techniques – particularly lithography and silkscreening — is essential for a designer working in the record industry. Most covers are produced by lithography using the four process colours or the Pantone Matching System. A single or album cover involves logotype design, cover, posters, press advertising and, occasionally, the supervision of related merchandising. The Fountainhead *So Good Now* sleeve was commissioned at 11 o'clock in the morning, the roughs were prepared over lunch and the paste-up was completed by an outside studio the following morning.

The group involved was working in Ireland on a tour and was unable to be in London for a meeting. The ideas for the sleeve were discussed over the telephone and roughed out on tracing paper in the manager's presence. The rather predictable approach of using a photograph was discarded, and the final layout included a block of justified Bembo type, with all the relevant information in different colours. It was also decided to use bright, solid Pantone colours and silver on an industrial textured card.

BOOK JACKET

The airbrush can be used for laying down large areas of flat or subtly gradated colour, or for modelling and highlights. Although often tricky and time consuming, it can give even the beginner's

work a professional polish, while in the hands of an expert it will produce a stunning array of tones and textures.

This project, the word AIRBRUSH, which was to appear as the focal point of the jacket of a book on the subject, gave the artist the opportunity to use the widest possible range of effects to show the technique's versatility. To emphasize and contrast with this freedom it was decided that the letterforms themselves should be kept as simple and hard-edged as possible and should be based on solid rectangles and semicircles. An instant lettering catalogue, such as that for Letraset, is a good source of reference for such standard shapes, since they can be traced directly from it and enlarged as necessary.

If a visualizer (camera lucida) is not available, then once the lettering has been traced, you can enlarge it by using a grid and simply redrawing the image freehand, guided by a diagonal line. The shadow should be drawn in with an outline, using a technical pen and black ink.

The artist chose to lay the background areas in first. The initial line work was already inked in, as were the shadows. Masking film was laid over the whole image and the outline of the letter forms followed with a scalpel (X-Acto knife) so that the background areas could be lifted off.

To create the background glow the artist used ink, which is a transparent medium, in black, blue and scarlet. Darker areas were worked up to the required depth by over-spraying. These should be applied first, since lighter colours are more prone to contamination by darker tones than vice versa. They may also be smudged or fingerprinted as you lift and replace masks. The black was sprayed first, gradually changing to blue and finally scarlet.

When the mask was lifted, the next step was to create the bevelled border. A matt masking film should be used here, since

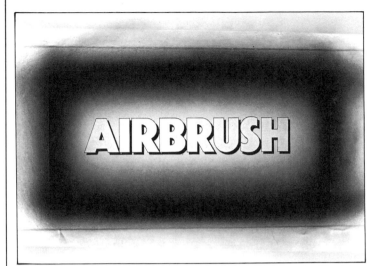

▲ *Darker areas should be worked on first because lighter colours are more easily contaminated by darker tones than vice versa.*

▼ *Use a scalpel (X-Acto knife) to lift the central part of the matt masking film from the letter.*

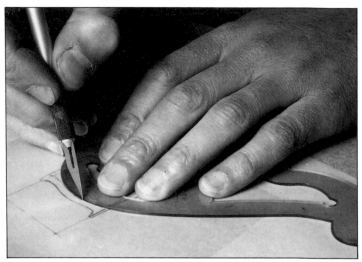

▲ *A French curve can be used to cut a smooth wavy line on the mask.*

▼ *Remove all the remaining masks and, if necessary, remove any imperfections by hand with a fine paintbrush.*

this will take the pencil lines that will have to be drawn directly onto it.

The pencil outlines are then followed with the scalpel (X-Acto knife) and the inner part of the letters lifted out. Do not throw these away, because they can be stored for later use.

The next special effect was the creation of the wavy line across the centre of the letters. Tracing paper was secured over the letters and the wave drawn freehand in pencil. The tracing was removed and reinforced with masking film before cutting to prevent it from tearing. The mask was then cut with the aid of a French curve. Tracing paper was used to create a soft edge, since it does not

adhere to the surface but lies loose, allowing some of the spray to spread underneath. The mask was cut away below the wave and vignetted down in violet and blue. Because the ink is transparent, it will not matter if the black wave is oversprayed.

The last step was repeated for the blue vignette in the upper part of the letters. Remember that the background mask is in position throughout this whole process. To complete the inner letters the bevelled borders had to be sprayed with shadows. The previously cut inner parts of the letters were replaced, fitting exactly against the border mask.

It had been decided that the light source for this title was from

Airbrushing can also be used to produce extremely detailed full-toned work, as this illustration of a truck shows.

above, so the bottom edge of the letters were the darkest. Remembering the rule for dark areas, you should cut out and spray these first, following them with the sides and finally the lightest area at the top.

Now all the remaining masks were removed and any imperfections touched up by hand using a good quality sable brush and a ruler for the sharp edges. Protect airbrushed artwork immediately, since moisture from the pores of your fingers will lift off the surface and leave white fingerprints, which are virtually impossible to repair.

BROCHURE

This project covers the full range of the graphic artist's skills, starting with the initial visuals and following through the various procedures that led up to the final artwork. The client, the Anglo-American Historical Society, required a brochure depicting the history of artillery through the ages. The purpose of the brochure was to show the subscribers the pewter scale replicas of guns and cannon that they would be receiving each month from the society.

The client decided that the title of the brochure was to be *The*

Remarkable History of Artillery. It would feature a full-colour cover (because this is the first thing that prospective buyers are drawn to and often purchase on the strength of), and three colours inside to keep costs down. The format was 12 pages, 8¼ × 6in (210 × 152mm), and the text and main visuals were supplied. The first stage for the artist was to arrange the text and visuals in such a way that the material was visually interesting, chronologically accurate and accessible to the subscriber. Once this was complete, the specialists in the studio, such as the Magic Marker visualizer, the lettering artists, the typographer and the finishing artists, made the final artwork ready for printing.

Using the photographic material supplied as reference, the artist used thumbnail sketches to play around with his ideas on the various ways of arranging the front cover. This method is quick and allows the artist to assess the different ways of arranging the necessary elements without incurring any great expense. Once one of the sketches has been selected, the artist can experiment with colour to give a clearer idea of what the final visual will look like.

To develop a presentation visual for the client, the artist used a visualizer (camera lucida) to trace the outline of the selected photograph onto layout paper. The exact dimensions of the front cover were ruled around the traced image, the artist using a set-square (triangle), to give precise right angles at the corners, and a

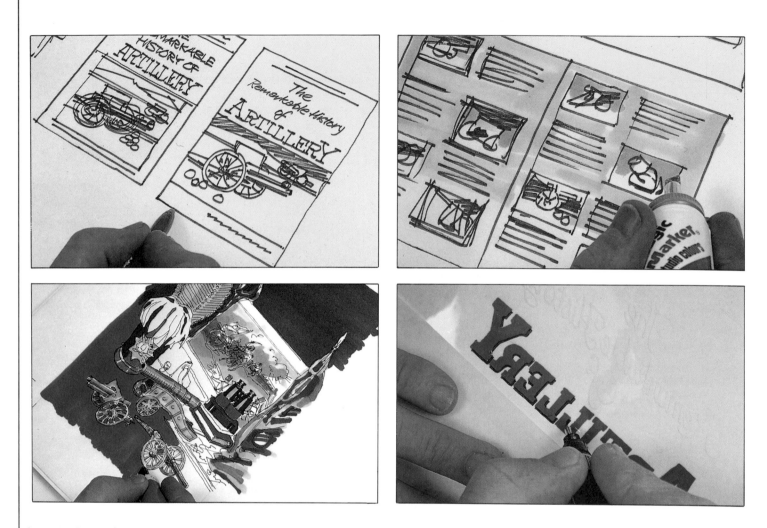

fine, bleed-proof pen. A Magic Marker was used to add colour, and the detail was worked on before the background was filled in. To make the colours look stronger, Magic Marker can be applied to the back of the paper as well.

To add the lettering the artist ruled a sheet of tracing paper with guidelines to contain the title and straplines and to show where they were to be positioned. The lettering was then drawn on the tracing paper in black. Then the artist fixed an acetate overlay over the tracing and painted the lettering directly onto the acetate in the selected colours. At this stage the small lettering does not need to be lettered in full, but the size and weight should be indicated. Because the word 'artillery' was chosen as the focal point of the cover and would run over several colours, the artist decided to add a black drop shadow on the reverse of the acetate so that the lettering did not get lost. The acetate was then aligned over the visual, and the edges of the acetate and visual were neatly trimmed.

◄▲ *Thumbnail sketches allow the artist to experiment with different layouts and lettering styles for the cover.*

▲▲ *When Magic Marker is used to colour visuals, the solid background should be applied with broad, horizontal strokes of the same pressure to give an even tone, while the background that has to fit around more detailed illustrations should be applied with shorter, vertical strokes to give greater control.*

◄◄ *For the inside spreads, which were to be printed in three colours, the artist chose an overall sepia background and a blue that would harmonize with the colours selected for the cover.*

▲ *The use of a drop shadow not only sharpens the appearance of the word 'artillery' but also creates an almost three-dimensional effect.*

To represent the inside of the brochure only one spread had to be presented to the client. The appearance of the inside pages was worked on in the same way as the cover, but the artist had the additional problem of where to place the text in relation to the

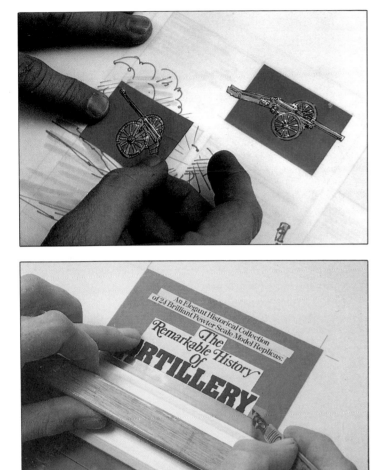

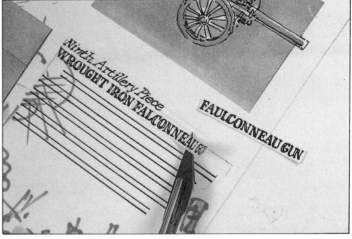

◄ ▲ *The illustrations for the spread were mounted on thin drawing paper with spray adhesive to give extra strength before being cut out and placed in position. The main headings for the captions were rendered in a fine-line, felt-tipped pen.*

◄ *Corrections to a layout can be easily stripped in at this stage. Cut carefully around the original and corrected captions and lift off the incorrect version. Remove any traces of adhesive from the backing paper with lighter fuel before* *spraying adhesive on the back of the corrected text and fitting it carefully in position.*

▲ *The final lettering for the cover is prepared in black and should be positioned accurately on the acetate overlay with a parallel motion drawing board.*

illustrations. Bearing in mind that the inside pages were to be printed in three colours, the artist chose two colours that would harmonize with the cover. A light sepia was chosen for the all-over background, while blue was used to lift the illustrations; the third colour was, of course, black.

To bring the pages to life and to get away from the rather rigid, box-like look, the artist decided at this point to remove the boxes and use cut-out illustrations and to have an overall background illustration running across the spread. The background illustration was traced onto layout paper using a visualizer (camera lucida), and the line illustrations were drawn on a separate sheet of layout paper so that the artist could experiment before deciding on their final positions.

Apart from the main headings, the text was represented by double parallel lines, which were drawn accurately by placing a ruler vertically down the side of the spread and then butting a set-square (triangle) against it so that it could be moved down in

regular widths, measured against the ruler.

The complete spread was then mounted on thin drawing paper to give it additional support. At this stage any corrections — such as a spelling mistake in a heading — can easily be made by re-drawing the correct lettering on a separate piece of layout paper. The corrected layout sheet should be laid exactly over the original and secured in position. Using a metal rule and a scalpel (X-Acto knife), the artist can cut through both layers of layout paper, being careful not to pierce the drawing paper. The original can then be peeled off and the correction stripped in its place.

The inside spread and front and back cover visuals were then made up into a dummy to show to the client. Any minor alterations that the client wants to make can be marked on an overlay and taken into consideration when the final artwork is produced.

The typesetting for the cover artwork was accurately positioned on a sheet of acetate over the illustrations. An overlay was placed over the entire artwork on which the instructions for the printer were written. Because the artwork was prepared in black and white, the printer had to be provided with specified colours — the Pantone system is invaluable here — and the original transparencies had to be sized and their positions indicated accurately on the overlay.

Because the inside pages were to be printed in three colours, the artist who prepared the pages for the printer treated each colour as an individual image and used separate overlays. The sepia background image was drawn on artboard. PMTs of the typeset text and black line illustrations were positioned on an overlay, and the solid backgrounds for the line drawings were filled in on the top overlay. All this work is completed in black and white, but the printer can produce a separate plate for each colour.

CORPORATE IDENTITY

The creation of an identity for a company or corporation gives the graphic artist the opportunity to put all his or her skills to the test. Nowadays many major advertising campaigns are aimed at promoting not a product or a service but a company itself. This is known as corporate advertising. The aim is to put forward a carefully constructed image of how a company sees itself and its concerns. This image is designed not only to attract new clients and customers, but to involve employees, to inform shareholders and potential investors and to educate the general consumer — corporation recognition as opposed to product recognition. A new corporate image may be necessary and a whole new advertising campaign will be launched if the products or services are familiar while the parent company itself remains virtually unknown, or if the current image lacks appeal and no longer coincides with what the company now represents.

Many corporations wish to move away from the facelessness associated with large business concerns and make their corporate strategy visible to the targeted audience. Once such an image has been created, of course, the company can diversify, even change the nature of its associated products, while its image remains constant.

American universities are much more attuned to their environment than their British counterparts. Aston University, Birmingham, in the UK, decided to follow their example and introduced a corporate redesign in order to counteract ailing student applications, and to improve the image and reputation of the college. The university is bounded by three roads — called the Aston triangle — which provides the central theme for the stationery. The design decided to celebrate Aston as a campus in the middle of Birmingham — a high-tech establishment rather than an ivory tower. The graphic artist threw out the 750 years of heraldic shields which had been the university's logo and accepted the new triangular, graffiti-like mark.

This logo was ideal as the university (which does most of its own printing) could use it at any size, in any position on the page, at any angle or in any colour. The triangle is blue for the university, red for the science park and split red and blue for the Aston triangle. For the letterhead it is used with a specially drawn alphabet creating the logotype Aston University, with Univers light condensed as a secondary typeface.

◀ *The new logo for Aston University's range of stationery can be used in various colours and in different positions to identify separate areas of the campus.*

Another brief that required a logo that could be used in several ways was to create an eye-catching and up-to-date identity for the 40-year-old Luncheon Vouchers, as a visual representation of their move up-market. The new identity had to be acceptable, especially in terms of a window display sticker, to new outlets such as wine bars and bistros. Although the new design kept a circle as a visual link with the old one, the original green, to which research had shown that people responded badly, was replaced by a strong red, white and blue combination.

Alto is a graphic design consultancy specializing in literature, packaging and company identity design. The design of Alto's own image was, therefore, extremely important, enabling it to demonstrate its creative abilities in this area. The brief called for a striking contemporary image that was used with style and flair.

Work began on designing the basic elements of the identity. The design team considered the problem from several different aspects. Should the image or logo be based on the name Alto, or on the initial letters ADG? Would a symbol be more appropriate? It was finally agreed that the logo should be based on a capital A, used along with ALTO in a contrasting formal serif typeface.

The main use of the new identity was to be for the company's stationery. Designs were produced for a letterhead, compliments slip and visiting card. The image was thought to work well with the A logo printed in strong colours, and ALTO blind embossed, running vertically along the righthand edge of the paper. The typeface used was Largo light, which has only a capital alphabet. The designer created a house style, combining large initial letters with smaller capitals, and, in conjunction with the typesetter, produced a master guide, illustrating usage in a variety of type sizes. The information — name, address, directors — and the company logo were positioned on the letterhead to leave the greatest area of the paper for typing. An alignment guide for the typist was provided by the lefthand edge of the typography at the top and bottom of the heading.

The final dummy was produced to closely resemble the printed heading. The type and A logo were produced using dry transfer coloured letters, and the blind embossed ALTO was imitated by cutting the letters from an identical style and weight of paper, and mounting them in position on the layout. This replica of the printed letterhead enabled the final decision to be made, and the design was adopted as the new company identity.

A limited-edition poster was produced to publicize the new identity. The company logo and namestyle were the main elements used on the poster, which was silkscreen printed using a matt black ink for the background with a combination of glossy orange and blue for the logo. The poster, together with an explanatory leaflet that was numbered and embossed with the company seal, was distributed by post in a matt black tube.

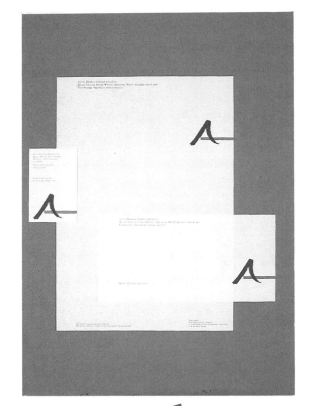

▲ *The main use of the new identity was for the company's stationery.*

▲ *The new style was also used on address and artwork labels.*

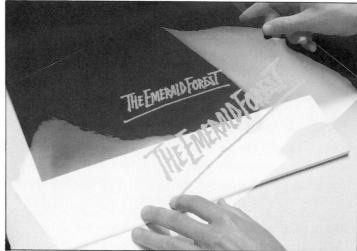

FILM PROMOTION POSTER

The art of creating a successful film poster is highly specialized. The story has to be captured in one illustration that will make the public want to go and see it and that will adapt to different formats of promotion — like any other form of advertising. The first step is to talk to the distributors and hear how they see the film; the second is for the graphic artist to see the film. The art is in marrying the two views successfully.

In this case the brief was fairly loose. The artist was told what the client did *not* want, but the choice of an image was left up to him. Magic Markers were used — the difference in this project is that in such a highly finished rough the artist will pay more attention to detail. The airbrushed look was achieved by mixing pastel crayons with the markers.

The lettering was first drawn freehand in various thicknesses using a Magic Marker on absorbent paper so that it would bleed and create a jagged edge. It was then photocopied on a larger scale to give the artist a crude idea of how it would look when reproduced. Two PMTs of different sizes were then taken.

The PMTs were covered with an overlay indicating the shade of red required with a Pantone swatch. This was then sent to a typesetter with an autotype facility. Autotype is a process whereby the PMT is transformed into dry transfer lettering. It is possible to have any colour you wish. The first lettering was rubbed onto an acetate overlay to enable the artist to experiment with positioning and the second was transferred onto a black background.

The artist decided to add an extra illustration, which was put on

◄◄ *The lettering for the film title was drawn freehand in various thicknesses using a Magic Marker.*

◄ *One of the autotypes of the lettering was rubbed down onto an acetate overlay.*

◄ *A black frame was used to crop the illustration to portrait format. The lettering for this version is placed on a separate overlay.*

► *The final poster, showing the commissioned illustration, the reversed-out type, the hand lettering and the symbols and logos that have to be incorporated in this kind of work.*

an overlay, since he felt there was too much space. This was taken from stills of the film. The finished posters were printed in both landscape and portrait formats to cater for the varied shapes of the chosen sites.

A border made from black cardboard was placed over the illustration to crop it down to a portrait format. The lettering on the black background was placed on another overlay. A further, alternative illustration was added, on another overlay, to give the client more choice. The final result was a combination of the two.

IN-FLIGHT MAGAZINE

British Airtours, the charter division of British Airways, wanted a new look for its in-flight magazine, which is distributed free to all passengers. This captive readership, not business travellers but people going on holiday or returning home, would determine both the style and content of the magazine and the type of consumer advertising attracted to it. Editorially and visually the product was to be cheerful, with a lively, holiday feel to it.

Several designs were prepared, based on a selection of new titles that were suggested by the agency. The name of the magazine would have the strongest influence on the overall visual styling, and so it was a title rather than a design that was finally chosen by the client.

A simple three-column page layout was devised, and the typefaces for text, headings, lead-ins and captions were selected. To give the editorial pages sufficient identity within the typographical variety of the advertising, which is outside the control of the designer but constitutes a powerful visual element within the magazine for the reader, it was decided to limit the display type to two styles.

Because each issue is planned around the advertising spaces — many advertisers have previously guaranteed positions — miniature, very rough flat plans are prepared. At this stage, no attempt is made to design individual pages, although, of course, copy length and number and size of illustrations and the editor's preferences are all considered when making the plan. The degree of pre-layout visualization varies from designer to designer, some preferring to prepare quite detailed thumbnail sketches, other going straight ahead from simple roughs.

The page layout and design are then produced in the form of a design paste-up — not as camera-ready artwork. Galley proofs have to be marked up to indicate headings and the position of illustrations to act as a guide for the printer and for the approval of the editor and client.

This paste-up goes both to the typesetter as the instruction for

▲ *It was eventually decided to call the magazine* Skylife, *which instantly suggested a more sophisticated style than* Sunbird, *the original name.*

◄ *The original visuals for the cover were as much an exercise in deciding a title for the magazine as in creating the graphic style. The name itself would dictate the style.*

▶ *These three spreads are from the first issue. Magazines develop and change gradually over time, but the basic style should show through. The use of a grid for the positioning of text, page numbers and captions will give an underlying impression of consistency, while allowing the designer flexibility to place illustrations and text at unexpected angles.*

the complete page make-up and to the reproduction house, which scans the original transparencies and illustrations and supplies colour proofs. The work of the typesetter and repro house is married together to produce an ozalid proof, which, with the colour proofs, is corrected and amended as required before printing.

PACKAGING

Crabtree & Evelyn decided that it needed a range of Sun Care products that would have both great cosmetic value and all the normal sun tanning properties.

It was decided that the products themselves would be made in Switzerland to achieve the best possible quality. The brief for the design of the packaging stressed that three aims were to be met. First, the high quality of the Swiss product had to be conveyed clearly in the design. Second, the products had to be instantly recognizable as a Sun Care range. Finally, the packaging was to reflect the fact that the new range was aimed primarily at a young market but at the same time the design was not to detract from the overall image of Crabtree & Evelyn's other products.

The designs went through three or four stages from initial flat roughs, to a three-dimensional dummy carton, to alternative rough illustrations and to the finished packs.

The central image of the palm tree was chosen for its obvious connections with hot sun, sea and sand, but it was treated in a different way to distinguish between the different types of products. The design was also altered within the groups of products so that some had an appearance that more closely resembled that of cosmetics. The range was accompanied by beach towels, T-shirts and counter display units.

◄◄ *Much product packaging is purely functional, but this range of Crabtree & Evelyn's product are so beautifully packaged that they become desirable objects in themselves. Crabtree & Evelyn have evolved a distinctive style of packaging that reflects tradition and quality, attributes that were to be reflected in the packaging of the new range.*

◄ *The initial ideas were produced as flat illustrations, the aim being to establish a style that would appeal to the youth market.*

► *When the style of the palm tree had been agreed, an illustrator was commissioned and colour roughs were presented.*

◄ *Three-dimensional dummy packs were made out of card similar in weight to the stock that was to be used for the finished cartons.*

► *The finished range of Sun Care products retains the Crabtree & Evelyn hallmark of sophistication yet creates a more relaxed, carefree style.*

POINT-OF-SALE PACKAGING

For this particular project the client had four products that required individual packaging and a point-of-sale counter display to contain them. While the artist had to bear in mind how the packaging would translate in terms of production costs, the main priority was to create a design that consumers would always relate to that specific product.

The studio initially supplied the client with a full three-dimensional mock-up, which was constructed from material of a type similar to that finally adopted. The point-of-sale has to be quite sturdy to protect the individual products while in transit yet must convert easily to an eye-catching display on arrival. The obvious solution was to use the box method, in which the lid converts into a crowner holding the client's message. The first client presentation did not carry any graphics. When the graphics were added they were drawn on a separate sheet that was attached to the dummy. This makes any changes or corrections far easier and does not spoil the pack.

Before embarking on a project of this nature, to avoid spending hours on working out the mathematics involved to obtain the correct folds and so on, the artist will usually find it profitable — for a simple project like this — to purchase an already existing similar pack and dismantle it. This will show immediately how a pack is folded, and all the artist has to do is roughly sketch the flat shape and work out the dimensions by scaling up or down.

From this initial rough the layout can be drawn accurately on the chosen material. Although this should be sturdy, it must be flexible enough to be folded without the surface cracking. Do not forget that the guide lines for the folds must be drawn on the side of the board that will eventually form the inside of the display. To make possible a clean, accurate fold, the vertical lines must run parallel to the grain of the board. Every artist has his or her own technique when it comes to scoring cardboard, from a used up ballpoint pen to the blunt end of a pair of scissors. Whatever the implement, a steel rule is always used.

The layout was then secured to a cutting board and the outlines carefully cut. Double-sided tape was applied to the flaps and the folds — made by placing a steel rule along the score lines and gently lifting the sides until they bent around to form the three-dimensional main body of the box. Finally the top and bottom flaps were folded in the same manner. The bottom flap was secured with double-sided tape and the securing flap for the top of the box fitted over and slit to allow for easier folding. This final artwork will be transposed onto an overlay, which will be placed over the graphics as a cutting guide for the printer.

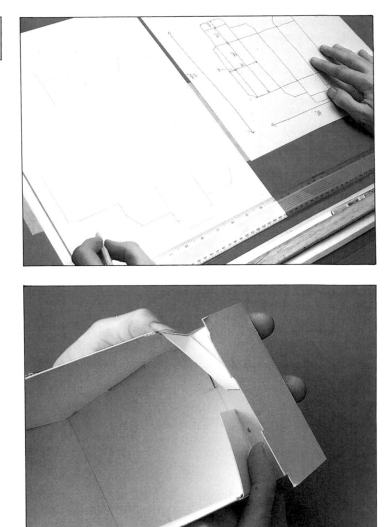

▲ ▲ Dismantle an existing package to work out the construction and dimensions before drawing an accurate layout on card, remembering that the guide lines for the folds should always be drawn on the side of the card that will, eventually, form the inside of the carton.

▲ The point-of-sale display itself was made in the same way as the individual packs. The flat pattern was worked out from an existing pack and drawn on card of the correct weight before being scored and cut.

▲ ▲ To give the display pack extra strength it was decided to use two layers of card rather than thicker cardboard. The double layers have to be precisely scored and cut so that they slot neatly together. The lines were drawn as parallel lines to ensure that they were absolutely exact.

▲ The final point-of-sale display with the packages for the individual products. The show card or crowner folds over to form a protective lid during transport. An advantage of this kind of display is that it can be printed on only one side.

The technique used to construct the individual packs was also employed for the point-of-sale display. First, the flat pattern was worked out; then, in this case, a small scale mock-up was made in order to make sure the design would work. Once this had been satisfactorily worked out, the artist drew the full-scale plan on the board and proceeded with the cutting out and scoring.

The display pack has to be quite sturdy, so instead of using thicker cardboard, the designer gave the pack strength by engineering the construction so that the sides were folded over to give double layers, which were secured by slots. These had to be absolutely precise. They were drawn on the plan as parallel lines, with the use of a triangle and parallel motion. When cutting the slots out, the designer cut the short edges before the long ones. All the folds were then made, finishing with the lid, which folds back to create the double layer and crown at the back of the pack.

PRESS ADVERTISEMENT

This type of project will usually come to the graphic studio via an advertising agency, so the majority of the groundwork will already have been carried out and in some cases the illustration itself commissioned. The agency will have discussed the client's needs in full and presented the initial roughs, so, by the time it reaches the studio there will be a very tight brief and specific instructions.

The skills involved in a project of this nature are those of a paste-up artist. The artist involved will not be creating an original drawing but laying down all the components supplied to him in such a way as to create a well-balanced advertisement that will draw the attention of the reader to the vital information immediately. This advertisement was specifically for reproduction in a newspaper and therefore in black and white only. To create the impact that is necessary without the use of colour and to accommodate the amount of information in a clear manner, various tricks and techniques, such as breaking up the type, have to be employed.

First, a PMT was made from the artwork and placed in position on the board. The type was set ranged left to keep things simple, and the artist repositioned it himself. Remember that when you move lines of type to run around an outline shape you must cut straight lines between every line, so that when they are moved the lines will still run parallel. Always cut towards yourself, since this makes it easier to apply even pressure and does less damage if the knife slips.

A sheet of tracing paper was placed over the illustration and the outline traced in black. The artist decided on the distance from the edge of the illustration to which the type would be fitted and drew this freehand on the sheet. The traced sheet was secured along one side over the type, and each line had to be lifted individually under the sheet and butted up to the drawn edge. Run-around type gives more unity to the text and illustrations.

The advertisement incorporated quotations from various large companies that had actually invested in the system. Rather than use straight boxes, the agency had decided to make it look as if the comments had been torn straight from the pages of the publications in which they had been printed. This procedure is started by drawing and plotting the box areas on the page in pencil. The boxes are then drawn over with a technical pen, since this will give an accurate fine line and constant width. The bottom line of the box will be the torn edge, so using the straight pencil edge as a guide, the artist draws the wiggly line freehand. To pull them out of the page and draw attention to the boxes he creates a three-dimensional effect by using a shadow. Luckily for the artist, the dots are available on a sheet of Letraset, so he does not have to draw them himself.

followed with the knife and the underneath trimmed freehand. The excess is lifted off with the help of the knife point. If any dots have stuck to the artwork they can be cleaned off by dabbing them with the sticky side of a piece of tape. Do not press hard, for this could damage the surface of the board — just keep applying a clean area of tape until they eventually come away. A piece of layout paper is then placed over the shadow and given a final rub down. The copy is trimmed, positioned and finally stuck down into the box.

To separate and draw attention to the special offer it was decided to use a rubber stamp effect. This adds to the feeling that the offer has been stamped on for that day only and must be taken up immediately. A quick, simple way of achieving a rubber stamp effect is to adapt a Letraset oval. Most people know that a rubber stamp very rarely produces a perfect image, so a piece of absorbent cotton with white paint is dabbed at irregular intervals to break up the solidity of the line.

The illustration is now cut out and positioned, this time using the type as a guide. The original photograph of the reference book will have been converted into a halftone. If, once the PMT has reduced to the required size, the print appears muddy, then you have chosen the wrong size of dots — that is, the screen ruling is incorrect. It is possible to change the screen at this stage.

The final component is the coupon to cut out and use to order the system. Both the broken lines and scissors are taken from Letraset and rubbed down into position. This time, as the corners of the coupon have to be exact, the excess Letraset can be gently scraped away with the tip of a scalpel blade (X-Acto knife). After protecting the finished artwork with a secure overlay, the artist can send it to the printer.

▲ *The black line illustration was to be the central focal point around which all the copy for the advertisement had to be fitted. It was obviously drawn in a horizontal format to fit a newspaper page, and its aim is to show the amount of staff time taken to search for specific information in an old-fashioned filing system that relies on the information* having been replaced in the correct place when previously used. The illustration reminds the reader of all these points instantly in visual terms and overcomes the need to refer to them in the text.

▶ *Each line of type has to be lifted individually and moved to align with the drawn edge on the overlaid tracing.*

The dry transfer dots are placed over the box and the amount needed cut out. At this stage the protective backing sheet for the Letraset must be kept in place, since this will prevent any of the dots from sticking to the artwork where they are not wanted. The piece is then positioned but not rubbed down with any pressure, since some areas will have to be removed.

The artist now has to do all the trimming. The black lines are

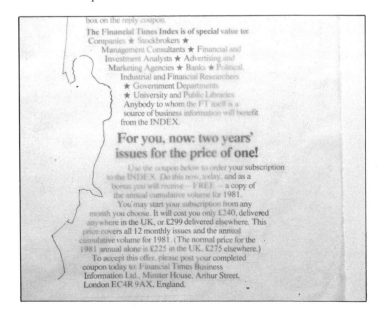

The finished artwork shows how the various elements and techniques were combined to achieve the final advertisement.

A Letraset oval was used to give the impression of a rubber stamp. The typesetting was cut to fit and stripped in, line by line.

A PMT of the original photograph of the book itself has to be reduced to fit, and the typesetting is again cut and repasted to run round the image area.

The dotted line and the image of the scissors for the coupon are available on Letraset sheets.

The copy for the quotation should be trimmed, positioned and stuck down in the box. Note how each box contains a different style of typesetting.

TELEVISION STORYBOARD

Television storyboards are presented as a series of still separate images in individual frames (rather like a comic strip), which represent a sequence for moving pictures or film. Although only roughs, they are taken to a very high standard, since they will be used both to talk the client through the idea and for market research at a later stage. Because of the high costs involved in producing an advertisement, the storyboards, rather than the finished film, are shown to a sample of the viewing public.

Here, we show how one frame is worked up. There was no brief, since the illustration used was purely an exercise to demonstrate Magic Marker techniques; however, this type of brief would usually come from an advertising agency which would supply the products and any ideas they have already discussed with the client in the form of crude, stick figure sketches, accompanied with a few gags or copy. Most storyboards are executed in colour, and every individual artist will have his or her own style, which the agency takes into consideration when making its choice of studio. On some occasions the client might want to see up to six different ideas — in which case they will be done in black and white.

The artist begins by making a very rough pencil sketch. A sheet of tracing paper is then placed over the top, and, using the initial sketch as a guide, the artist makes the image more positive and rubs out the superfluous lines. This might be done several times. An overlay is then placed over the final pencil sketch and the background laid down. The quickest way to cover large areas of background with Magic Marker is to cut off the top and extract the piece of fibre which is soaked in the colour. This way a far more even tone is achieved.

The artist follows the pencil rough underneath and adds the figures and various components, always working in stages and constantly building up to darker, more positive, strokes. By splitting a marker nib into three the artist can achieve a series of lines that are the same but of varying width — which is very useful for producing images of things such as hair and water.

The artist gradually introduces different colours, and as the illustration builds up so does the artist's confidence. When working with markers, speed of line is vital, and the artist must always be bold and brutal. The blacks and darker shades are now laid down. When a straight edge is required, a sheet of paper is placed along the edge as a mask so that the artist's bold strokes are not suddenly interrupted and a constant weight of colour is achieved.

Because the overall aim is to create the impression of heat, orange shades are added to produce a glow. Any fine details are

▶ By splitting the nib of a Magic Marker into three, the artist can achieve a series of lines that are the same colour but of varying widths, which is very useful for producing images of things such as hair and water.

added with a black felt-tipped pen at this stage, but the artist keeps these details to a minimum. Highlights are added at the final stage. White paint is used, except for the softer highlights, where coloured pencils are much more effective.

Television Storyboard

◄ *The first step in creating a frame for a storyboard is to make a very rough pencil sketch.*

► *Speed of line is vital when you work with Magic Markers so that no hard lines appear in blocks of colour. A straight edge can be achieved by placing a piece of paper as a mask.*

► *By standing back and viewing the illustration as a whole, it is possible to see that the artist has succeeded in creating the illusion of a detailed image using sketchy lines and simple squiggles. This is the advantage and the attraction of Magic Marker work. The last stage is to add highlights in white paint or coloured pencil.*

◄ *A complete storyboard for a proposed television commercial.*

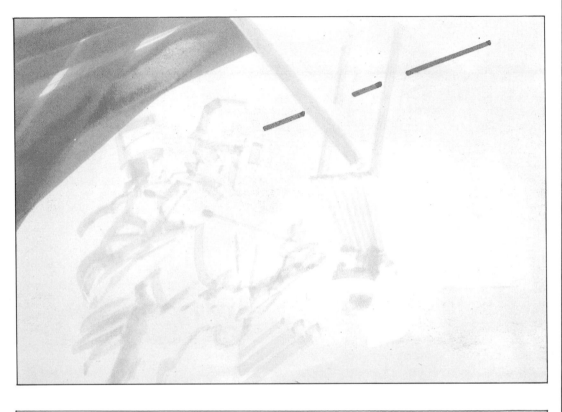

▲ *If an artist is not sure at which angle an image will have the most impact, he can use a simple cropping aid. This consists of two large L-shapes cut from cardboard. They are placed over the illustration and can be moved around to any position.*

APPENDIX 1: PAPER SIZES

ISO A SERIES

(UNTRIMMED)

The A series system of sizing paper was first adopted in Germany in 1922, where it is still referred to as 'DIN A'. The sizes were calculated in such a way that each size is made by dividing the size immediately above into two equal parts. The sizes are all the same geometrically, as they are made using the same diagonal. The basic size (A0) is one square metre in area. It is important to remember that the A series sizes refer to the *trimmed* sheet.

The untrimmed sizes are know as 'RA'. About 26 countries have now officially adopted the A system and it is likely that this system will gradually replace the wide range of paper sizes still used in Great Britain and the USA. B sizes are used when intermediate sizes are required between any two adjacent A sizes.

Unlike the metricated A series of paper sizes, the British and American systems refer to the untrimmed size. In Britain sizes are usually referred to by name, but this can lead to confusion, both the name and the size should be given in any specification.

	inches	mm		inches	mm
A0	33.11 × 46.81	841 × 1189	*A6*	4.13 × 5.83	105 × 148
A1	23.39 × 33.11	594 × 841	*A7*	2.91 × 4.13	74 × 105
A2	16.54 × 23.39	420 × 594	*A8*	2.05 × 2.91	52 × 74
A3	11.69 × 16.54	297 × 420	*A9*	1.46 × 2.05	37 × 52
A4	8.27 × 11.69	210 × 297	*A10*	1.02 × 1.46	26 × 37
A5	5.83 × 8.27	148 × 210			

RA0	33.86 × 48.03	860 × 1220	*SRA0*	38.58 × 50.39	980 × 1280
RA1	25.02 × 33.86	610 × 860	*SRA1*	25.20 × 35.43	640 × 900
RA2	16.93 × 24.02	430 × 610	*SRA2*	17.72 × 25.20	450 × 640

ISO B SERIES

(UNTRIMMED)

	inches	mm		inches	mm
B0	39.37 × 55.67	1000 × 1414	*B6*	4.92 × 6.93	125 × 176
B1	27.83 × 39.37	707 × 1000	*B7*	3.46 × 4.92	88 × 125
B2	19.68 × 27.83	500 × 707	*B8*	2.44 × 3.46	62 × 88
B3	13.90 × 19.68	353 × 500	*B9*	1.73 × 2.44	44 × 62
B4	9.84 × 13.90	250 × 353	*B10*	1.22 × 1.73	31 × 44
B5	6.93 × 9.84	176 × 250			

BRITISH PAPER SIZES

(UNTRIMMED)

Sizes of printing papers	**inches**	**mm**
Foolscap	17 × 13½	432 × 343
Double Foolscap	27 × 17	686 × 432
Crown	20 × 15	508 × 381
Double Crown	30 × 20	762 × 508
Quad Crown	40 × 30	1016 × 762
Double Quad Crown	60 × 40	1524 × 1016
Post	19¼ × 15½	489 × 394
Double Post	31½ × 19½	800 × 495
Double Large Post	33 × 21	838 × 533
Sheet and ½ Post	23½ × 19½	597 × 495
Demy	22½ × 17½	572 × 445
Double Demy	35 × 22½	889 × 572
Quad Demy	45 × 35	1143 × 889
Music Demy	20 × 15½	508 × 394
Medium	23 × 18	584 × 457
Royal	25 × 20	635 × 508
Super Royal	27½ × 20½	699 × 521
Elephant	28 × 23	711 × 584
Imperial	30 × 22	762 × 559
Size of bound books		
Demy 16mo	5⅝ × 4⅜	143 × 111
Demy 18mo	5¾ × 3¾	146 × 95
Foolscap Octavo (8vo)	6¾ × 4¼	171 × 108
Crown 8vo	7½ × 5	191 × 127
Large Crown 8vo	8 × 5¼	203 × 133
Demy 8vo	8¼ × 5⅝	222 × 143
Medium 8vo	9½ × 6	241 × 152
Royal 8vo	10 × 6¼	254 × 159
Super Royal 8vo	10¼ × 6⅞	260 × 175
Imperial 8vo	11 × 7½	279 × 191
Foolscap Quarto (4to)	8½ × 6¾	216 × 171
Crown 4to	10 × 7½	254 × 191
Demy 4to	10¼ × 8¾	260 × 222
Royal 4to	12½ × 10	318 × 254
Imperial 4to	15 × 11	381 × 279
Crown Folio	15 × 10	381 × 254
Demy Folio	17½ × 11¼	445 × 286
Royal Folio	20 × 12½	508 × 318
Music	14 × 10¼	356 × 260

APPENDIX 2:

AMERICAN PAPER SIZES

(UNTRIMMED)

inches	mm	Bible	Bond/writing	Book (coated and uncoated)	Cover (coated and uncoated)	Gravure	Ledger	Newsprint	Offset (coated and uncoated)	Onionskin and manifold	Opaque circular	Text	Wedding
16 × 21	406.2 × 533.4						●						
17 × 22	431.8 × 558.8		●				●			●	●		●
17 × 28	431.8 × 711.2		●				●			●	●		
19 × 24	482.6 × 609.6		●										
20 × 26	508.0 × 660.4				●	●							
21 × 32	533.4 × 812.8								●				
22 × 24	558.8 × 609.6						●						
22 × 34	558.8 × 863.6						●	●	●		●		●
22½ × 35	571.5 × 889.0								●				
23 × 35	584.2 × 889.0					●							
24 × 36	609.6 × 914.4						●						
24 × 38	609.6 × 965.2		●										
25 × 38	635.0 × 965.2	●		●		●	●		●		●		
26 × 34	660.4 × 863.6									●			
26 × 40	660.4 × 1016.0			●		●						●	
26 × 48	660.4 × 1219.2			●									
28 × 34	711.2 × 863.6		●					●	●		●		
28 × 42	711.2 × 1066.8	●	●			●		●	●				
28 × 44	711.2 × 1117.6		●						●				
32 × 44	812.8 × 1117.6	●	●			●							
34 × 44	863.6 × 1117.6		●										
35 × 45	889.0 × 1143.0	●	●				●		●		●	●	
35 × 46	889.0 × 1168.4				●								
36 × 48	914.4 × 1219.2		●			●							
38 × 50	965.2 × 1270.0	●				●			●		●	●	
38 × 52	965.2 × 1320.8								●				
41 × 54	1041.4 × 1371.6		●						●				
44 × 64	1117.6 × 1625.6								●				

CONVERSION TABLES

USA WEIGHTS TO g/m²

500 sheets 25×38in		500 sheets 24×3×in		500 sheets 20×26in		500 sheets 17×22in	
lb	g/m²	lb	g/m²	lb	g/m²	lb	g/m²
20	30	25	41	50	135	8	30
25	31	30	49	55	148	10	38
30	44	35	57	60	162	12	45
35	52	40	66	65	176	14	53
40	59	45	73	70	189	16	60
45	66	50	82	75	203	18	68
50	74	55	90	80	216	20	75
55	81	60	98	85	230	22	83
60	88	65	105	90	243	24	90
65	96	70	114	95	256	26	98
70	104	75	122	100	270	28	105
75	111	80	130	105	284	30	113
80	118	85	138	110	298		
85	126	90	147	115	310		
90	133	95	155	120	324		
95	140	100	163	125	338		
100	146	125	204	130	352		
105	155	150	244	135	366		
110	162	175	285	140	379		
115	170	200	325	145	392		
120	178	225	365	150	406		
125	185	250	400				
130	193	275	450				
135	200	300	490				
140	208						
145	215						
150	222						

Instruction to printer	Textual mark	Marginal mark
Correction is concluded	none	
Leave unchanged	typeface groups	
Remove unwanted marks	typeface groups	
Push down risen spacing material	typeface groups	
Refer to appropriate authority	typeface groups	
Insert new material	typeface groups	New matter followed by
Insert additional material	typegroups	Copy A
Delete	typeface groups	
Delete and close up	typeface groups	
Substitute character or part of one or more words	typeface groups	
Wrong fount: replace with correct fount	typeface groups	
Correct damaged characters	typeface groups	
Transpose words	groups typeface	
Transpose characters	typeface groups	
Transpose lines	the dimension of / is disastrous when	2 / 1
Transpose lines (2)	the dimension of / is disastrous when	
Centre type	typeface groups	[ ]
Indent 1 em	typeface groups	1em
Range left	typeface groups	R/L
Set line or column unjustified	typeface groups	
Move matter to right	typeface groups	
Move matter to left	typeface groups	
Take down to next line	typeface groups	t.o.
Take back to previous line	typeface groups	t.b.
Raise matter	typeface groups	
Lower matter	typeface groups	
Correct vertical alignment	typeface groups	
Correct horizontal alignment	typeface groups	
Close up space	typeface groups	
Insert space between words	typeface groups	#
Reduce space between words	typeface groups	T
Reduce or insert space between letters	ty pe face groups	Y
Make space appear equal	typeface groups	equal #

Instruction to printer	Textual mark	Marginal mark
Insert space between lines	aerobic movement / The dimensions of	
Reduce space between paragraphs	aerobic movement / The dimensions of	
Insert parentheses or brackets	typeface groups	
Figure or abbreviation to be spelled out in full	12 point / twelve pt	sp out
Move matter to position indicated	are called The set points dimension	trs
Set in or change to italics	typeface groups	itals
Set in or change to capitals	typegroups	
Set in or change to small capitals	typeface groups	
Capital for initials, small caps for rest of word	typeface grooups	
Set in or change to bold type	typeface groups	
Set in or change to bold italic type	typeface groups	
Change capitals to lower case	typefACE groups	
Change small capitals to lower case	typeface GROUPS	
Change italics to roman	typeface groups	
Invert type	typeface groups	
Insert ligature	filmsetter	fi
Substitute separate letters for ligature	filmsetter	fi
Insert period	typeface groups	
Insert colon	typeface groups	
Insert semicolon	typeface groups	;
Insert comma	typeface groups	
Insert quotation marks	typeface groups	
Insert double quotation marks	typeface groups	
Insert character in superior position	typeface groups	
Substitute character in inferior position	typeface groups	
Insert apostrophe	typeface groups	
Insert ellipsis	typeface groups	
Insert leader dots	typeface groups	
Insert hyphen	typeface groups	
Insert rule	typeface groups	2pt —
Insert oblique	typeface groups	
Start new paragraph	are called points. The questions	
Run on	are called points. The question is	

Key *com:* computer; *pho:* photography; *pri:* printing; *typ:* typography/typesetting. Terms that have their own entries in the glossary are written in SMALL CAPS

Absorbency The ability of a material to take up liquid or moisture.

Accordian fold *(US)* see CONCERTINA FOLD

Acetate see CELLULOSE ACETATE.

Acrylic A polymer based on synthetic resin. Most paints with an acrylic emulsion base can be mixed and diluted with water. They dry to a tough, flexible waterproof finish.

Additive colours The primary colours of light — red, green and blue — that may be mixed to form all other colours in photographic reproduction.

Aerate To use an air stream or manual riffling to separate paper SHEETS to be fed mechanically through a printing machine.

Against the grain Folding or marking paper at right angles to the GRAIN (1).

Agate *(US)* Type size of 5½ POINTS.

Agate line *(US)* Measurement of space in newspaper advertising, denoting ¼in depth by one COLUMN (1) width.

Air *(US)* A large amount of white space in a LAYOUT.

Airbrush/airbrushing A pen-shaped pressure gun, invented by Charles Burdick in 1893. Compressed air mixes with paint to produce a fine spray. Used for photographic retouching and for creating effects of graduated tone.

Albion press Heavy iron, hand-operated printing press, still often used in printing WOODCUTS and LINOCUTS.

Album paper Antique finish paper made from wood PULP, used mainly for the pages of photograph albums.

Albumen plate Lithographic plate with PHOTOSENSITIVE surface coating, originally made from albumen.

Aligning numerals see LINING NUMERALS.

Alignment The arrangement of type or other graphic material to level up at one horizontal or vertical line.

All in hand A term referring to a TYPESETTING job when it is in the hands of the compositors.

All up A term referring to a print job when COPY setting is completed.

Alphabet/alphabet length A measure derived from the length in POINTS of the 26 alphabet letters set in LOWER CASE. Thus 39 CHARACTERS (1) have a measure of 1½ alphabets.

Angle bar The metal bar of a WEB-FED printing press that turns paper between two units of the press.

Animal sized Describes paper that has been hardened or sized with animal glue or gelatin, by passing the finished SHEET through a bath of glue.

Animation A method of film-making that produces movement by rapid projection of a series of sequential still images, usually drawings or cartoons.

Annotation (1) A type label added to an illustration. (2) Explanatory notes printed in the MARGIN of a text.

Anodized plate A plate used in OFFSET printing, specially treated to harden the surface so it will resist wearing down in the press.

Antihalation backing A protective coat on the non-EMULSION side of a film or plate that prevents light reflecting back into the emulsion.

Antiqua (1) Early TYPEFACE based on the 11th- and 12th-century Italian scripts. (2) A German term for ROMAN type.

Antiquarian The largest known size of handmade paper, 53 × 31in (1350 × 790mm).

Antique paper Paper with a rough, lightly sized finish used mainly for books, booklets and folders.

Aperture *(pho)* The opening behind a camera lens that allows light to penetrate to the film. The size of the aperture is variable, governed by the DIAPHRAGM and measured by the F NUMBER.

Aperture card A card mount for the storage of MICROFILM.

Application software *(com)* SOFTWARE including basic computer routines and also special user requirements.

Apron *(US)* Extra white space allowed at the MARGINS of text and illustrations forming a FOLDOUT.

Aquatint An INTAGLIO process that allows reproduction of even or graded tones.

Arrowhead *(typ)* Symbol shaped like an arrowhead used in illustration to direct a LEADER LINE, or as a reference in conjunction with a figure or letter related to CAPTION material.

Art paper Paper with a hard, smooth surface caused by an even coating of china clay on one or both sides.

Artwork MATTER other than text prepared for reproduction such as ILLUSTRATIONS (2), DIAGRAMS and PHOTOGRAPHS.

ASA *abb* (1) Advertising Standards Authority. The organization that handles public complaints about advertising (apart from TV and radio) and is also responsible for administering the application of the British Code of Advertising Practice. (2) American Standards Association. An ASA number appears on film stock to provide a basic quantity from which the length and f number of an EXPOSURE can be calculated.

Ascender The section of a LOWER CASE letter rising above the x-HEIGHT — e.g., the upper part of an h or d.

Assembled negative Negative of line and HALFTONE COPY used in preparing a printing plate for PHOTOLITHOGRAPHY.

As to press Term used in production of gravure printed magazines for proofs showing final position of colour images.

Author's proofs GALLEY PROOFS checked and marked by the printer's reader to be read by the author.

Auto indent Instruction entered in a machine for PHOTOCOMPOSITION indicating that text should be automatically indented until the command is cancelled.

Autolithography Printing from an image hand drawn directly on a lithographic stone or plate.

Automated publication *(US)* Published work of which a COPY is kept on tape, disk or film for future publication with revised MATTER or format.

Autopositive Photographic materials designed to provide a POSITIVE (1) image without a NEGATIVE being required.

Autospacer Mechanism in a TYPESETTING machine designed to include automatic QUADDING.

Autotype A process that converts a PHOTOMECHANICAL TRANSFER (PMT) of original lettering into dry transfer form.

Auxiliary roll stand A second stand holding a paper roll in a WEB-FED press, allowing continuous printing while the first roll is replaced.

Azure Term for the colour of light blue LAID or WOVE PAPERS.

B

Back the part of a book nearest the fold or the edge at which the pages are bound.

Background In an illustration or photograph, the part of the image that appears furthest from the viewer, or on which the main subject is superimposed.

Background art Part of a design such as a pattern or texture forming a background for type and illustrations.

Back jacket flap Section of a BOOK JACKET folded inside the back COVER of a HARDBACK book.

Back lining A strip fixed to the back of a book before CASING IN.

Back margin The MARGIN of a page nearest to the SPINE of the book.

Back projection Projection of a TRANSPARENCY onto the back of a translucent screen by bouncing the image off a mirror surface.

Back step collation To COLLATE a book by reference to marks printed on the back fold of each SECTION (1).

Back to back *(US)* Printing on both sides of a SHEET. See BACK UP.

Back up To print the second side of a SHEET of paper. Backed refers to the sheet when it has been backed up.

Balance In a LAYOUT or design, an arrangement that is visually pleasing — e.g., an equal relationship between text and illustrations on facing pages.

Bank paper A light, uncoated paper used for making carbon copies.

Bar code A pattern of vertical lines identifying details of a product, such as country of origin, manufacturer and type of product, conforming to the UNIVERSAL PRODUCT CODE. The pattern is read by a computer-controlled sensor for stock control purposes.

Barrel printer *(com)* A high speed PRINTOUT (1) mechanism attached to a computer, making information visible in a form legible to the eye.

Baryta paper Paper coated with barium sulphate gelatin. It is used for text impressions on TYPESETTING machines.

Base alignment System of PHOTOCOMPOSITION giving automatic ALIGNMENT of different type sizes from one BASE LINE (1).

Base artwork ARTWORK requiring the addition of other elements — e.g., HALFTONE positives — before reproduction.

Base film The basic material for contact film in platemaking for PHOTOMECHANICAL (1) reproduction, to which film positives are stripped.

Base line (1) An imaginary line on which the bases of CAPITALS rest. **(2)** *(US)* The last line of space on a page containing type MATTER.

Base material Material forming the support for a coating or plating.

Base stock Accumulated material from which different papers can be made.

Basic weight *(US)* The designated weight of a REAM of paper cut to a given standard size.

Bastard (1) *(pri)* A substandard or abnormal element. **(2)** *(pri)* A letter foreign to the FOUNT in which it is found. **(3)** A general term meaning a non-standard size of, e.g., type or paper.

Batter Type which is damaged or worn and thus gives a defective IMPRESSION (2).

Bearoff *(US)* Adjusting spacing in type MATTER to correct JUSTIFICATION and COMPOSITION of the COPY.

Bed The steel table of a printing press on which the FORME is placed for LETTERPRESS printing.

Begin even Instruction to printer to set first line of COPY FULL OUT.

Below the line Advertising term describing costs of promotional items other than the advertisement itself.

Benday prints A series of mechanical tints in the form of celluloid sheets that are used in blockmaking and LITHOGRAPHY to add texture, shading and detail to line drawings.

Bible paper A very thin paper that is also tough and opaque, used mainly in printing Bibles and prayer books.

Billboard Outdoor advertising sign or poster, often large scale.

Bimetal plate LITHOGRAPHIC plate used in long runs; the printing area is of copper while the non-printing sections are of aluminium or steel.

Binder A medium of some liquidity that forms paint when mixed with powder pigment. It largely fixes the properties of a particular type of paint.

Binder's board *(US)* Heavy paperboard covered with cloth, used in binding HARDBACK BOOKS.

Binding edge see SPINE.

Blackletter Old style of typeface based on broad-nib script, also called Gothic *(UK)* and Old English *(US)*.

Blackline *(US)* Text for ARTWORK in black line reproduced by the WHITEPRINT process.

Black out *(US)* see BLACK PATCH.

Black patch A piece of black (or red) material used to mask the image area on reproduction LINE COPY, leaving a WINDOW **(2)** in the NEGATIVE for STRIPPING in a HALFTONE.

Black printer *(pri)* Term for the film printing black in the COLOUR SEPARATION process.

Blad Sample pages of a book produced in booklet form for promotional purposes.

Blank *(US)* Thick paper used for posters and advertising display.

Blanket A sheet made of rexine or rubber that covers the impression cylinder of a printing machine. Also, a similar sheet used to cover the FLONG when casting a STEREOTYPE.

Blanket cylinder The cylinder of an OFFSET press that transfers the ink image to the paper.

Blanket to blanket press *(US)* An OFFSET printing press in which paper is fed between two blanket cylinders to print both sides at once.

Bleach out An underdeveloped bromide print used as the basis for line drawing. It is later bleached away.

Bleed (1) That part of an image that extends beyond the TRIM MARKS on a page. Illustrations that spread to the edge of the paper allowing no MARGINS are described as bled off. **(2)** When ink or paint is applied to an unsuitable surface and the lines run and blur.

Blind emboss To make an impression without foil or ink — e.g., on the CASE (1) of a book.

Blind folio Page number counted for reference or identification but not printed on the page itself.

Blinding Poor surface condition on an apparently sound printing plate that causes a substandard image.

Blind punching In an automatic LINECASTER, making a perforated tape without running off printed COPY.

Blind stamping *(US)* see BLIND EMBOSS.

Blister card *(US)* Form of display packaging in which goods are mounted on card and protected by a transparent plastic bubble.

Block (1) *(pri)* HALFTONE or line illustration engraved or etched on a zinc or copper plate, for use in LETTERPRESS printing. **(2)** A metal stamp used to impress a design on a book COVER. The verb to block means to emboss a book cover. **(3)** *(US)* *(pri)* Metal or wood base on which a plate is mounted to TYPE HEIGHT.

Block book A book made by RELIEF PRINTING from page-sized wood blocks, before the advent of movable type.

Block letter A SANS SERIF CHARACTER (1) cut in a wooden block, that can be used for embossing or printing.

Blockmaker A person producing plates for LETTERPRESS printing by the technique of PHOTOENGRAVING.

Blowback *(US)* An enlarged print made from MICROFILM, Thus 'blown up' 'back' to its original scale or larger.

Blow up *(US)* To make photographic enlargement of COPY or image.

Blueline *(US)* COPY made by the WHITEPRINT process in blue lines on a white background.

Blues, blueprints *(pri)* Low quality PROOFS for initial checking, printed as white lines on a blue ground. See also OZALID.

Blue sensitive *(pho)* Quality of film that is sensitive to blue or ultraviolet light.

Body (1) The shank of a type. **(2)** The main portion of a book, excluding prelims or appendices.

Body copy/matter/type (1) Printed MATTER forming the main part of a work, but not including HEADINGS, etc. **(2)** *(US)* body type refers to the actual type used in setting a text.

Body size POINT measurement of a body of type as cast.

Bold, bold face Type with a conspicuously heavy, black appearance. It is based on the same design as medium weight type in the same FOUNT.

Bolts The folded edges of a SHEET or SECTION (1) that will be trimmed off.

Bond paper Standard grade of evenly finished paper used for writing and typing. It can also be printed upon.

Bookbinding see PERFECT BINDING, SADDLE-STITCH, SECTION-SEWN, SIDE-STITCH.

Book block A book that has been FOLDED AND GATHERED and stitched but not CASED IN.

Book face Old term for a particular TYPEFACE, but now used to mean any type suitable for the text of a book.

Book make up *(US)* The collation and identification of COPY prepared for printing.

Book paper A general classification of papers suitable for book printing.

Book proof IMPOSED PROOFS or PAGE PROOFS put together in book form.

Bottom out *(US)* To arrange text so there are no unsuitable breaks at the bottom of a page, or so that the page does not end with a WIDOW.

Bowl The curved part of a type CHARACTER (1) that encloses the COUNTER.

Boxhead In a table arranged in COLUMNS (2), the HEADING to each column appearing under the main heading.

Bracketed type type in which the SERIF is joined to the main stem in an unbroken curve.

Brass A bookbinder's engraved plate used to block a book COVER.

Break up for colour *(pri)* Instruction to reconstruct a FORME that is to be printed in more than one colour as separate formes for each colour.

Bristol board Fine board made in various thicknesses and qualities, used for drawing and printing.

Broad fold Method of paper folding in which the GRAIN (1) runs along the shorter dimension after folding.

Broadside/broadsheet Old term for a sheet of paper printed on one side only.

Bromide (1) A photographic print on bromide paper. **(2)** A PROOF from PHOTOCOMPOSITION, made on paper rather than on film.

Bronzing Producing a gold or metallic effect by applying powder to a SHEET treated with special printing ink.

Buckram A sized, coarse cloth used in bookbinding.

Buffing The final polishing of a reproduction plate before ETCHING.

Bulk (1) The thickness of the assembled pages of a book, excluding the COVERS. **(2)** The thickness of a SHEET of paper related to its weight.

Bullet *(typ)* A large dot used to precede listed items or to add emphasis to particular parts of a text.

Bundle *(US)* Two REAMS of paper.

Bundling In bookbinding, the tying together of SIGNATURES.

Burnisher A smooth curved metal tool used (1) for removing rough spots from printing plates and (2) for rubbing down dry transfer forms.

Burnout The MASKING (2) of COPY being exposed in a reproduction process, to make space for new insertions.

Burn through Exposure of film caused by light penetrating a MASK (1).

Burr A rough edge left on a block by a rotating machine.

●

Calender A column of metal rollers at the dry end of a papermaking machine through which the paper passes under pressure. This action closes the pores and smooths the surface.

Caliper (1) A measurement of thickness in paper or board expressed as thousandths of an inch (mils) or millionths of a metre (microns). (2) The instrument that can measure such a thickness.

Cameo (1) (UK) A term for TYPEFACES in which the CHARACTERS are reversed to show white on a dark ground. (2) (US) A brand of dull, coated paper suitable for the printing of HALFTONES or ENGRAVINGS.

Camera lucida An electronically powered piece of equipment for scaling an image up or down. The image is placed on a lit copyboard below a lens and glass viewing screen. The sized image is projected through the lens up onto the screen, where it can then be traced. Also known as VISUALIZER.

Camera ready A term applied to ARTWORK, COPY or PASTE-UP that is ready for reproduction.

Cancel To cut out and replace a wrongly printed LEAF (2) or leaves.

Canvas board A prepared board with simulated canvas texture, suitable for oil or acrylic painting.

Capital, cap The term for UPPER CASE letters, deriving from the style of inscription at the head, or capital, of a Roman column.

Caption board Artwork for film titles or studio use when making videotape titles.

Carbro A colour printing process using sensitized gelatine matrices carrying the printing colours separately and transferred by IMPRESSION (2).

Cardboard As distinct from the common type of paperboard, a thick paper made in various colours for display graphics.

Card to paper printout A method by which paper copies of a MICROFILM image can be produced from an APERTURE CARD.

Carry forward/over See TAKE OVER.

Cartridge paper A general purpose, rough surfaced paper used for drawing, wrapping, OFFSET printing, etc.

Case (1) The stiff COVER of a book, consisting of two boards, a HOLLOW and a binding material. (2) (typ) A box with separate compartments in which pieces of type are kept. This is the origin of the terms LOWER and UPPER CASE.

Cased/case bound A HARDBACK BOOK, that is, one with stiff outer COVERS.

Casing in To insert a book into its CASE (1) and paste it down.

Cast coated paper Art paper with an exceptionally glossy enamel finish.

Casting-off Making a calculation as to how much space MANUSCRIPT COPY will take up when printed in a given TYPEFACE.

Cast up Printer's calculation of the cost of setting MATTER in type.

Catchline The temporary HEADING for identification at the top of a GALLEY PROOF.

Cathode ray tube Vacuum tube producing information display electrostatically.

Cel (1) abb CELLULOSE ACETATE. (2) In ANIMATION, a transparent SHEET, the proportion of the film frame, on which one stage of the sequence is drawn.

Cell (1) (pri) A recessed DOT in a PHOTOGRAVURE plate forming part of the image for inking. (2) (US) see CEL. (3) (US) A MASK (1) used in photographic methods of reproduction.

Cellophane Transparent CELLULOSE ACETATE film that is thin and very flexible.

Cellulose acetate Plastic sheet material, usually transparent or translucent, available clear or coloured and with a shiny or matt finish. It is used as the basis of ARTWORK and OVERLAYS and is the base material of some photographic films.

Centrefold/spread The centre opening of a SECTION (two pages) where one plate may be used to print facing pages with following page numbers. Centre spreads are also called 'naturals'.

Centred TYPE which is placed in the centre of a sheet or type measure.

Centred dot (US) A raised dot used as a decimal point between figures.

Chain lines/marks (UK/US) Lines running through LAID paper, caused by the wires of the papermaking machine.

Chalking A printing fault caused by ink soaking into the paper leaving pigment deposited on the surface.

Chancery italic A 13th-century style of handwriting on which ITALIC type designs were based.

Change bar A vertical rule in the MARGIN of a revised technical publication indicating a part that varies from the original text.

Chapter drop The level at which text begins underneath a chapter heading.

Character (1) (typ) An individual item cast in type — e.g., a letter, figure, punctuation mark, sign or space. (2) (com) A set of symbols in data processing which represents a figure, letter, etc.

Character assembly An alternative term for TYPESETTING, especially in methods not using metal type.

Chase A metal frame into which type and blocks are fitted to make up a page. The type is held in place by furniture and quoins.

Chemical pulp Processed wood PULP used in high quality printing papers.

Choke A method of altering the thickness of a letter or solid shape by overexposure in processing.

Chroma The intensity or purity of a colour.

Chromo A printing paper heavily coated on one side.

Chromograph A machine for producing copies of plans, MANUSCRIPTS, etc, using ANILINE dye instead of ink.

Chromolin A fast proofing system in which powder is used instead of ink.

Chromolithography Lithographic printing in several colours by traditional techniques.

Chuck The core supporting a paper roll in a WEBB-FED printing press.

Cibachrome Agfa process, a direct method of obtaining photographic colour prints.

Cicero A European unit for measuring the width, or MEASURE, of a line of type and the depth of the page. One Cicero = 4.511mm or 12 DIDOT POINTS. See also PICA.

Circular screen A photographic screen that can be adjusted to prevent MOIRÉ patterns in colour reproduction.

Clean proof A PROOF free from errors.

Cliché The French term, used also elsewhere in Europe, for a block, STEREOTYPE or ELECTROTYPE.

Closed section/signature In either case, one where BOLTS are uncut.

Coated paper A general term for ART, CHROMO and enamel papers or similar groups, in which the surface has a mineral coating applied after the body paper is made; also known as surface paper.

Cock-up figure/letter see SUPERIOR FIGURE/LETTER.

Cold composition/type Typewriting or TYPESETTING in which no molten metal is used and including methods of PHOTOCOMPOSITION.

Cold-pressed A categorization of a type of paper surface. See NOT.

Collate To put the SECTIONS (1) or pages of a book in correct order.

Collotype A PHOTOMECHANICAL printing process suitable for fine detail reproductions. Printing is done from a raised gelatine film on glass support and gives CONTINUOUS TONE.

Colour (typ) The light or heavy appearance of a particular TYPEFACE.

Colour bar/codet A standard set of bars on PROOFS in FOUR-COLOUR PROCESSING, showing the strength and evenness of ink, and the registration of colours.

Colour blind emulsion Photographed EMULSION sensitized to blue, violet or ultraviolet light only.

Colour break The edge between two areas of colour in an image.

Colour burnout A deterioration in the colour of printing ink caused by chemical reactions in mixing or drying.

Colour coder An instrument capable of comparing the intensity of printed colours, ensuring correct reproduction.

Colour control bar (1) The set of small marginal marks placed on each of the three NEGATIVES used in making blocks for colour printing, which enable the printer to superimpose them when building up a picture. (2) The set of progressive PROOFS supplied by the plate- and blockmaker as a guide to the printer.

Colour correction The adjustment of colour values in reproduction to obtain a correct image.

Coloured edges The edges or top of a book which have been coloured with a brush-on fluid.

Colour filters Thin SHEETS of coloured glass, plastic or gelatine placed over a

C

C

camera lens to absorb or allow through particular colours in the light entering the camera.

Colour negative film Film which provides a colour image in NEGATIVE form after processing.

Colour positives A set of screened positive COLOUR SEPARATIONS.

Colour proofs Printed sheets that are run off to enable the artist, client and printer to check colour accuracy and register prior to final printing.

Colour reversal film A film which provides colour images in positive form after processing.

Colour separation Division of colour of a CONTINUOUS TONE multicoloured ORIGINAL or LINE COPY into basic portions by a process of photographic filtration. The portions are reproduced by a separate printing plate carrying a colour.

Colour separations The number of images or pieces (SUBJECTS) to be separated in the COLOUR SEPARATION process.

Colour sequence The accepted order of LETTERPRESS printing.

Colour transparency A positive photographic image produced in colour on transparent film.

Colour value The TONAL VALUE of a colour as compared to a light-to-dark scale of pure greys.

Column (1) A section of a page divided vertically, containing text or other MATTER. It is measured by the horizontal width. **(2)** A vertical section in tabulated work.

Comb binding Mechanical binding method in which slots are driven through the cover and pages, then secured with plastic fingers. Also known as coil binding.

Combination line and halftone A combined block or plate used to reproduce photographs with super-imposed figures, letters, diagrams, etc.

Commercial art A term used to describe ARTWORK intended for use in advertising or promotion, as distinct from fine art.

Compose To set COPY in type.

Composing room The area of a printing works specifically designated for TYPESETTING and MAKE-UP (2).

Composite artwork ARTWORK combining a number of different elements.

Composition Type which has been set

in a form ready for reproduction by LETTERPRESS printing or PHOTOLITHOGRAPHY.

Composition size A description of any type up to a size of 14 POINTS, used mainly in setting text.

Computer input devices Methods of transmitting instructions, queries and information to a computer in a prescribed form — e.g., keyboard, punched cards, paper tape, OPTICAL CHARACTER RECOGNITION.

Computer typesetting/ computerized composition The use of computers to control various aspects of PHOTOCOMPOSITION such as CHARACTER (2) assembly. The computer can be programmed with details of format, tabulation, rules of punctuation, type sizes, measures, etc.

Concertina fold/fan fold Method of paper folding in which each fold runs in the opposite direction to the one before to form a pleated effect.

Condensed A TYPEFACE with an elongated, narrow appearance.

Contact print, contacts Photographic print or prints made by direct contact with an original POSITIVE (1) or NEGATIVE at same size.

Contact printing frame see VACUUM FRAME.

Contact screen A HALFTONE SCREEN made on a film base which has a graded DOT pattern. It is used in direct contact with a film or plate to obtain a halftone NEGATIVE from a CONTINUOUS TONE ORIGINAL. They provide better definition than the conventional glass screen.

Continuous fold A paper folding system to convert rolls of paper into CONCERTINA FOLDS.

Continuous tone Photographs or coloured ORIGINALS in which the subject contains continuous shades between the lightest and darkest tones, without being broken up by dots.

Contrast The degree of separation of tones in a photograph in the range from black to white.

Controlling dimension The width or height of an image taken as the basis for enlargement or reduction.

Copperplate printing An INTAGLIO process used in short run printing, producing a sharp, but very black image.

Copyboard (US) see VACUUM FRAME.

Copyfitting see CASTING-OFF.

Copywriting A term applied to writing

of COPY specifically for use in advertising.

Corner marks The marks on a printed SHEET acting as TRIM MARKS, and also sometimes as REGISTER MARKS.

Corporate identity/house style The elements of design by which a company or other institution establishes a consistent and recognizable identity through communication, promotion and distribution material.

Correction overlay A TRANSLUCENT OVERLAY, registered to ARTWORK, on which corrections are made.

Counter The inside area of the TYPEFACE — e.g., the centre of an o or space between the vertical strokes of an n.

Counter-mark A WATERMARK of the papermaker's initials, placed opposite the normal watermark.

Counting keyboard A PHOTOCOMPOSITION keyboard that shows the position of CHARACTERS (1) in a line to indicate the need for an END OF LINE DECISION.

Cover The paper, board, cloth or leather to which the BODY (2) of a book is secured by glue and thread.

Cover papers Papers for the COVERS of books, pamphlets, etc.

Crash finish Paper which has a coarse, linen-like finish.

Crease see SCORING.

Creasing (1) A linear indentation made by machine in thick paper providing a hinge. **(2)** A printing fault producing deep creases.

Crimping (US) see CREASING.

Crop, cropmark The part of a photograph or illustration that is discarded after it has been trimmed.

Cropped A term applied to a book with overtrimmed MARGINS.

Cropping aid Two L-shaped pieces of cardboard which can be moved over an image until the most complimentary position for cropping is found.

Cross front The description of a camera in which the lens can be moved laterally in relation to the film.

Cross-head Subsection, paragraph HEADING or numeral printed in the BODY (2) of text, usually marking the first subdivision of a chapter.

Cross section Illustrator's view of an object showing it as if cut through to expose the internal workings

Crown Standard size of printing paper 15 × 20in (381 × 508mm).

Crowner The lid of a point-of-sale display that folds back to make a show card.

C-type A term for a photographic colour print produced directly from a NEGATIVE. It refers to a method of processing developed by Kodak.

Curved plate A plate used in a ROTARY PRESS that curves around the PLATE CYLINDER.

Curves Templates for designers and draftsmen, made of plastic or metal. French curves combine several curves in one shape while others are produced for specific purposes, to be used in technical drawings.

Cut (1) A shortened version of WOODCUT, used to describe a relief or block print. **(2)** (US) A metal relief plate from which an image is printed. **(3)** An instruction to an editor meaning 'cut text to fit'.

Cut dummy Cut PROOFS of illustrations used in sequence as a guide to MAKE-UP (2) of pages.

Cut edge The three edges of a book which are cut with a GUILLOTINE.

Cut flush A term describing a book with even COVER and pages as the cutting is done after the cover has been attached.

Cutline (US) **(1)** A CAPTION to an illustration. **(2)** An instruction to the printer to insert an illustration during MAKE-UP (2).

Cutout (1) A term referring to a SILHOUETTE HALFTONE where the background dots have been removed. **(2)** (US) A shape cut out of paper stock with a steel DIE, — e.g., in the soft COVER of a book to expose COPY on the page below.

Cylinder press A printing press in which the FORME is carried on a FLAT BED under a paper-bearing cylinder for an IMPRESSION (2) to be made at the point of contact.

●

Dampening Necessary process in LITHOGRAPHY of dampening the printing plate to prevent ink spreading.

Dark field illumination A method of checking the quality of HALFTONE DOTS on film by viewing them in angled light against a dark background.

Dead matter Leftover MATTER that is not used.

Dead metal In LETTERPRESS ENGRAVING, the areas of a plate that do not print.

Decal A printed transfer image.

Deckle edge The rough uneven edge of handmade paper.

Deep-etch halftone A HALFTONE plate with unwanted screen dots removed, leaving areas of plain paper.

Deep-etching The removal, by ETCHING, of unwanted material on HALFTONE plates to give a white background.

Delineate To accentuate outlines in line ARTWORK by making them heavier.

De luxe edition A smarter edition than the standard one, printed on higher grade paper with specially cast type and expensive binding.

Demy A standard size of printing paper 17½ × 22½in (445 × 572mm).

Densitometer An electronic precision instrument used to measure the quantitive colours or density in a colour TRANSPARENCY.

Density Of type, the amount and compactness of type set within a given area or page. Of a TRANSPARENCY or printed image, the measure of tonal values.

Descender The part of a LOWER CASE letter that falls below the X-HEIGHT.

Detail paper/layout paper a thin TRANSLUCENT paper with a hard surface used for LAYOUTS and sketches.

Developer The chemical used to bring up an image on photographic film, paper or plate.

Diapositive A photographic TRANSPARENCY in which the image is positive.

Diazo *abb* Diazonium. A method of reproducing in limited quantities from a transparent or TRANSLUCENT ORIGINAL on paper, cloth or film. The image is exposed on to a light-sensitive coating of diazo salts and dyestuff and the print may be blue, black or another colour.

Didot point The continental unit for type. It measures 0.0148in whereas an English POINT is 0.013888in.

Die An INTAGLIO engraved stamp used for impressing a design.

Die cutting To cut paper, card or board to a particular design with a metal DIE, for packaging and display work.

Dielectric coated paper Paper on which an image is printed through the action of a liquid toner on an electrostatically charged DOT pattern. It is used in computer work.

Die-stamping A form of printing where all the CHARACTERS (1) are in relief.

Differential spacing The spacing of each CHARACTER (1) of type according to its individual width.

Diffusion transfer process A method of reproduction used in various types of copying machines to transfer an image to paper or a flexible printing plate.

Digitize To convert an image into a form that can be processed, stored and electronically reconstructed.

Dingbat *(US)* A general term for ORNAMENTS.

Dinky A term referring to a half roll (WEB) of paper, halved by width not diameter.

Diploma paper A fine paper made specially for printing of certificates, official documents, etc.

Direct colour separation COLOUR SEPARATION in which a HALFTONE SCREEN is used in the original separation to produce screened NEGATIVES directly.

Direct entry photocomposition A computer typesetting system in which INPUT and OUTPUT are combined in one unit.

Direct image master/plate A plate used in LITHOGRAPHY, often made of paper, on which COPY can be typed or drawn directly. It is only suitable for short runs.

Display board Heavy, dull finish, coated board in various colours.

Display matter/type Larger TYPEFACES designed for HEADINGS, etc, usually above 14 POINT in bookwork.

Display size The size of type used for HEADINGS, advertising MATTER, etc. It is always greater than 12 POINT so clearly distinguishable from BODY TYPE (2).

Distribution rollers The rollers on a printing press that control an even distribution of ink to the roller that contacts the FORME.

Doctor blade A device used in INTAGLIO printing processes to wipe excess ink from the surface of a plate. The blade is made of flexible metal.

Dodging *(pho)* A method of obtaining greater contrast when printing a photograph by the selective use of MASKING (3).

Dot The smallest basic element of a HALFTONE.

Dot area The pattern of a HALFTONE, that is both the DOTS and the spaces in between.

Dot etching A method of reducing the size of HALFTONE DOTS by chemical action in processing.

Dot for dot reproduction A direct method of producing printing film by photographing a previously screened image. A maximum of 10 per cent enlargement or reduction can be achieved.

Dot formation The pattern of DOTS in a HALFTONE SCREEN.

Dot gain An aberration occurring in the making of HALFTONE film or plates, when the DOTS become slightly enlarged. A dot gain scale is included in PROOFS to check this occurrence.

Dot loss The devaluation or disappearance of a HALFTONE DOT on a printing plate.

Double burn To expose two or more NEGATIVES to expose an image on to a sensitized plate.

Double coated paper Paper with a heavy coating on one or both sides.

Double digest fold One of the four basic folds forming a SHEET into a SIGNATURE in WEB OFFSET printing.

Double image The appearance of two impressions of an image on one surface in printing or photography.

Double spread/page spread Two facing pages of a publication.

Down stroke A heavy stroke in a type CHARACTER (1), originally the downward stroke of a pen in calligraphy.

Drawdown (1) The evacuation of air from a VACUUM FRAME. **(2)** A smear of ink produced by a smooth blade on paper, used to check quality and tone.

Drawn on Describes a paper book COVER glued to the back of the book.

Drawing out Arranging the spaces in a line of type to fill the line.

Drop The number of lines of text in a COLUMN as allowed on the GRID.

Drop cap *(typ)* A large initial at the beginning of a text that drops into the lines of type below.

Drop down see CHAPTER DROP.

Drop folios The numbers printed at the bottom of each page.

Drop letter see DROP CAP.

Drop out/dropped out halftone Areas removed from a HALFTONE NEGATIVE, print or plate by MASKING (2). See also HIGHLIGHT HALFTONE and SILHOUETTE HALFTONE.

Dropped shadow A shadow behind an image designed to bring the image forward.

Drum (1) A drum-shaped image carrier used in some machines for PHOTOCOMPOSITION. **(2)** An image carrier or recording device used in electronic scanners.

Drum plotter A COMPUTER OUTPUT DEVICE that marks information on a roll of paper rotating on a drum, by means of a moving writing tool.

Dry ink Powder used in some copying machines to create the image. It is sealed by heat or chemical action.

Dry offset see LETTERSET.

Dry transfer lettering CHARACTERS (1) transferred to a page by rubbing them off the back of a SHEET.

Dual roll stand A stand supporting two WEBS fed simultaneously through a press to increase production.

Duct The ink reservoir in a printing machine.

Ductor roller *(pri)* A roller carrying ink or water between the FOUNTAIN roller and the DISTRIBUTION ROLLER.

Dull finish A matt paper finish. See also COATED PAPER.

Dull seal *(pri)* A term for paper stock having an adhesive backing.

Dummy The prototype of a proposed book in the correct format, paper and bulk but with blank pages.

Duotone Also called a duplex HALFTONE, an illustration process using two colours. Two NEGATIVES are made from a MONOCHROME ORIGINAL, one for the darker shade with the greater detail, the other for the lighter flat tint.

Duplex board/paper Paper or board of two layers pasted together to give a different colour or surface quality on each side.

Duplex halftone see DUOTONE.

Dutch paper Describes any DECKLE-EDGED paper produced in the Netherlands.

Dye transfer print A method of making photographic colour prints using gelatin relief matrices. A MATRIX is made for each of the three PRIMARY COLOURS, red, yellow and blue, and soaked in appropriate dye solution. These are then placed in turn on a gelatine COATED PAPER which absorbs dye from each to produce the full image.

Dyeline see DIAZO.

Edition The whole number of copies of a work printed and issued at one time.

Edition bound *(US)* see CASED BOOK.

Eggshell finish The rough finish found on drawing paper and notepaper as a result of omitting CALENDERING.

Egyptian A group of display types with heavy SLAB SERIFS and little contrast in the thickness of strokes.

Eight sheet A poster size measuring 60 × 80in (1524 × 2032mm).

Electrostatic processes A copying or printing process using static electricity to deposit powder ink on a support to make the image.

Electrotype A duplicate printing FORME made in a galvanic bath by precipating copper on a MATRIX (2).

Elliptical dot screen A HALFTONE SCREEN with graduated DOT pattern that includes elliptical dots forming middle tones.

Em A unit of linear measurement, 12 POINTS or 4.5mm.

Em quad A space in type that is the square of the type size.

Em rule/dash A dash used in punctuating text, the length of one EM.

Embossing RELIEF PRINTING or stamping in which DIES are used to raise letters above the surface of paper, cloth or leather.

Emulsion The light sensitive coating of a photographic material.

Emulsion down In making a printing plate, the direct contact of film with EMULSION side down on the plate. If the emulsion is uppermost the image formed is slightly haloed due to the thickness of the film.

En A measurement half the width of an EM, used in CASTING-OFF.

En quad A space in type half the width of an EM QUAD.

En rule/dash A dash (–), approximately half an EM.

Enamel paper see COATED PAPER.

End even Instruction to a typesetter to end a section of COPY with a full line.

End of line decisions Decisions made by a COMPOSITOR as to JUSTIFICATION of type and WORD BREAKS at the end of a line. In computer TYPESETTING this function may be included in the computer PROGRAM.

End papers The leaves of paper at the front and end of a book which cover the inner sides of the boards, securing the book to its CASE.

Engine sizing A method of sizing paper by the addition of emulsified resin to cleaned paper PULP.

Engraving The design or lettering etched on a plate or block and also the print taken from such a plate.

Etching A metal plate treated with acid and with certain parts protected by the application of a GROUND. It is also a print taken from the etched plate.

Even smalls SMALL CAPITALS used without a larger sized CAPITAL at the beginning of a word.

Even working A printed work divided into a number of SECTIONS of equal size — e.g., 16, 32, 48 pages.

Exception dictionary A list of WORD BREAKS that are exceptions to the standard guidelines, stored in a computer used in PHOTOCOMPOSITION.

Expanded/extended type Type with a flattened rectangular appearance.

Exposure The amount of light allowed to contact a PHOTOSENSITIVE material. The exposure is the combination of length of contact and intensity of light acting upon the material.

●

Face The printing surface of any type CHARACTER (1). It also refers to the group or FAMILY to which any particular type design belongs, as in TYPEFACE.

Fade out blue A light blue used in marking reproduction COPY. The blue is not registered by the camera.

Family A group of printing types in series with common characteristics in design, but of different weights such as BOLD, CONDENSED, EXPANDED, ITALIC, etc.

Fan fold see CONCERTINA FOLD.

Fashion boards Simple body boards lined with good RAG PAPER on one side, and thin paper on the other to prevent warping.

Fat face A TYPEFACE with extreme contrast in the widths of thin and thick strokes.

Fat matter *(pri)* Term for COPY with a large proportion of spacing allowing rapid setting. Dense copy is known as lean MATTER.

Fatty A mask with INTERNEGATIVES to enlarge COPY slightly. This allows for exact registration of butted elements by lapping one over the other.

Feathering The method of biting areas of a plate using drops of acid, controlling their movement with a feather.

Featherweight paper A light, bulky paper with a high esparto content made with little or no CALENDERING.

Feeder Apparatus for feeding and positioning paper SHEETS in printing presses and paper processing machines.

Feet The base of a piece of type. It is recessed at the centre to form two 'feet' on which it stands.

Felt finish Paper finish applied in the manufacturing machine by felt that marks the paper roll.

Felting The binding together of FIBRES in the wet PULP.

Felt side The top side or printing side of paper. See also WIRE SIDE.

Ferrotype A photographic print made on thin metal plate.

Figure title The title given to an illustration as distinct from a CAPTION describing the picture.

Figures An alternative name for numbers. arabic numerals are used more frequently than Roman ones.

Filler An extra figure or piece of COPY in a magazine or newspaper put in to fill space in a page or COLUMN (1).

Filling in/up A fault in printing when ink fills spaces between HALFTONE DOTS or the COUNTERS of type to produce small areas of solid tone.

Film (1) Transparent plastic material, usually CELLULOSE ACETATE. **(2)** Cellulose acetate coated with light-sensitive EMULSION for photographic recording of an image.

Film assembly FILM NEGATIVES or POSITIVES (1) assembled in correct positions to make plates for PHOTOLITHOGRAPHY.

Film negative A photographic image on film in which the HIGHLIGHTS and SHADOWS are reversed; also used extensively in REPROGRAPHIC PRINTING.

Film positive (1) A black image on a background of clear or TRANSLUCENT film. **(2)** A POSITIVE image on a film base made as a contact print from stripped NEGATIVES. It is used as a MASK in INTAGLIO platemaking.

Filmsetting see PHOTOCOMPOSITION.

Film sizes Standard measurements for sheet film or numerical codings for roll film corresponding to usual film widths.

Filmstrip A section of roll film from which images may be projected separately as stills.

Filter A gelatine, glass or plastic sheet which may be placed over or in front of a camera lens to alter the colour or quality

of light passed through to the film.

Final draft COPY fully prepared for TYPESETTING.

Fine rule A line of hairline thickness.

Finial letter A CHARACTER (1) in certain TYPEFACES devised as the end letter in a word or line, not used elsewhere.

Finish The surface given to paper during manufacture.

Finisher An artist or illustrator who inks over or finishes ARTWORK drawn up by another artist.

Fit The ALIGNMENT and registration of individual images within a page.

Fit up halftones A term in LETTERPRESS describing separately made HALFTONE plates placed together on a MOUNT.

Fix, fixer Colloquial term for a chemical used in photographic processing to make an image permanent. See HYPO.

Fixed word spacing A method of TYPESETTING employing a standard size for spaces between words, leaving lines UNJUSTIFIED.

Flange An edging on a HALFTONE plate used in LETTERPRESS printing. It is below type height and allows space for securing the plate to a MOUNT.

Flare (1) Non-image-forming light caused by reflection and scattering so that the quality of a photographic image is degraded. **(2)** Reflected light in PHOTOMECHANICAL reproduction that distorts or obscures the true image.

Flash exposure A second exposure in HALFTONE processing that reinforces the DOTS in dark areas. These would otherwise run together and print solid.

Flat An opaque based material with cut-out WINDOWS, in which are inserted NEGATIVES of COPY to be printed by PHOTOLITHOGRAPHY. The flat is then used as a composite image in preparing the printing plate.

Flat bed cylinder press This press has the printing FORME on a plane surface, as opposed to a curved printing surface. The form is placed and moved to and fro under the cylinder.

Flat bed plotter A COMPUTER OUTPUT DEVICE using a WRITING HEAD to draw on paper or film laid over a flat support.

Flat colour Solid areas of colour without any tonal value.

Flat copy A PHOTOMECHANICAL image without a wide range of tonal values, such as LINE COPY.

Flat plan (1) A diagrammatic plan of the pages of a book used to establish the distribution of colour, chapter lengths, etc. **(2)** A diagram or chart showing the sequence of events involved in a process or activity.

Flat tint halftone A HALFTONE printed over a background of flat colour.

Flexography A method of LETTERPRESS printing from rubber or flexible plates.

Flocking A decorative slightly three-dimensional effect obtained in printing by blowing fibres over an adhesive ink base.

Flong The sheet of papier-mâché used to make a MOULD from a FORME for casting a STEREOTYPE PLATE.

Flop A PHOTOMECHANICAL image that has been deliberately or accidently REVERSED LEFT TO RIGHT.

Flow chart (1) A schematic diagram showing the sequence of a process or related series of events. **(2)** See FLAT PLAN. The plan of a book shown as a sequential drawing of the proposed design and LAYOUT of pages.

Flow line A line indicating the relationship of parts in an object when they are drawn separately — e.g., as an exploded view.

Flush cover The COVER of a book cut to the same dimensions as the pages.

Flush left, right COPY aligned at left or right MARGINS. See RANGE.

Flush mount In LETTERPRESS printing, the mounting of a plate and type, or two plates, in close fit, requiring removal of the FLANGE.

Flush paragraphs Paragraphs in which the first word is not indented but set flush with the vertical line of text. See also FULL OUT.

Fly fold A folding method producing four pages from a SHEET.

Flying paster An automatic mechanism on a WEB-FED press for running in a new web without interruption to the printing process.

Fly leaf Another term for END PAPERS, the part which is not stuck down.

Focal length A property of a camera lens indicating its focusing ability. It is a measurement between lens and film when the image of a distant object is in sharp FOCUS in the camera.

Focus A point at which light rays converge. In photography, light rays are bent by the camera lens to converge on

the film in such a way as to produce a sharp, clearly defined but much reduced image of the subject.

Foil An extremely thin, flexible metal sheet applied as decoration to a blocked or embossed design.

Folded and gathered sheets/F and Gs COPY which is collated but not trimmed and sent to the publisher for approval of printing before binding begins.

Folding methods see CONCERTINA FOLD, FRENCH FOLD, GATEFOLD, PARALLEL FOLD and RIGHT-ANGLE FOLD.

Fold out An extension to the LEAF of a book making it wider than the standard page width so it must be folded back onto the page.

Fold to paper A method of folding a SECTION **(1)** after printing by aligning the edges of the SHEET.

Fold to print A method of folding a SECTION **(1)** after printing by reference to page numbers or other matter printed on the SHEET.

Foliation In book publishing, the practice of numbering leaves, that is alternate pages, rather than each page.

Folio (1) The book size formed when a SHEET is folded making the pages half the size of the sheet. **(2)** A LEAF of paper numbered only on the front. **(3)** A page number and the RUNNING HEAD of a page.

Follow copy Instruction to the COMPOSITOR to follow the spelling and punctuation of a MANUSCRIPT, even if unorthodox, in preference to the HOUSE STYLE.

Follow on see RUN ON.

Foolscap Standard size of printing paper 13½ × 17in (343 × 432mm).

Foot (1) The MARGIN at the bottom of a page or the bottom edge of a book. **(2)** The undersurface of a piece of type.

Foot margin The MARGIN at the bottom of the page in a publication.

Fore edge/foredge The outer edge of a book parallel to the back.

Foredge margin The outer side MARGIN of a page in a publication.

Format the general appearance, size or style of a book.

Forme, form Type matter and blocks assembled into pages and locked up in a CHASE ready for LETTERPRESS printing.

Forty-eight sheet A standard poster size measuring 120 × 480in (305 × 1220cm).

Forwarding The binding of a book after sewing and before CASING IN.

Foundry proof A PROOF from a FORME prepared for stereotyping or electrotyping.

Fount A complete supply of a TYPEFACE.

Fountain A reservoir for ink supply in a printing press. The term is also used for a similar mechanism that supplies a solution for dampening the rollers of an OFFSET press.

Four-colour process A method of printing in full colour by COLOUR SEPARATION, producing four plates for printing in cyan, yellow, magenta and black.

Foxed The term is applied to book pages discoloured by damp which has affected impurities in the paper.

Free line fall see RAGGED RIGHT and UNJUSTIFIED.

French curves see CURVES.

French fold A term used to describe a SHEET of paper that has been printed on one side only and then folded twice to form an uncut four-page section.

French folio Thin smooth, sized paper.

Friction feed A paper feeding mechanism in a printing or copying machine using rubber rollers.

Fringe A halo seen to surround HALFTONE DOTS in the early stages of processing.

Front jacket flap The part of a BOOK JACKET that folds inside the front COVER of a book.

Front lay edge see LAY EDGES.

Front matter *(US)* see PRELIMS.

Front projection A method of superimposing images in a photograph by projecting one image onto a two-way mirror placed between camera and subject.

Fugitive colours Colours or inks which are not permanent and change or fade when exposed to light.

Full binding A BOOKBINDING made completely of leather.

Full measure The width of a line of type as measured in PICAS.

Full out An instruction to the printer to set type with lines starting at the MARGIN, that is, not indented.

Full shadow A heavy outline to a letter or line of type.

Full space The horizontal space between two lines of type.

Full word wrap In PHOTOCOMPOSITION,

the transfer of a full word to the following line to avoid a WORD BREAK.

G

g/m²/gsm, grams per square metre A unit of measurement for paper used in printing.

Galley Long, shallow, metal tray used to hold type after it has been set.

Galley proofs PROOFS taken from the GALLEY before COPY is divided into pages.

Gang shooting In PHOTOLITHOGRAPHY, to make one NEGATIVE containing several pages of COPY for transfer to a printing plate. The pages are arranged to form a sequence that can be folded into page order.

Gang up (1) To print a SHEET of paper with several different jobs, to be divided appropriately. **(2)** To place a group of ORIGINALS of the same proportions together for camera work or scanning.

Gatefold A paper fold in which both sides are folded across the middle of the SHEET in overlapping layers.

Gathering Placing the SECTIONS of a book in the correct order for binding.

Gelatine process A duplication method using gelatine as the medium for transferring a carbon image as in GRAVURE printing.

Ghosting (1) To decrease the tonal values of the surrounding parts of an image to make the main object stand out more clearly. This can be done by photographic processing or by AIRBRUSHING. **(2)** In technical illustration, to depict parts of an image that would not normally be visible — e.g., parts of an engine covered by its casing.

Gilt edges/top The three edges, or top of a book, which are covered with gold leaf and rubbed down preventing the absorption of dust.

Glassine A TRANSLUCENT, grease-resistant paper used for wrappings and stationery.

Gloss ink A printing ink consisting of a synthetic resin base and drying oils. These inks dry quickly, without penetration, and are suitable for use on COATED PAPERS.

Glossy print A photographic print with a glossy surface.

Glued back only Reference to a paper COVER which is glued to the back of a book only, leaving the sides loose.

Glued or pasted down to ends A paper COVER glued at back, with each side glued to the first and last leaves of the book.

G

Glyphic A TYPEFACE originating from carved rather than scripted letters.

Gold blocking The stamping of a design on a book COVER using gold leaf and a heated DIE or block.

Goldenrod An opaque, orange paper ruled with a GRID used in preparing FLATS for PHOTOLITHOGRAPHY.

Golfball A colloquial term for the printing head of a typewriter in the form of a faceted ball, originally a feature of IBM machines.

Gothic see BLACKLETTER.

Gouache Opaque watercolour for which the pigments are mixed with white lead, bone ash or chalk.

Gradation The smooth transition from one tone or colour to another, or the range of values between black and white.

Grain (1) In paper, the pattern of fibres in a manufactured SHEET. **(2)** *(pho)* The density of tiny silver crystals in a photographic EMULSION.

Grain direction The direction the fibres lie in a SHEET of paper.

Graining The process by which a LITHOGRAPHIC plate is given a moisture-retaining surface. Abrasive powder and either glass or steel marbles are used. Mechanical agitation produces the required surface.

Grammage see g/m².

Graphic (1) *(typ)* A TYPEFACE originating from drawn rather than scripted letter forms. **(2)** A general term meaning related to written or drawn symbols.

Graphic design Design based on or involving two dimensional processes — e.g., ILLUSTRATION, PHOTOGRAPHY, ILLUSTRATION and PRINTING METHODS.

Graphoscope A magnifier used for close viewing of photographs or ENGRAVINGS.

Graticule A linear GRID placed over an image giving reference to points on the image — e.g., lines of latitude and longitude on a map.

Gravure An INTAGLIO printing process. See PHOTOGRAVURE.

Grey scale A tonal scale included in a TRANSPARENCY enabling the printer to check reproduction of tones.

Grid Transparent sheet representing a double-page spread of a publication designed to insure consistency. It is printed with ruled lines and shows the exact page size, margins and trim marks over which all the components of the

spread can be positioned accurately. Alternatively, it can be used to scale an image up or down. The image is traced and divided into equally ruled boxes. The key points are plotted and transferred onto a correspondingly larger, or smaller, boxed grid.

Gripper edge The edge which is caught by the GRIPPERS as a SHEET of paper is fed into a CYLINDER PRESS.

Gripper margin An extra MARGIN on a SHEET where it is gripped on the press, later trimmed away.

Grippers On job presses these are the iron fingers attached to the PLATEN to keep the SHEET in place and take it off the type after the IMPRESSION **(2)**. On CYLINDER PRESSES, they are short curved metal fingers attached to an operating rod which grip the sheet and carry it round the impression.

Ground A thin coating made from pitch, gum-mastic, asphaltum and beeswax which protects the non-image-bearing parts of an ETCHING plate from the action of the acid.

Groundwood A cheap wood PULP, such as that used to make NEWSPRINT.

Guards Narrow strips of linen or paper to which the inner MARGINS of single plates are pasted before sewing them with the SECTIONS of a book.

Guillotine A machine for cutting a large number of SHEETS of paper accurately.

Gum arabic A liquid used in platemaking processes. It dries to form a protective finish.

Gutter A term used in imposition for the space made up of FOREDGES of pages plus the trim. Commonly, the channel down the centre of a page is incorrectly described as the gutter.

Gutter bleed An image allowed to extend unbroken across the central MARGINS of a DOUBLE SPREAD.

●

Hairline rule The thinnest RULE that is possible to print.

Hairlines The very fine strokes of a TYPEFACE.

Hairspace Mainly used for letter spacing, the very narrow space between type.

Halation The spreading of lights around the HIGHLIGHTS of an image.

Half-bound A book with its back and

corners bound in one material, the sides in another.

Half sheet work The construction of FORMES so that each SHEET will be printed with two whole SECTIONS, half a sheet folding to one section.

Half-title The title of a book as printed on the LEAF preceding the title page.

Halftone Process by which CONTINUOUS TONE is simulated by a pattern of dots of varying size. A halftone block is a zinc or copper printing plate prepared by this process.

Halftone blow up The enlargement of a HALFTONE NEGATIVE to coarsen the screen DOT pattern.

Halftone screen A sheet of glass or film bearing a network of lines ruled at right angles. The screen is used to translate the subject to a HALFTONE illustration into DOTS.

Half up ARTWORK completed at one and a half times the size at which it will be reproduced.

Hand press A printing press in which the plate is inked and the paper is fed and removed by hand.

Hanging indent A setting where the first line of each paragraph is set FULL OUT to the COLUMN measure and the remaining lines indented by 1 EM.

Hanging punctuation Punctuation marks are allowed to fall outside the MEASURE of a piece of text.

Hardback book/hardcover book *(UK/US)* A CASED book with a stiff board COVER.

Hard copy (1) A copy on paper of MATTER prepared for printing, used for revision or checking. **(2)** A computer printout for checking INPUT to the machine.

Hard dot A HALFTONE DOT in the second or third stage of processing, with good density and sharpness.

Hard size Paper which contains the maximum amount of SIZE

Hardware A term for equipment. It generally applies to the physical apparatus in a computer.

Head The MARGIN at the top of a page.

Head bolt The thickening of a fully folded SHEET before it is trimmed.

Head to foot arrangement The placement of COPY on either side of a SHEET to align the top of the first page with the bottom of the page overleaf.

Headband A cotton or silk cord sewn

to the top of the back of a book.

Headless paragraph A paragraph set apart from other text but without a separate HEADING.

Heat-set inks Ink designed to dry particularly quickly when the printed MATTER is passed through a drier.

Hectography A duplication process based on the use of gelatine plates.

Hickie, hickey A spot with a blank halo appearing in printing due to a speck of dust or hard substance adhering to the printing plate or BLANKET.

High gloss ink A viscous ink that does not soak into paper and dries to a glossy surface.

High key A photographic image exposed or processed to produce light tones overall.

Highlight halftone A HALFTONE plate in which DOTS appearing in HIGHLIGHT areas are etched out. See DROP OUT HALFTONE.

Hollow The strip of brown paper placed in the centre of a CASE to stiffen the SPINE.

Hologram/holograph (1) An image with three-dimensional illusionism created by the action of lasers. **(2)** In publishing, the term holograph refers to a manuscript hand-written by the author.

Honing A technique of removing image areas from a printing plate by mechanical means.

Hooking A method of attaching a single LEAF to a SECTION **(1)** by means of a GUARD.

Hot metal General term for composing machines casting single pieces of type from molten metal.

Hot press lettering A method of laying down CHARACTERS **(1)** in metal foil on board, using type under heat and pressure.

Hot-pressed Paper glazed by heated metal plates.

Hue The distinguishing property of a pure colour, not including any white or black.

Hygroscope A device for measuring how much humidity is picked up from the air by paper.

Hypo *abb* Hyposulphate. A term applied to the FIXER used in photographic processing, though the solution used is in fact sodium thiosulphate.

●

Ideal format A size of photographic NEGATIVE measuring 60 × 70mm.

Illustration (1) A drawing, painting, diagram or photograph reproduced in a publication to explain or supplement the text. (2) A term used to distinguish a drawn image from one that is photographed.

Image The SUBJECT to be reproduced as an illustration on a printing press.

Image area The amount of space given to a particular image in design and printing, assumed to be square or rectangular even if the image is not.

Imitation cloth/leather A bookbinding material, usually of paper, made to simulate the appearance of leather or cloth.

Imperial A size of printing and drawing paper 22 × 30in (559 × 762mm).

Impose/imposition To arrange pages of type in a FORME so that when the SHEET is folded the text will read continuously.

Impression (1) All copies of a book printed at one time from the same type of plates. (2) The pressure applied to a frame of type by the cylinder or PLATEN.

Impression cylinder The cylinder of a ROTARY PRESS carrying paper into contact with the inked plate or BLANKET CYLINDER.

In camera processs Photographic process in which the print is developed inside the camera. See POLAROID.

Indentation Any setting short of the COLUMN measure.

Index board Coloured board made by machines.

India paper A very thin but strong opaque paper, made from rags and used for printing Bibles and dictionaries.

Indirect letterpress see LETTERSET.

Inferior figure/letter A small figure or letter printed at the foot of ordinary letters and cast partly below the base line, for example in chemical formulae, such as H_2O.

In-house A process or service carried out within a company, not bought in from an individual or organization.

Initial A large CAPITAL often found at the beginning of a 'chapter. It is usually dropped to a depth of two or three lines below the first line.

Initial caps Instruction to the printer to set the first letter of a word or phrase as a CAPITAL.

Ink duct The FOUNTAIN supplying ink to a printing press.

Ink jet printer A printing device attached to a computer, that uses high speed ink jets to form an image.

Ink squash A spread of ink outside the required details of an image, occurring during printing.

Inked art ARTWORK drawn up first in pencil for checking and then completed in ink.

Inkers The rollers on a printing press which apply to the type and block surfaces.

Inking roller A printing machine roller that carries ink from the FOUNTAIN to the plate of FORME.

Inline lettering TYPEFACE with a white line inside the shape, following the outline of the letter.

Inner forme The FORME that includes the pages of a CENTRE SPREAD.

Insert A SHEET or part of a sheet placed inside another which is not part of the book's normal PAGINATION.

Instant art Images or letters created by the use of dry transfer forms.

Intaglio A printing image below the surface of the plate.

Intensification Chemical methods of improving the DENSITY of a NEGATIVE.

Interlaying Placing SHEETS of paper between a printing plate and its block or MOUNT.

Interleaved (1) A book with blank leaves between the printed pages for handwritten notes. (2) A book with thin tissue inserted to protect the illustrations. (3) A plate with a thin LEAF bearing a descriptive caption pasted to its inner MARGIN.

Interlinear spacing The method of establishing space between lines of type in PHOTOCOMPOSITION.

Interlock An effect produced by joining together type CHARACTERS (1) in PHOTOCOMPOSITION.

Intermediate A transparent or TRANSLUCENT COPY of an ORIGINAL from which other copies can be made.

Internegative A photographic NEGATIVE forming the intermediate stage in making a print from a flat ORIGINAL.

ISBN *abb* International Standard Book Number. A reference number given to every published work, identifying area of origin, PUBLISHER, title and check control, encoded in a 10-digit number. A new ISBN is given to each new EDITION of a book.

Italic Type with sloping letters. Indicated by a single underline.

Ivory board A smooth white board used for ARTWORK and display printing.

●

Jacket The paper wrapper in which a book is sold.

Jaw folder A paper folder attached to a WEB-FED printing press, that cuts and folds a SIGNATURE.

Jobbing work Small everyday printing such as display cards, letter-headings, etc.

Job press A hand-fed, small scale printing press.

Jogging To vibrate paper stock to bring the edges into line before trimming. A jogger may be attached to a printing press or form a separate unit.

Joint The flexible part of a CASE between the boarded side and the SPINE.

Jump In a publication MATTER carried over to continue on a succeeding page.

Justification Spacing of words and letters so that each line of text finishes at the same point.

●

Keep down Instruction used in newspaper printing to keep text in LOWER CASE type.

Keep in An instruction to a COMPOSITOR to keep spaces narrow between words.

Keep out The opposite of KEEP IN, to use wide spaces between words.

Keep standing To keep plates ready for possible REPRINTS.

Keep up Instruction to keep text in UPPER CASE type.

Kern The part of a letter which overhangs the next.

Kerning Deliberate reduction of spacing between specified characters to improve the letter fit, legibility and evenness of a line of typesetting.

Key The block or plate containing the main outlines of the design. It acts as a guide for the position and registration of the other colours.

Keyboarding A term referring to the first procedure in PHOTOCOMPOSITION, that of typing in COPY to be recorded in the machine for setting.

Key letters/numbers (1) References used to key in COPY to a LAYOUT. (2) Numbers forming references between a technical drawing and description of parts in the CAPTION.

Keyline An outline drawing in ARTWORK that shows the size and position of an illustration or HALFTONE image.

Key plate see BLACK PRINTER.

Kiss impression An IMPRESSION (2) in which ink is put on paper by the lightest possible surface contact and not impressed into it. This technique is necessary when printing on COATED PAPERS.

Klischograph A German electronic PHOTOENGRAVING machine which produces a plastic, zinc, copper or magnesium HALFTONE plate.

Knocking up (UK) The adjustment on one or two edges of a pile of SHEETS so that they can be cut squarely.

Kraft paper Strong brown paper made from sulphate PULP. It is often used for packing books.

●

Lacquer A clear coating applied to the surface of a printed job to protect against marking and improve appearance. See VARNISH.

Laid paper Paper showing the wire marks of the mould or dandy roll used in manufacture.

Laminate To protect paper or card and give it a glossy surface by applying a transparent plastic coating through heat or pressure.

Landscape/horizontal format (UK/ US) An image in which the width is noticeable greater than the height.

Lap The slight overlapping of two printed colours to ensure there is no fault in the REGISTER. See also FATTY.

Larger face The larger version of type cast in two sizes on one BODY (1).

Latent image A photographically recorded image that can be made apparent by chemical processing.

Lateral reversal The transposing of an image from left to right, as in a mirror reflection. See also FLOP.

Latin A term for TYPEFACES derived from letter forms common to western European countries, especially those with heavy wedge-shaped SERIFS.

Latitude (pho) The range of EXPOSURES that all produce an acceptable image on a given type of film.

Lay edges The two edges of a SHEET which are placed FLUSH with the side and front lay gauges or marks on a printing machine to ensure that the sheet will be removed properly by the GRIPPERS, and have uniform MARGINS when printed.

Layout An outline or sketch which gives the general appearance of the printed page, indicating the relationship between text and illustration.

L

Layout paper Translucent tough paper used for paste-up or illustration at the rough stage.

Lead (1) Spaces less than type height which are used to space out HEADINGS and text. **(2)** The main story in a newspaper or the opening story.

Leaded Type which is set with LEADS (1) between the lines.

Leader line/rule A line on an image keyed into ANNOTATION (1).

Leaf (1) Refers to newly formed SHEETS of paper before they are dried and finished. **(2)** Each of the folios which result when a sheet of paper is folded. Each side of a leaf is called a page.

Leaf edge The opposite edge to the GRIPPER edge.

Letraset Proprietary name for DRY TRANSFER LETTERING on a plastic sheet that is rubbed down on paper or board in preparing ARTWORK, ANNOTATION (1) etc.

Letterpress A printing process. The image is raised and inked to produce an impression. It also refers to the text of a book, including line illustrations but excluding plates.

Letterset A term deriving from LETTERPRESS and OFFSET, describing a method of printing from a relief plate.

Letterspacing The insertion of space between the letters of a word to improve the appearance of a line of type.

Library binding BOOKBINDING strong enough to endure continual handling.

Library shot/pic A picture or illustration taken from an existing source, not specially commissioned.

Lift The number of SHEETS of paper that can be cut all together or handled in a single operation.

Lifted matter Type MATTER already set which is taken out of one job to be used in another.

Lifting see PICKING.

Light face The opposite of BOLD FACE.

Light-fast ink Ink that is not susceptible to fading colour when exposed to light over a period.

Light table/box A table or box with a TRANSLUCENT glass screen top illuminated from below, used for viewing or working with any photographically produced material — e.g., STRIPPING, RETOUCHING.

Limp binding A form of binding using a flexible COVER — e.g., paper, cloth or leather — and no board stiffener.

Line and halftone An illustration

process in which line and halftone NEGATIVES are combined into a plate and etched as a unit.

Line block A printing plate made of zinc or copper consisting of solid areas and lines. It is reproduced directly from a line drawing without tones. It is mounted on a wooden block to type height.

Line board A smoothly finished support suitable for line illustrations and ARTWORK.

Linecaster This is the generic term for all keyboard-operated slug-casting composing machines, LINOTYPE or Intertype.

Line conversion A photographic process of converting HALFTONE or CONTINUOUS TONE COPY into line images. Middle tones are eliminated to increase contrast.

Line copy COPY consisting of black line or solid masses on white, with no intermediate tones.

Line feed The measure, expressed in POINTS, of the movement of paper or film from one line to the next in PHOTOCOMPOSITION.

Line gauge The printer's rule. It is calibrated in PICAS and is 72 picas (11.952in) long.

Line increment The smallest allowable increase in the basic measure between lines in TYPESETTING.

Line interval The distance between the BASE LINES of following lines of type. Where metal type is used, the BODY SIZE dictates the interval.

Linen tester A magnifying glass designed for checking the detail of a HALFTONE DOT pattern.

Line original An original image prepared for line reproduction.

Line printer A printing device attached to a computer that prints one line at a time at very high speed.

Line up When two lines of type, or a line of type and a block, touch the same imaginary horizontal line.

Line weight The relative thickness of RULES or lines used in illustration.

Lining figures/numerals A set of numerals aligned at top and bottom.

Lining up/lineup table (UK/US) A table used in preparing and checking the ALIGNMENT of PASTE-UP, FLATS, etc. It has an illuminated top with a gridded surface and movable scales.

Linocut A RELIEF PRINTING surface of

linoleum on which the background to the design is cut away with a knife, gouge or engraving tool.

Linotype The first keyboard-operated composing machine to employ the principle of the circulating MATRIX (1) and cast type in solid lines or slugs. It was invented by the German/American engineer Ottmar Mergenthaler and first used in 1886.

Linting The adhesion of loose scraps from the surface of paper to the BLANKET CYLINDER in OFFSET printing. See also PICKING.

Lith film A film used in preparing PLATES in PHOTOCHEMICAL reproduction. It omits middle tones and increases contrasts.

Lithography Printing from a dampened, flat surface using greasy ink, based on the principle of the mutual repulsion of oil and water.

Live matter A FORME awaiting printing, stereotyping or electroplating.

Loading The addition of a substance such as china clay in papermaking, to give better opacity and finish.

Logic mode A method of automatic programming used in PHOTOCOMPOSITION that can be overriden by the keyboard operator if necessary.

Logotype A word of several letters cast as one unit.

Long descenders The DESCENDERS of a TYPEFACE that are extended compared to the usual design of the face.

Long ink Ink mixed to a consistency of flow that can be drawn out in a thread without breaking.

Long letters Type CHARACTERS (1) that extend right across the shank.

Long page A page with type extended by one or two lines to avoid an inconvenient break.

Look-/see-through (US/UK) The visibility of an image through paper when seen against the light.

Loose leaf A BINDING METHOD that allows the easy removal of individual leaves.

Lower case The small letters in a FOUNT of type.

Low key A photographic image given dark tones overall by the lighting or processing methods applied.

● **Machine composition** Methods of TYPESETTING involving the use of keyboard operated machines.

Machine direction The path of paper through a papermaking machine that dictates the GRAIN (1) of the paper.

Machine glazed paper Machine finished paper with a high gloss surface on one side.

Machine-made paper The continuous WEB of paper made on cylinder machines.

Machine proof A PROOF taken when corrections marked on the GALLEY PROOF and PAGE PROOF have been made and the FORME is on the printing machine. This is the last opportunity for correcting mistakes before the final printing.

Machine sheet A general term for any printed SHEET coming off the press.

Magic Markers Brand of felt-tip markers.

Magnet ink characters (com) CHARACTERS (1) printed in magnetizable ink which are readable both by humans and by appropriately equipped machines.

Main exposure The first exposure in the processing of a HALFTONE image.

Make-up (1) The SHEET indicating the placing of the various items on a page. **(2)** The actual assembling of the page.

Making A term referring to one whole batch of MACHINE-MADE PAPER.

Making ready In printing, the surface on which the paper or plate rests has to be built up in places to given overall evenness of impression. This is called making ready, the build-up backing is known as make ready.

Manilla A tough, buff coloured paper used in the manufacture of stationery.

Marbling Decorative paper used for binding books and sometimes the book EDGES. It is done by dipping the SHEET in a bath of colours floating on a surface of gum. The colours do not mix but can be combined into patterns with the use of a comb, and transfer readily to the paper.

Marching display A display unit used in PHOTOCOMPOSITION allowing the operator to check the most recent INPUT up to about 40 CHARACTERS (1).

Margins The blank areas on a printed page which surround the MATTER.

Marked proof The PROOF, usually on GALLEYS, supplied to the author for correction. It contains the corrections and queries made by the printer's READER.

Mark up To mark up is to specify every detail needed for the COMPOSITOR to set the COPY.

Mask (1) A material used to block out part of an image in photography, illustration or LAYOUT. **(2)** A photographic image modified in tone or colour.

Masking (1) Applying a protective layer to an illustration to cover an area while other parts are painted or AIRBRUSHED. **(2)** Blocking out part of an image with opaque material to prevent reproduction or to allow for alteration in COPY. **(3)** A technical method of adjusting values of colour and tone in PHOTOMECHANICAL reproduction.

Masking film A transparent film with a low-tack adhesive backing widely used in airbrushing. The mask can be cut in position on the surface, allowing greater accuracy.

Masking tape Tape coated with a low-tack adhesive. It can be used as a mask and is ideal for attaching transparencies to layouts because it can be peeled off.

Master cylinder The cylinder of a printing press that transfers ink from reservoir to plate.

Master plate The plate containing the image for OFFSET printing.

Master proof A printer's PROOF read and marked with corrections and queries.

Matrix (1) The brass DIES used in HOT METAL composition. **(2)** The impression in papier mâché taken from a page of type for stereotyping and the stereotyper's FLONG after moulding.

Matt art A clay-coated printing paper with a dull finish.

Matter Either MANUSCRIPT or COPY to be printed, or type that is composed.

Mean line The imagined line showing the top limit of X-HEIGHT.

Measure The width of a setting, usually measured in PICA EMS.

Mechanical (US) A term for CAMERA-READY COPY or ARTWORK.

Mechanical binding BINDING METHOD securing leaves through punched or drilled holes by means of a metal or plastic device, for permanent or LOOSE LEAF binding.

Mechanical pulp Untreated paper pulp used as the basis of NEWSPRINT and low quality papers.

Mechanical tints DOT or line patterns that can be laid down on ARTWORK before or during reproduction processing.

Medallion An illustration printed on paper, pasted to the front of the CASE of a book.

Medium (1) A standard size of printing paper 18 × 23in (457 × 585mm). **(2)** The liquid, usually linseed oil, in which the pigment of a printing ink is dispersed. **(3)** An alternative name for BENDAY tint. **(4)** The weight of TYPEFACE midway between light and bold.

Metallic ink A printing ink which produces an effect of gold, silver, copper or bronze.

Mezzotint INTAGLIO printing process producing a range of tones.

Microfilm The sensitized vehicle for recording of MICROFORMS.

Microform An image reproduced photographically on an extremely small scale. It may be positive or negative, transparent or opaque. Microforms are generally used to store published information without bulk and can be read through equipment specially designed to enlarge the images to a legible form.

Microimage see MICROFORM.

Middle space In handset type, a standard word space measuring one quarter of an EM.

Mill brand The trademark and brand name of the manufacturer.

Mill ream A bulk quantity of handmade or MOULDMADE PAPER (472 SHEETS).

Millboards Strong grey or black boards of good quality used for the COVERS of a book.

Minus leading/linespacing see NEGATIVE LINESPACING.

Mixing The combination of TYPEFACE designs and sizes contained in a single PHOTO MATRIX.

Mock-up The rough visualization of a publication or packaging design showing size, colour, type, etc.

Modern face A TYPEFACE with vertical stress, strong stroke contrast and unbracketed fine SERIFS.

Moiré A printing fault where HALFTONES appear as a mechanical pattern of DOTS.

Mono adoption A single-coloured image taken from a full-colour original.

Monochrome An image made up of varying tones but in only one colour.

Monograph A publication dealing with a single person or subject.

Monophoto The trade name of the PHOTOCOMPOSITION system produced by the manufacturers of MONOTYPE.

Monotype (1) The trade name for composing machines which cast single

types. **(2)** The process of making a painting on glass or metal and then taking an IMPRESSION **(2)** on paper. Only one impression can be taken.

Montage Assembling portions of several drawings or photographs to form a single ORIGINAL.

Mordant An adhesive for fixing gold leaf. It is also any fluid used to etch lines on a printing plate.

Morocco Tanned goat-skin which is finished by glazing or polishing and used in BOOKBINDING.

Mottling An uneven IMPRESSION **(2)**, especially in flat areas. It is usually caused by too much pressure or unsuitable paper or ink.

Mould A flat impressed SHEET made by beating or pressing a FLONG onto a type, for casting a STEREOTYPE.

Mouldmade paper A manufactured, imitation handmade paper.

Mount The base used to support a printing plate and bring it type high.

Mounting and flapping A method of presentation for ARTWORK, involving mounting the finished work on strong board and protecting the surface with a hinged SHEET of CELLULOSE ACETATE or tissue.

Mounting board A heavy board used for mounting photographs or ARTWORK.

Movable type The principle of an old fashioned method of TYPESETTING in which single pieces of type were used rather than slugs.

Mull Coarse variety of muslin which forms the first lining of a CASE BOUND book. Also known as scrim.

Multiple exposure In photography, stages of the same subject or separate images superimposed to form one image in EXPOSURE or PROCESSING.

Multiple flats FLATS used in printing successive pages where it is required that some elements of the design are matched from page to page.

Multi-ring binder BINDING METHOD using a number of closely spaced rings to secure leaves.

Multisheet drawing ARTWORK requiring more than one drawing to make up the whole image.

Munsell colour system A system of colour measurement and notation that defines all colours in terms of hue, value and CHROMA.

Mutton, mutt The term for an EM QUAD.

Neck line The amount of white or leading under a RUNNING HEAD.

Needle printer A computer output device printing CHARACTERS **(1)** based on a dot matrix.

Negative Photographic film that has been exposed and processed to fix a reverse tone or colour image from which POSITIVE **(1)** prints can be made.

Negative line feed see REVERSE LINE FEED.

Negative line spacing In PHOTOCOMPOSITION, a LINE INTERVAL smaller than the POINT size of the type.

Newsprint The paper used for printing newspapers, characteristically absorbent because it is unsized.

Next reading/text matter An instruction to place advertisement COPY next to editorial copy in a publication.

Nickel facing A deposit applied to blocks, usually STEREOTYPES, which gives a harder and longer-lasting surface.

Nipping Pressing a book after sewing but before FORWARDING. This flattens the BOLTS and expels air from between the SHEETS.

Non-counting keyboard A keyboard used in PHOTOCOMPOSITION that does not provide the operator with details for making END OF LINE DECISIONS.

Non-impact printing PRINTOUTS produced without a plate or cylinder — e.g., by a writing head.

Non-lining figures/numerals A set of numerals designed with DESCENDERS, therefore not of standard height and ALIGNMENT as are LINING FIGURES.

Nonpareil The name of an old type size (approximately equal to 6 POINTS). It is still used as an alternative term to indicate spacing.

Not A finish in high quality RAG PAPERS, which is midway between ROUGH and HOT-PRESSED.

Octavo A SHEET of paper folded in half three times, to make eighths or sixteen pages. It also refers to a standard BROADSIDE divided into eight parts.

Off-line Work done in relation to a computer process but not as direct use of the computer.

Offprint A REPRINT of an article or other part of a publication produced as a separate item.

Offset lithography A method of lithography by which the image is not

O printed direct from the plate but 'offset' first onto a rubber covered cylinder, the BLANKET, which performs the printing operation.

Offside The part of the CASE which comes at the end of the book.

Old face/old style *(US)* Type form characterized by diagonal stress and sloped, bracketed SERIFS.

On-line Interconnected functions in computer work under the direct control of a central computer.

Onion skin A thin, TRANSLUCENT paper with a glazed finished used for carbon copies and OVERLAYS.

Opacity The term used to describe non-transparency in printing papers.

Opaline A semi-opaque paper, fine and with a highly glazed finish.

Opaquing To paint out unwanted areas in a NEGATIVE with opaque solution before processing the image.

Optical alignment An arrangement of CHARACTERS (1) allowing a degree of projection on the left-hand MARGIN so the main strokes of the letters are aligned.

Optical centre A point within a rectangle slightly higher than the actual geometric centre, at which an object or image appears to be centrally placed.

Optical character recognition (OCR) Device for the electronic scanning of COPY and its conversion into photoset MATTER without keyboard operation.

Optical/optically even spacing The adjustment of letterspaces between CHARACTERS (1) to give an even appearance to a line of type.

Order *(US)* The relative importance of HEADINGS in a text, determining the style in which they are set.

Orphan A single work that stands at the top of a page when COPY has been set.

Orthochromatic Refers to photographic materials sensitive to green and yellow as well as blue light.

Outer forme The FORME containing MATTER, for the outer pages of a folded SECTION.

Outline letters TYPEFACES in which the letters are formed of outlines rather than solid strokes.

Overexposure A fault caused when the light source is too close to the VACUUM FRAME.

Overhang cover A book COVER that projects past the trimmed edges of the leaves.

Overhead projector A machine for projecting images drawn on a transparent ACETATE slide or roll, by passing the image through an overhead lens and turning it through 90 degrees on to a flat surface.

Overlay (1) A transparent SHEET used in the preparation of multicolour ARTWORK. **(2)** A TRANSLUCENT SHEET covering a piece of ORIGINAL ARTWORK, on which instructions may be written.

Overmatter MATTER set which does not come within the appropriate space.

Overprint Printing over an already printed area.

Overs, overruns Paper issued beyond the bare requirements to allow for MAKING READY, SPOILS, etc. It also refers to the quantity produced above the ordered number.

Oversize A description of COPY made at a larger size than that intended in reproduction.

Ozalid A trade name referring to a method of copying PAGE PROOFS by the DIAZO process.

●

Packing To place paper under a PLATE or BLANKET in printing to ensure firm contact of surfaces to produce an even quality of print.

Page frame A page printed with details, such as a FIGURE NUMBER, page number or RUNNING HEAD, leaving space for an illustration to be inserted.

Page make up (1) See MAKE UP. **(2)** In PHOTOCOMPOSITION, a display showing COPY as it will appear on a page.

Page printer A COMPUTER OUTPUT DEVICE capable of printing a complete page at high speed. See also LINE PRINTER.

Page proofs PROOFS of type which have been PAGINATED. It refers to the secondary stage in proofing, after GALLEY PROOFS and before MACHINE PROOFS.

Pages to view The number of pages visible on one side of a SHEET that has been printed on both sides.

Pagination The term given to numbering the pages of a book.

Pallet (1) A wooden storage device on which SHEETS of paper are stacked. **(2)** The brass finishing tool used for impressing straight lines on COVERS. **(3)** A small hand-tool in which letters are placed and heated to stamp the COVER of a book.

Panchromatic Photographic material which is sensitive to all visible colours and to ultraviolet light.

Pantograph An instrument for copying a design. The COPY can be the same size, reduced or enlarged.

Pantone Matching System A registered trade name for a system of colour matching in designer's materials such as inks, papers, marker pens. Known as PMS.

Paper plate A photosensitized plate used in OFFSET printing for short RUNS, on which MATTER can be typed or drawn.

Paper to paper see FOLD TO PAPER.

Paperback A book with a soft outer COVER made of paper.

Parallel A type CHARACTER (1) in the form of a double vertical bar, used as a reference mark for FOOTNOTES.

Parallel fold A SHEET (1) folded in half widthways and then in half again, the second fold parallel to the first.

Parallel motion A drawing board that holds counterweights and has a straight edge to ensure accurate measurement and positioning.

Parchment Goat or sheepskin, scraped and dressed with lime and pumice and used for writing on.

Paring In hand-binding, paring is thinning and chamfering the edges of leather to give a neat turn-in over the boards.

Pass The full operational cycle of a machine used in printing or PHOTOCOMPOSITION.

Pastel Drawing material in the form of sticks made from PIGMENT bound in glue and allowed to harden.

Paste-up A LAYOUT of a number of pages used to plan the positioning of ILLUSTRATIONS, CAPTIONS and TEXT.

Pasting in/on see TIPPED ON.

Peculiars Type CHARACTERS (1) for non-standard accent-bearing letters used when setting certain foreign languages.

Perfect binding A binding method in which the leaves of a book are trimmed at the back and glued, but not sewn.

Perfecting see BACK-UP.

Perfecting press, perfector A press which prints both sides of the paper at a single PASS. All LETTERPRESS rotaries and WEB-OFFSET machines are perfectors.

Perforate (1) Print perforation is to make broken slotted rules so that MATTER can be torn off. **(2)** Pin-hole perforation is to punch holes – e.g., in postage stamps.

Perspective Systems of drawing objects in three-dimensional representation on the basis of a fixed point, or points of view.

Photocomposition The production of DISPLAY LINE and text by photographic means on film or paper. Photocomposing machines assemble lines of letters from various forms of PHOTO MATRIX.

Photocopy A COPY produced immediately from an ORIGINAL by one of several methods involving photographic techniques.

Photodirect The description of a method of producing plates for PHOTOLITHOGRAPHY from ORIGINAL ARTWORK without an INTERNEGATIVE being made.

Photoengraving A PHOTOMECHANICAL method of producing etched line or HALFTONE plates.

Photogram An image made by the direct action of light on sensitized paper.

Photograph A representational image formed by the action of light on a sensitized material.

Photogravure The process of printing from a PHOTOMECHANICALLY prepared surface, which holds the ink in recessed cells.

Photoheadliner A machine designed to arrange display type and produce an image by photographic methods.

Photolithography A method of lithographic printing in which the image is transferred to the plate photographically and printed on a lithographic printing machine. This is sometimes known as OFFSET.

Photomechanical (1) Methods of making printing PLATES that involve photographic techniques. **(2)** The assembly of type or illustrations for transfer to a printing plate.

Photomechanical transfer An extremely versatile process camera with functions that include changing black to white and vice versa, converting colour to black and white, and producing screened HALFTONES. The standard is high enough for use in ARTWORK. Commonly known as PMT.

Photomicrography A technique of photographing minute objects using a combination of camera and microscope.

Photomontage The use of images from different photographs combined to produce a new composite image.

Photo-opaque A general term for opaque solutions used to paint out parts of process NEGATIVES.

Photopolymer plates Sensitized plastic plates on which NEGATIVES can be printed down; a RELIEF PRINTING surface is formed by a chemical WASH-OUT. PHOTOCOMPOSED pages can thus be converted into LETTERPRESS printing surfaces, either by printing direct from the photopolymer plate or moulding from it to make STEREOTYPE PLATES.

Photoprint (1) In PHOTOCOMPOSITION, a PROOF of type MATTER of suitable quality for reproduction. **(2)** A print of an image produced photographically.

Photosensitive A material treated chemically to become light-sensitive.

Pica The old name for 12 POINTS, the unit of measurement used in setting.

Picking Lifting of small scraps of the paper surface in printing caused by tacky ink or poor quality paper.

Pigment Finely ground solid matter forming the colouring agent of paints and printing inks.

Pinhole An unexposed speck on a photographic NEGATIVE, sometimes caused by dust on a lens or film.

Planographic Methods of printing from a flat surface, as in LITHOGRAPHY

Plastic film Materials used for lamination and packaging, such as CELLOPHANE, varying in properties such as thickness and flexibility.

Plate (1) An electro or stereo of set-up type. **(2)** A sheet of metal bearing a design, from which an IMPRESSION **(2)** is printed. **(3)** A full page book illustration, printed separately from the text often on different paper. **(4)** A photographic plate; a whole plate measures 8½ × 6½in (216 ×165mm), a half plate measures 6½ × 4in (165 × 102mm).

Plate cylinder On a printing press, the cylinder that supports the inked plate.

Platen press A printing press in which a flat plate, or platen, is lowered and pressed against a horizontal FORME.

Plot To mark the main reference points on a GRID or GRAPH.

Plugging A condition in platemaking when COPY is marked or damaged and DOT areas have filled in.

Ply A measurement of the thickness of board stock, deriving from the number of layers in the composition of a SHEET.

Point Standard unit of type size. In the British-American system it is 0.013888in, or 72 to the inch. The Continental (DIDOT) point is calculated differently.

Point of sale The term for display equipment and advertising matter placed in a sales area close to the commodity it describes.

Polaroid A trade name of photographic materials capable of self development. The term also covers equipment used with such materials.

Portrait An upright image or page.

Positive (1) An image made photographically on paper or film, usually derived from a NEGATIVE. **(2)** A photographic colour TRANSPARENCY or film with a positive image used in platemaking.

Posterization A method of separating the tones of a CONTINUOUS TONE ORIGINAL, making one NEGATIVE for each grade of flat tone. The series of negatives is then reassembled to form a composite print.

Powderless etching A process which gives a faithful reproduction, greater depth between the fine lines and a smooth, even shoulder. The plates print well, and are ideal for subsequent electro or stereotyping.

Prelims, preliminary matter The pages preceding the BODY **(2)** of a book. They usually consist of half title, title, preface and contents.

Pre-make-ready The checking and preparation of printing plates or FORMES before they are made ready on the press.

Preprint (1) Any MATTER printed separately and pasted to CAMERA-READY COPY or ARTWORK. **(2)** A SHEET, or sheets, printed in advance of a publication to form a loose INSERT in bound copies.

Presentation visual Material prepared as a sample of the proposed appearance of a printed work. Also called a FINISHED ROUGH, it may consist of drawings, typeset COPY, photographically produced prints, or a combination of such elements.

Press proof The last PROOF to be read before giving authorization for printing.

Press run In the printing of a publication, the total number of copies produced in one printing.

Primary colours Pure colours from which all other colours can be mixed. In SUBTRACTIVE COLOUR MIXING, used in printing, they are magenta, cyan and yellow. The primary colours of light, or ADDITIVE COLOURS, are red, blue and green.

Printing down frame see VACUUM FRAME.

Printing processes The main classes of printing processes are INTAGLIO, PLANOGRAPHIC, RELIEF and STENCIL. All these rely on the contact of surfaces under pressure.

Printmaking A term referring to printing processes used in making fine art print editions.

Print origination In printing, all preparatory work completed prior to proofing.

Printout (1) *(com)* A general term for the record of information made by a printing device attached to a computer. **(2)** An enlarged COPY made from a MICROFORM.

Print run The number of copies required from a printer and the process of printing the copies.

Print to paper An instruction to print a quantity according to the supply of paper available without fixing the number of copies required.

Process camera A camera designed for process work in PHOTOMECHANICAL reproduction techniques.

Process colours Cyan, magenta and yellow. See PRIMARY COLOURS.

Process engraving The name given to several PHOTOMECHANICAL methods of producing relief blocks or plates for printing illustrations.

Process inks Printer's inks in the PROCESS COLOURS.

Process white An opaque white GOUACHE for correction and MASKING **(2)** of ARTWORK intended for reproduction.

Progressive proofs The PROOFS taken in colour printing as a guide to shade and registration. Each colour is shown separately and also imposed on the preceding colour.

Promotion Presentation and advertising intended to encourage the production and marketing of a product.

Proof An IMPRESSION **(2)** obtained from an inked plate, stone, screen, block or type in order to check the progress and accuracy of the work. It is also called a pull.

Proof correction marks A standard set of signs and symbols commonly understood by all those involved in preparing COPY for publication.

Proof reader A person who reads PROOFS to correct and revise COPY where necessary.

Proofing press A press, sometimes hand-operated, usually smaller than that used in the full PRINT RUN, on which COPY is proofed.

Proportonal spacing A method of

spacing CHARACTERS **(1)** in COLD COMPOSITION, to accommodate the different widths of the letters and figures.

Publisher's ream A bulk quantity of paper (516) SHEETS.

Pull see PROOF.

Pull out see FOLD OUT.

Pull out section Pages of a periodical that can be detached altogether and kept as a separate entity.

Pulp The basic material used in papermaking, broken down chemically or mechanically.

Punch register A device used in close REGISTER work, requiring holes punched in COPY, film or plate so they can be assembled on register pins.

Put down/up An instruction to the printer to change CHARACTERS **(1)** to LOWERCASE (down) or CAPS (up).

Put to bed The state of printing plates or FORMES when they are secured to the press ready to print.

●

Quad Four times the normal paper size — 35 × 45in (890 × 1143mm).

Quadding Filling out a line of type by extending spaces with EN or EM QUADS.

Quarter-bound A case-book using a stronger material for the back than the sides.

Quarto A piece of paper folded in half twice, making quarters or eight pages.

Quire 24 or 25 SHEETS of paper or ¹⁄₂₀th of a REAM.

Quires, quire stock The SHEETS of a book which are printed but not folded.

●

RA paper sizes The designation of untrimmed paper sizes in the series of INTERNATIONAL PAPER SIZES.

R-type A direct process of producing photographic colour prints, developed by Kodak. R19 is the production of a print from ARTWORK. R14 from a TRANSPARENCY.

Ragged left/right Typeset COPY in which the lines of type are not aligned at left/right. See UNJUSTIFIED.

Rag paper High quality writing paper made from rag PULP.

Raised point/dot *(typ)* A point printed at half the height of CAPITALS rather than on the BASE LINE.

Ranged left/right A form of setting in which lines of unequal length form a vertical either on the lefthand side of the COLUMN **(1)** or the right.

Ranging figures see LINING FIGURES.

R

R

Rapidograph Brand of technical pens.

Reader screen A display device for the enlargement of MICROFORMS.

Ream 500 SHEETS of paper.

Rear projection see BACK PROJECTION.

Reducer A chemical which acts upon a photographic image to reduce its intensity.

Reel-fed see WEB-FED.

Reflection copy (US) COPY/ARTWORK which is reproduced by photographic means, using light reflected from its surface.

Register The correct ALIGNMENT of pages with the MARGINS in order. It is also the correct positioning of one colour on another in colour printing.

Register marks In colour printing, the crosses, triangles and other devices used to position the paper correctly.

Registered design A design officially registered by a PATENT office, to give some protection against plagiarism.

Relief printing Printing methods in which the image is obtained from a raised surface. See FLEXOGRAPHY, LETTERPRESS, LINO-CUT, WOODCUT, WOOD ENGRAVING.

Relief stamping see DIE STAMPING.

Reprint The second or subsequent printing of a publication.

Reproduction copy see CAMERA READY.

Reproduction proof/repro High quality PROOFS on art paper which can be used as ARTWORK.

Reprographic printing Techniques of copying or duplicating printed material.

Resin coated paper Paper for photographic printing in which the sensitized surface is strengthened with a layer of polyethylene.

Retouching Methods of altering the image in ARTWORK or photography, to make corrections, improve or change the character of the image.

Retree A term referring to a batch of paper that is of substandard quality.

Retroussage The term given to flicking a soft rag lightly over a wiped INTAGLIO PLATE, to draw out the ink slightly and give a softer line.

Reversal film (1) Colour film producing a positive image. **(2)** A contact film reproducing the tonal values of an original image.

Reverse b to w *abb* Reverse black to white. An instruction to the printer to reverse the tones of an image.

Reverse indent see HANGING INDENT.

Reverse leading/line feed In PHOTOCOMPOSITION the device for returning to a line already set on film or paper to add in COPY.

Reverse out see SAVE OUT.

Reverse reading COPY that reads backwards as it may appear on a LETTERPRESS printing surface. It is the opposite of RIGHT READING.

Rider roller Printing press cylinder that rotates under the force of another cylinder.

Right-angle/chopper fold (UK/US) The standard method of folding a SECTION **(1)**. A SHEET is folded in half, then halved again at right angles to the first fold.

Right reading COPY that reads as normal — e.g., text reading from left to right.

Ring binder A mechanical binding device in which leaves are secured through punched holes by means of metal rings.

RIP *abb* Rest in proportion. Instruction in SIZING UP ARTWORK or photographs where the other dimensions or images are to be reduced or enlarged in proportion to a given dimension.

Rivers The streaks of white spacing produced when spaces in consecutive lines of type coincide.

Roll stand A stand supporting the WEB of a WEB-FED printing press.

Roman Ordinary vertical type as distinct from ITALIC.

Rotary press A REEL- or WEB-FED newspaper press which uses a cylindrical printing surface. The papers are delivered folded and counted, ready to be dispatched.

Rotogravure INTAGLIO printing performed on a ROTARY PRESS.

Round and back Refers to a concave appearance at the FOREDGE of a book and a convex back with a projecting SHOULDER.

Router A machine which uses a rotating cutter to remove the superfluous parts of a wood or metal HALFTONE block.

Royal A size of printing paper 20 × 25in (508 × 635mm).

Ruling pen A drawing instrument with two tapering metal fingers between which ink or paint is held.

Runaround Text set to fit around an illustration smaller than page or COLUMN width.

Run-in heading A HEADING leading into text starting in the same line, as distinct from a heading placed above text.

Runners Numbers placed in the MARGIN of a text to form references for identifying particular lines.

Running head The line of type which repeats a chapter HEADING, etc., at the top of a page.

Running text A BODY of text which runs over from one page to another even when there are breaks for illustrations and diagrams.

Run of paper (1) See PRINT TO PAPER. **(2)** position of advertising matter in a newspaper or periodical which gives no display advantages.

Run of press Colour printing included as a standard feature of printing for newspapers, journals or trade publications.

Run on Instruction to printer that the text is continuous and no new paragraph is to be made.

Run ragged see RAGGED RIGHT.

Run through work The printing of even parallel lines across a SHEET, using a machine designed for the purpose.

●

Saddle-stitch/wire A method of stitching brochures: they are opened over a saddle-shaped support and stitched through the back.

Sans serif A TYPEFACE without SERIFS and usually without stroke contrast.

Satin finish A smoothly finished paper with a sheen to the surface.

Save out Also called reverse out, to reproduce text, lettering or line illustration as a white image on a solid or HALFTONE ground, by PHOTOMECHANICAL techniques.

Scaling, scaling up To determine the degree of enlargement or reduction necessary to reproduce an original image within a given area of a design. The scaling may be represented as a percentage of the image area or in figures proportionate to the dimensions of the original, using a diagonal bisection of the image to govern the increased or reduced measurements.

Scamp A rough sketch showing the basic idea for an advertisement or design.

Scanner A device used in PHOTOMECHANICAL reproduction to identify electronically the density of colours in an image for COLOUR SEPARATION.

Scatter proofs PROOFS for checking the quality of illustrations in PHOTOMECHANICAL reproduction. To reduce proofing costs, as many images as possible are proofed altogether, with no reference to correct positions in a LAYOUT.

Score To make a crease in paper or card so that it will not be damaged by folding.

Scraperboard/scratchboard (UK/US) A prepared board with a gesso surface. First it is inked and then scraped or scratched with a point or blade to give the effect of a white line engraving.

Screen see HALFTONE SCREEN.

Screen angle The position of a HALFTONE SCREEN as arranged in converting images to HALFTONE when two or more must be overprinted to avoid MOIRÉ.

Screen clash A disruptive pattern in an image produced when two or more HALFTONE SCREENS have been positioned at incorrect angles.

Screen printing Printing method in which ink is forced through the fine mesh of a fabric or metal screen. The image is formed by a stencil made photographically on the screen or a cut stencil that adheres to the screen fabric.

Screen ruling The grid on a CONTACT or HALFTONE SCREEN.

Screen tester A device for identifying the screen size used in a printed HALFTONE image.

Scumming A condition when the non-printing areas of a PHOTOMECHANICAL PLATE attract ink and transfer it to paper.

Second cover The page area on the inside of the front COVER of a publication.

Secondary colours Colours obtained when two PRIMARY COLOURS are mixed.

Section (1) A SHEET folded to create four or more book pages. See also SIGNATURE. **(2)** (US) A division of a publication, either smaller than a chapter or consisting of more than one chapter.

Section-sewn book A book in which SECTIONS **(1)** are sewn together with thread after GATHERING.

See through see LOOK/SEE THROUGH.

Self cover A book with a COVER of the same paper stock and printed at the same time as the leaves.

Self-ends ENDPAPERS formed from a LEAF from the first SECTION **(1)** at the front, and the last section at the back of a book.

Self quadder A mechanism of LINOTYPE machines providing automatic QUADDING.

Separation artwork ARTWORK in which a separate layer is created for each colour to be printed.

Sepia toning A method of changing black-and-white photographic prints to sepia (brown) tones with chemical bleach and dye.

Serif The small terminal stroke at the end of the main stroke of a letter.

Set (1) The width of a type BODY (1). **(2)** It is used as an instruction in 'set to 12 PICAS' or as a description — e.g. 'handset'. **(3)** It has a special sense to describe the proportions of the EM of a size of type.

Set and hold An instruction to the printer to set MATTER in readiness for future use.

Set close Describes type set with the minimum of space between the words and no extra space between sentences.

Set off (1) The accidental transference of an image from one SHEET to the back of the next impression. **(2)** In LITHOGRAPHY, it refers to an impression taken from a KEY outline of a design which is powdered with a non-greasy dye while the ink is damp, then placed on the stone or plate and passed through the press.

Set solid refers to type set without leading (line spaces).

Sewn book Any book, the SECTIONS (1) of which have been sewn together with thread.

Sexto, 6to A SHEET trimmed or folded to one sixth its basic size.

Shaded letter *(typ)* **(1)** Letterforms, such as OUTLINE LETTERS, given a three-dimensional appearance by heavy shadows beside the main strokes. **(2)** Letterforms filled with hatched lines rather than solid tone.

Sheet A single piece of paper.

Sheeter a device that cuts SHEETS from a WEB in a WEB-FED printing press.

Sheet-fed A printing machine into which SHEETS are fed singly.

Sheetwise Printing the pages of a SECTION (1) by printing first one side, then the other of a SHEET.

Sheet work The SECTIONS (1) of a book printed by backing up a SHEET with a different FORME from the front.

Short ink Printing ink with a heavy texture that does not flow easily.

Short page A page with text shorter than usual length, adjusted to improve the LAYOUT or accommodate a break.

Shoulder The projection down each side of a book's SPINE, obtained by ROUNDING AND BACKING.

Shoulder notes The marginal notes at the top outer corners of a paragraph.

Show through The fault in which a printed impression on one side of the paper is visible on the other side through the paper.

Side-stab/stitch A method of securing the SECTIONS (1) of a book, with wires passed through close to the BACK.

Signature The letter at the TAIL of the first page of each SECTION (1) in a book, running in alphabetical order, which serves as a guide to the binder in GATHERING.

Silhouette halftone A HALFTONE image in which background tones have been reduced or eliminated to emphasize the outline of an object.

Silkscreen printing SCREEN PRINTING using a screen made of silk, the traditional method often still used in printing fine art editions.

Single-colour press A printing press that has the facility to print only one colour at a time, requiring separate runs for prints of more than one colour.

Single printing Printing a SHEET on both sides by the WORK AND TUMBLE or WORK AND TURN methods.

Sixteen mo, 16mo A SHEET folded or trimmed to one-sixteenth its basic size.

Sixteen sheet A standard poster size measuring 120 × 80in (3050 × 2030mm).

Size A gelatinous solution used to coat paper, to glaze or seal the surface and render the paper less porous. Size may be based on glue, casein or a similar substance.

Size/sizing up see SCALING UP.

Slab serifs Square serifs of almost the same thickness as the uprights, used in most EGYPTIAN TYPEFACES.

Slip The broad strip of paper on which a GALLEY PROOF is printed.

Slip case An open sided CASE to hold one or more books, with their SPINES showing.

Slip page A GALLEY PROOF containing MATTER for one page.

Slit A cut made on the printing press by a rotary knife between IMPRESSION CYLINDER and delivery.

Sloped roman A TYPEFACE commonly termed ITALIC but actually a sloping version of ROMAN type.

Slur This results from movement between type and paper during IMPRESSION **(2)**.

Small capitals Capital letters which are smaller than the standard and usually aligned with the ordinary line of type. They are indicated by a double underlining in manuscript.

Soft A description of photographic paper that produces an image with low tonal contrast.

Soft copy (1) In PHOTOCOMPOSITION, the COPY displayed to the keyboard operator on a viewing screen. **(2)** *(US)* Typed copy used for checking a text before CAMERA READY copy is produced.

Soft cover A book COVER which is neither a CASE nor a SELF COVER. See also PAPERBACK.

Soft dot A HALFTONE DOT with a soft EMULSION, and thus softer edges, which makes ETCHING correction easier.

Solarization A method of creating photographic prints which are part positive and negative, by exposing the PHOTOSENSITIVE material to light during processing of a negative or print.

Space A non-printing graded unit for spacing out a line of type.

Spaceband In mechanical methods of TYPESETTING, a wedge-shaped piece used to vary the space between words.

Special sort Type CHARACTERS (1) not normally included in a FOUNT — e.g., fractions, musical symbols, etc.

Specification, spec A description of the components, characteristics and procedures of a particular job, product or activity.

Spine The centre of the CASE of a book which runs down the BACK when it is cased in.

Spiral binder A spiral wire holding the leaves of a book together.

Spirit duplicating A method of printing up to 100 copies from a master image typed or drawn directly on a SHEET backed with aniline dye. COPY paper damped with a spirit solvent is placed in direct contact with the master sheet to transfer the dye image.

Split boards Boards used for LIBRARY BINDING. A thick and thin board are pasted together, leaving a split about 1½in (37.5mm) wide for inserting END PAPERS and tapes.

Split duct/fountain A FOUNTAIN supplying inks of more than one colour to a printing press for simultaneous printing on one SHEET.

Spoils/spoilage Badly printed SHEETS which are discarded before delivery of a job.

Spotting RETOUCHING of photographic prints to cover tiny spots and blemishes affecting the image.

Spraygun A painting tool that emits a fine spray of liquid medium, paint or ink, similar in effect to an AIRBRUSH but a larger and less delicate instrument.

Sprinkled edges The edges or top of a book speckled with splashes of colour.

Square The portion of the inside of a CASE which projects beyond the CUT EDGES of a book.

Square back book A binding which is collated and sewn, but not ROUNDED AND BACKED.

Squared-up halftone A HALFTONE image confined to a rectangular shape.

SRA paper sizes The designation of untrimmed paper for bled work in the series of INTERNATIONAL PAPER SIZES.

Standing type/matter/forme Type MATTER composed by any method, that is held for reprinting if required.

Stem The most distinctive vertical stroke, or that closest to vertical, in a type CHARACTER **(1)**.

Stencil duplication A simple method for printing a relatively small number of copies using a paper stencil cut on a typewriter or with a scribe.

Step and repeat A PHOTOMECHANICAL method of using negative or positive images to produce a repeated image.

Stereotype plate A duplicate LETTERPRESS plate made by casting from a MOULD.

Stiff leaves END PAPERS attached by glue to the full width of the first and last leaves of a book.

Stipple A mechanical method of obtaining a background which could not be achieved by hand in the original. These areas are indicated by blue shading on the original.

Stock (1) The metal part of a printing roller, covered with COMPOSITION. **(2)** The printer's term for paper, etc. to be used for printing.

Stop out A chemical treatment for printing plates that removes any unwanted COPY or marks.

Storyboard A series of illustrations, rather like a comic strip, which represents a sequence of events that will eventually be filmed.

Strap/strapline A subheading that appears above the main HEADLINE of a newspaper or magazine story.

S

Strawboard A thick board manufactured from straw PULP, sometimes used to make the CASE of a book.

Stress The apparent direction of a letterform, given emphasis by the heaviest part of a curved stroke.

Strike-on composition see DIRECT IMPRESSION.

Strike through The effect of printing ink soaking right through a SHEET.

Stripping Assembling two or more images to produce a composite or multiple image for PHOTOMECHANICAL reproduction.

Stripping up as one Assembling two or more images to combine them into a single image for PHOTOMECHANICAL reproduction.

Subhead The HEADING for the division of a chapter.

Subject Term for any image which is to be reproduced or originated.

Subtractive colour mixing The reproduction of colours by overprinting PRIMARY COLOURS in different relative densities, thus gradually subtracting the reflection of light from the white of the paper.

Suction feed Mechanical paper feeding device using air suction to pass paper into a press or machine.

Super-calendered paper Smooth-surfaced paper produced by rolling it between metal CALENDERS or rollers.

Superior figure/letter Small figures or letters set above normal CHARACTERS (1) as in $12^2 = 144$.

Surprinting (1) (US) see OVERPRINT. **(2)** (US) The addition of line ARTWORK to a plate already bearing a HALFTONE image.

Swash characters OLD FACE ITALIC types with calligraphic flourishes.

Swatch A colour specimen supplied to the printer to which the ink can be matched.

Swell Extra bulking at the back of a book caused by the way the SECTIONS (1) have been sewn together.

Swelled dash/rule A RULE which prints as a thick line in the centre, tapering at both ends.

●

Tabloid A page half the size of a BROADSHEET.

Tabular work Type MATTER set in COLUMNS (1).

Tabulate, tabulating To arrange COPY such as text or figures in the form of a columnar table, according to fixed measures.

Tack The adhesive quality of a medium — e.g., printing ink — and of adhesives and adhesive tape.

Tail The bottom edge of a book.

Tail margin The MARGIN at the bottom of a page, also called FOOT MARGIN.

Tail piece A design at the end of a SECTION (2), CHAPTER or book.

Take back An instruction to the printer, marked on a PROOF, to take back CHARACTERS (1), words or lines to the preceding line, COLUMN (1) or page.

Take in An instruction to the printer, marked on a PROOF or MANUSCRIPT, to include extra COPY supplied.

Take over An instruction to the printer, marked on a PROOF, to carry CHARACTERS (1), words or lines forward to the following line, COLUMN (1) or page.

Tape perforator The machine in mechanical composition systems, such as LINOTYPE and INTERTYPE, that encodes keyboarded information on tape, which is then used to control the TYPESETTING.

Technical illustration A specialist branch of GRAPHIC DESIGN dealing with illustrations of all types depicting technical machines, systems and processes.

Technical pen A pen with a tubular nib designed to draw lines of an even width.

Template Shape or SHEET with cutout forms and designs, used as a drawing aid.

Text The written or printed MATTER forming the main BODY (1) of a publication.

Text type/matter Any TYPEFACE of a suitable size for printing text, usually up to 14 POINT.

Thermocopy A COPY produced by the action of heat, rather than light as in a PHOTOCOPY.

Thermography The process in which freshly printed SHEETS are dusted with resinous powder which forms a raised surface when fused with heat.

Thick The description of a word space used in hand-set type, measuring one-third of an EM.

Thin A word space as above measuring one-fifth of an EM.

Third-dimension printing Methods of producing a three-dimensional illusion in printed MATTER.

Thirty-two mo, 32mo A SHEET cut or folded to one thirty-second of its basic size.

Thirty two sheet A poster size measuring 120 ×160in (3048 × 4064mm).

Threadless binding see PERFECT BINDING.

Thread sewn Method of binding in which a sewing-machine inserts threads through each folded back section and sews them together.

Three-dimensional (1) In illustration an image creating the illusion of physically standing out from the page. **(2)** An object, such as a package, which has depth as well as height and width.

Throw out see FOLD OUT.

Thumbnail sketches Small, rough sketches used to work out an idea.

Tint (1) The effect of the admixture of white to a solid colour. **(2)** Also, the effect achieved by breaking up colour into a percentage using dots which allow white paper to show through.

Tip in/on An illustration printed on a single page and inserted separately in a book by pasting one edge.

Tonal value The relative densities of tones in an image. See also COLOUR VALUE.

Tone line process A method of producing line art from a CONTINUOUS TONE ORIGINAL by combining a negative and positive film image.

Tone separation see POSTERIZATION.

Tooling A method of impressing decorations and lettering on the COVERS of books by hand, using brass letters, PALLETS, rolls and DIES.

Tooth The surface quality of paper that enables it to hold a painting, drawing or printing medium.

Tracing materials TRANSLUCENT forms of paper, cloth and ACETATE used as the basis of ARTWORK for direct reproduction.

Transfer A film or ACETATE SHEET bearing an image for transfer to a printing PLATE.

Transfer lettering Pre-printed lettering or other images stored on a transparent sheet of CELLULOSE ACETATE. Dry lettering is transferred to paper or art board by burnishing; wet transfers are applied using water.

Transitional Type forms which are neither OLD FACE nor MODERN, including Fournier and Baskerville.

Translucent The description of materials that transmit light but are not fully transparent, that is, an image cannot be seen clearly through the material.

Transparency A photographically developed image on transparent film. The term usually refers to a positive image in colour, though it is also applicable to any image on a transparent base.

Transpose To correct the wrong order of CHARACTERS (1), words, lines or images on a MANUSCRIPT or PROOF.

Trim marks Marks incorporated in a printed SHEET to indicate where paper STOCK (2) is to be trimmed or cut.

Tungsten film Photographic colour film intended for use in artificial light created by tungsten bulbs.

Turnaround (1) The length of time elapsing between the start and finish of a particular job. **(2)** (com) A document containing computer output that is used in clerical activity separate from the computer and returned to the computer file as updated or corrected input.

Turned over cover The COVER of a book with FLAPS turned inside at the FORE EDGE.

Turn up A piece of type inserted upside down in composition to show where a specific CHARACTER (1) is temporarily unavailable.

Twelve mo, 12mo A SHEET folded or cut to one-twelfth its basic size.

Twice up ARTWORK or COPY prepared at twice the size at which it will be reproduced.

Twin-wire paper A machine manufactured paper with a smooth finish on both sides.

Two revolution press A printing press with a cylinder rotating twice for each IMPRESSION (1) without interruption for inking of the plate or FORME.

Two up, three up Printing method in which more than one image, or a multiple of the same image, is printed on one side of a SHEET by one process.

Type, typeface The raised image of a CHARACTER (1) cast on a rectangular piece of metal used in LETTERPRESS printing.

Type area The area of a page designed to contain text MATTER and illustrations forming the BODY (2) of the work.

Type family A term covering all the variations and sizes of a basic TYPEFACE design. See BOLD FACE, CONDENSED, EXPANDED, LIGHT FACE.

Type mark up Instructions marked on COPY to be printed giving the COMPOSITOR details of POINT size, TYPEFACE, etc.

Type scale/gauge A rule marked with a scale of type measurements, POINTS, EMS, PICAS, etc., used by designers and COMPOSITORS.

Type series Manufacturer's identification of type families and sizes by designation of a series number.

Typesetting Methods of assembling TYPE for printing, by hand, machine or photographic techniques.

Type specimen sheet A sample SHEET showing the forms of letters, figures, punctuation marks, signs, etc., available in a given TYPEFACE, often including an example of the type as set.

Type to type see FOLD TO PRINT.

Typo (US) abb Typographical error. A term referring to an error in typewritten or typeset COPY.

Typographer One whose occupation is TYPOGRAPHY.

Typography The art, general design and appearance of typeset MATTER.

●

Ultraviolet Lightwaves beyond the visible portion of violet waves in the electromagnetic spectrum, which can be absorbed by some PHOTOSENSITIVE materials.

Uncoated book paper Paper used in printing books, catalogues, etc., in a range of finishes including ANTIQUE (rough) and SUPER-CALENDERED (smooth).

Undercutting Faulty ETCHING of a block which results in weakening the metal of the block.

Underlay Colour, tone or pattern effect laid in underneath ARTWORK or a photograph or illustration.

Underscore/underline A RULE printed beneath a word or portion of text.

Unit system A system of machine composition in which CHARACTER (1) widths conform to unit measurements associated with the set.

Unjustified Lines of type which are centred or which align only at one MARGIN and are not adjusted in spacing to fill out the full measure of the line.

Unsewn binding see PERFECT BINDING.

Upper case The CAPITAL letters in a FOUNT of TYPEFACE.

Uprating film To calculate the EXPOSURE of a film based on a higher ASA number than is standard for the film.

●

Vacuum forming A method of shaping plastic sheet by heating it until it softens and forcing it down over a relief MOULD by creating a vacuum beneath the mould.

Vacuum frame A frame for making positive or negative process images by direct contact with an ORIGINAL. The frame is illuminated and creation of a vacuum ensures stable contact between surfaces.

Vandyke print A print of PHOTOCOPY producing the image as a dark brown print, either negative or positive.

Varnish A transparent solution mixed with ink or printed over ink to produce a glossy surface finish.

Vellum The treated skin of a calf, kid or lamb, used as a writing surface.

Velox A print of COPY from a CONTINUOUS TONE ORIGINAL that has been pre-screened as a HALFTONE image and may be used in PASTE-UP or CAMERA-READY COPY.

Vertical page (US) A page in which COPY is RIGHT READING when the page is held in a vertical position.

Vignette A small illustration or decoration without a BORDER.

Vignetted halftone A HALFTONE image in which tones gradually BLEED out into the background.

Visual A mock up of the proposed appearance of a design or LAYOUT presented as a rough drawing, or if more highly finished, as a PRESENTATION VISUAL.

Visualizer A device for producing immediate prints from an original in enlargement or reduction.

●

Walk off The deterioration of the image on a printing plate, occuring during printing.

Wallet fold see GATEFOLD.

Wash-out The rinsing, cleaning and drying of NEGATIVES, film, plates, etc., during processing.

Watercolour printing Printing process using water-based inks and relatively porous paper so that colours are absorbed and can be mixed by overlapping the layers printed.

Watermark A design incorporated in paper during manufacture.

Web A continuous roll of paper.

Web-fed A printing press supplied with paper from a WEB rather than in separate SHEETS.

Web-set An OFFSET press working from a WEB or reel of paper.

Weight The degree of boldness of a TYPEFACE.

Wet on wet Colour printing in which the first colour of ink is still wet when the subsequent colours are printed.

Wet stripping The stripping away of a film base when the image has been processed but while the film is still wet.

White line A space between lines of type equivalent to the spacing between lines of type plus the height of an additional line.

Whiteprint A reproduction method producing copies at the same size as the ORIGINAL by direct contact, the image being formed by a light-sensitive dye. The original for this process must be on transparent or TRANSLUCENT material.

Widow A single word standing as the last line of a paragraph in typeset COPY.

Window (1) (typ) see RIVER. (2) An opening cut in a FLAT for insertion of a negative image.

Wire binding Method of mechanical binding where slots are drilled through the cover and pages, then secured with ringed wire fingers. Also known as 'wiro'.

Wire side The side of paper which has been carried on the wire mesh of a manufacturing machine and is lightly marked by the wire.

Wire stitch/stab One of a line of wire staples passed through the back of a printed SECTION used as a method of binding.

Woodcut A RELIEF PRINTING method using the side GRAIN (1) of a wood block. areas not intended to print are cut away below the surface of the block leaving a raised image that can be inked.

Wood engraving RELIEF PRINTING method similar to WOODCUT, but using the end GRAIN (1) of a wood block and finer tools, to produce a more delicate image.

Woodfree/freesheet (UK/US) Paper made from chemical PULP, containing no wood fibre.

Word break A division of a word at the end of a line of type to fit the line measure and avoid excessive space between words in the line.

Word spacing The adjustment of space between words in COPY being set, using fixed or variable space widths according to the method of composition.

Work and tumble To print one side of a SHEET and turn it from front to back to print the second side, keeping the same ALIGNMENT of the side edges on the press.

Work and turn When MATTER for both sides of a SHEET is set in one FORME. After one side of the sheet has been printed it is turned over end for end and backed up from the same forme.

Work and twist To print the same FORME twice on the same side of a SHEET, turning the sheet through 90 degrees between printings.

Work up A type space displaced upwards in LETTERPRESS printing.

Working A single operation performed by a printing machine.

Wove paper This is made on a roll of closely-woven, finely-textured wire, and leaves no marks on the paper surface.

Wrap around plate A curved printing plate that wraps around the cylinder of a ROTARY PRESS.

Wrap around press A LETTERPRESS printing machine using a WRAP AROUND PLATE.

Wrap round/wraparound A printed SECTION (1) of 4 or 8 pages folded round a full sized section when work is GATHERED.

Wrapping cover A paper COVER glued to the SPINE of a publication.

Wrong reading see REVERSE READING.

●

x-height The height of letters with neither ASCENDERS or DESCENDERS — e.g., x.

Xerography A photocopying process in which the image is formed by an electrostatic charge that allows adhesion of power ink. The ink is sealed by heat processing.

●

Yapp binding A BOOK BINDING method in which a limp COVER is applied which projects over the edges of the book's leaves.

●

Zigzag book A book made up of a continuous strip of paper folded in a CONCERTINA FOLD If secured at the BACK, printing is only applied to one side of the SHEET. If printed both sides the book must be left unstitched and opened out from either side.

Zinco, zincograph A zinc PLATE used in LETTERPRESS line printing.

Zip-a-tone Mechanical tints printed off CELLOPHANE and used in the preparation of ORIGINAL ARTWORK.

INDEX

Page numbers in *italics* refer to captions to illustrations